Southern Baptist

Southern Baptists

A History of a Confessional People

SLAYDEN A. YARBROUGH *and*
MICHAEL KUYKENDALL

McFarland & Company, Inc., Publishers
Jefferson, North Carolina

This book has undergone peer review.

ISBN (print) 978–1–4766–8456–7
ISBN (ebook) 978–1–4766–4478–3

LIBRARY OF CONGRESS AND BRITISH LIBRARY
CATALOGUING DATA ARE AVAILABLE

Library of Congress Control Number 2021039769

Cover photograph: a Southern Baptist Church in rural surroundings
(Shutterstock/Sean Pavone)

Printed in the United States of America

*McFarland & Company, Inc., Publishers
Box 611, Jefferson, North Carolina 28640
www.mcfarlandpub.com*

To Dr. Warren McWilliams,
colleague and friend for more than forty years.

For Terry Kuykendall,
my brother and true friend.

Table of Contents

Preface
by Slayden A. Yarbrough

Why am I and Mike Kuykendall publishing this book on Southern Baptists? What do we hope to accomplish? The simple answer is to provide a helpful resource tool for anyone wishing to learn about the people called Southern Baptists and to encourage the reader to contribute to the ongoing history of the denomination. This book is designed to provide a wealth of historical information from the beginning of Baptists and Southern Baptists up to the time of this writing. Baptists have been around for more than 400 years. Southern Baptists have existed for 175 years as this book was being completed. This book also contains a wealth of recommendations from credentialed historians for those wishing to go into more depth on the Baptist movement.

At the same time, this book is written from the premise that every generation writes its own history in a manner relevant to the contemporary circumstances. My most recent effort at this history was published in AD 2000, entitled *Southern Baptists: A Historical, Ecclesiological and Theological Heritage of a Confessional People* (Brentwood, Tennessee: Southern Baptist Historical Society and Nashville, Tennessee: 2000). A significant contribution was the examination of "The Controversy" in the Southern Baptist Convention (SBC) during the last quarter of the twentieth century that resulted in denominational conflict, a major restructuring of the convention, and a redefinition of the character of SBC.

During the first two decades of the twenty-first century in the SBC new leadership has appeared, new structures established, and new challenges and issues faced. Contemporary Southern Baptists have not only the freedom but the responsibility to define and record the history of the SBC for their generation. Baptist and Southern Baptist history is a

1

record of constant change, conflict, and creativity. That change will and must continue.

So this expanded and updated volume is dedicated to encouraging the current generation of leaders, churches, and lay people to courageously and vigorously accept the challenge of knowing from where they came, cherish the responsibility to shape their faith in accord with God's leadership, and like the early church after Pentecost, follow the spirit where ever she leads.

The recent history of any group is not the final word. It is only one phase which contributes to the foundation of the contemporary participants and the contemporary historians. If this book fulfills its purpose, the next chapter is ready to be written. And, if those who make this history do it right, then the people called Southern Baptists will become an even better people.

With these principles in mind, the following comments based upon my earlier writing published in 2000 will provide foundational material for this book. After more than two decades and with the excellent input from my friend Mike Kuykendall, the time is now for an update and expansion.

The Southern Baptist Convention is the largest non–Roman Catholic denomination in the United States. Yet, the term "Southern Baptist" defines much more than simply the national denomination.

A relevant question is "Who are the Southern Baptists?" Certainly, a positive and clear answer needs to be formulated for the benefit of those who are not among SBC ranks. But even more important, those who call themselves Southern Baptists must know without question what the foundation, the fiber, and the fruit are of their identity.

In recent times many voices have claimed to represent the historic Baptist tradition or position on issues of theology and ecclesiology, the Bible, church and state questions, and ethical concerns. Only Southern Baptists who know who they are through profession, practice, and precedent can unapologetically separate the music from the noise among the uncertain sounds around us. At issue is the desire to continue the old ways and the manner in which Southern Baptists will respond to the opportunities of ministry and mission in contemporary society and the foundation which they will lay for future generations. As Southern Baptists are clear on their identity of the past and in the present, they will be able to determine those essential priorities which will shape their response to the future.

Preface (Slayden A. Yarbrough)

Almost five decades ago I began preaching a sermon entitled "Southern Baptists: Who Are We?" The sermon went through a constant state of revision during the years as I added and deleted material and as I focused upon current issues facing Baptists at particular moments in the denomination's history. I am convinced that most Baptist lay people and many ministers are limited in their knowledge of who we are. J.M. Gaskin, former editor of *The Oklahoma Baptist Chronicle*, after hearing my presentation on the topic to a senior adult group at Oklahoma Baptist University, asked me to expand my material and to put it in a written form for publication in the *Chronicle*. I agreed to do so in the form of three articles. These articles were published in subsequent volumes of the *Chronicle* and were reprinted in 1984 in the book *Southern Baptists: Who Are We?* The volume was revised and updated in two subsequent editions in 1985 and 1990.

In answering the question, "Who are Southern Baptists?" I proposed that three areas must be examined carefully. The first concern was to establish who Baptists are historically. This necessitated going beyond our beginnings and history as Southern Baptists to an examination of the history of Baptists in general to uncover those qualities and characteristics which have appeared in Baptist life. A second concern was to know who Baptists are theologically. Determination of how they develop and express their theology, as well as what they believe, was of utmost importance. Finally, Southern Baptists must know who they are practically in terms of our mission cooperation and efforts. Only as Baptists understand all three of these expressions of Baptist life as they blend together can we answer the question, "Who are the Southern Baptists?"

As the twentieth century drew to a close it became necessary to address anew the question of identifying and defining Southern Baptists. Two decades of controversy and change resulted in a woefully outdated volume in the third edition of *Southern Baptists: Who Are We?* In order to respond to this need I decided to revise the contents of the volume thoroughly. I reversed the order of Chapters 2 and 3. I then included between these two chapters a completely new one which examined "The Controversy" which began in 1979 and the restructuring of the Southern Baptist Convention (1995–1997).

I observed, participated in, researched, and taught Southern Baptist history for almost fifty years. My goals for *Southern Baptists: A Historical, Ecclesiological, and Theological Heritage of a Confessional*

Preface (Slayden A. Yarbrough)

People were that the average Southern Baptist could read and understand its contents clearly and that the Baptist scholar and researcher could appreciate its contributions. This present book edits and updates the 2000 volume in light of key events, personalities, institutions, and issues arising during the first two decades of the twenty-first century. As you read the pages that follow, may you appreciate those who came before us for their contributions and forgive those whose human failures compromised the high standards of the Baptist heritage.

Those who have contributed to my development and career are many. Two are professors who taught me about the importance of history. H.K. Neely was my first church history and Baptist history professor while I was a student at Southwest Baptist College, Bolivar, Missouri. His influence is evident throughout the pages of this book. Glenn O. Hilburn, my major professor at Baylor University, was patient with me as he directed me into becoming a good researcher.

J. M. Gaskin, director of history of the Baptist General Convention of Oklahoma, took me under his wing after I came to Oklahoma Baptist University. He assigned me several writing and speaking projects that whetted my appetite for publishing. He opened doors for me to participate in and contribute to Baptist history work at the state and national levels.

Lynn E. May, Jr., executive director of the Historical Commission of the Southern Baptist Convention (1971–1995), taught me important lessons that I never anticipated having to use until I became interim and then executive director of the agency during its dissolution from 1995 to 1997. His assistant for many years, Charles Deweese, a fellow Baptist historian gave many of us an opportunity to publish in *Baptist History and Heritage.* I am indebted also to Rosalie Beck, religion professor at Baylor University, and Alan Lefever, historian and archivist for the Texas Baptist Collection, who served consecutively as president of the Southern Baptist Historical Society (SBHS) during the years when its very existence was being threatened. Their encouragement and assistance kept me going during my tenure as executive director of the SBHS, which is now named the Baptist History and Heritage Society.

Most importantly for this current volume, I acknowledge the contributions of my friend Mike Kuykendall. As I shared my desire to update my book published in 2000, Mike provided significant material for the last twenty-five years of Southern Baptist life. Specifically, Chapter 4 and the Conclusion were produced with major input from Mike.

He edited each chapter and pointed me to resources from all spectrums of Southern Baptist life that he provided to his students in his Baptist history class at Gateway Seminary. Moreover, Mike critiqued and made recommendations for improvements to all drafts leading up to this final product. This volume could not have been completed without his contributions and critiques. Mike's experience as a student, a seminary professor, and a researcher of Baptist and Southern Baptist history, as one who knows the past and contemporary literature on the topics, and as simply a good friend, made him a superb choice with whom to collaborate on this important project.

Finally, thanks to Janis, my wife. Her service to the Southern Baptist Historical Society during the above-mentioned years will not receive much notice. But she contributed enormously.

Introduction
Southern Baptists:
A Denominational Identity

Why should you read this book on the history of Baptists and Southern Baptists? Why should any Baptist minister, church vocation student, missionary, denominationalist, or lay person read any book on Baptist history?[1]

There are many traditional reasons for studying one's history. One is to remember our past, good and bad. Another is to interpret the present in light of one's history. A third is to continue affirming and drawing from the good in our history. A fourth is to study the challenges faced in the past in order to face contemporary issues. If the contemporary church is to have a relevant prophetic voice, its people must understand its history. Knowing one's history provides an irreplaceable foundation for prophetic proclamation.

Finally, and possibly most importantly, is that knowledge of one's history equips a person and institutions to be prepared to make their own history. Making history never stops with any generation. Every generation must face its unique world, its distinctive culture, and its specific challenges.

We conclude that as historians we must believe in and trust the current and succeeding generations to draw from their history in order to be relevant. Looking back is extremely valuable. But observing and participating in the present and anticipating the future is essential. Making history is a right and it is a responsibility for every generation, every individual, and every organization or institution. Baptists must know their history. They must interpret that history. And most importantly they must have the freedom which characterizes the Baptist heritage to become history makers for themselves and for future generations.

Thus, the essential question of this book becomes "Who are the people called Southern Baptists?" The purpose of this study is to answer this question. The answer is historical, as seen in Chapter 1. It is practical, as identified in Chapter 2, which describes the ecclesiological development of the denomination up to the "Covenant for a New Century" (1845–2000). Chapter 3 characterizes Southern Baptists in terms of the "Controversy" that engulfed the attention of the movement during the last two decades of the twentieth century and resulted in the most comprehensive restructuring in the history of the Southern Baptist Convention. Chapter 4 updates the ecclesiological developments that have occurred up to 2021. Denominational agencies and entities are discussed in light of the changes produced by the Controversy and the Covenant for a New Century. Southern Baptist theology as addressed in Chapter 5 is also an essential factor in understanding the people called Southern Baptists. Finally, the study concludes by mapping out what Southern Baptist challenges there are for the twenty-first century. The chapters are in many ways standalone studies. There will be noticeable overlapping at times. Treat these sections as review.

Another way to characterize Southern Baptists is to examine the issue of Baptist identity, not just Baptist distinctions. The following suggestions contribute to an understanding of a Baptist identity and will help to introduce the issues and information found in this book.

A People of Faith

Southern Baptists are a committed people of genuine faith. They are committed to the Lordship of Christ through faith. There is no doctrine, which in reality is a confessional faith statement that can be expressed theologically, which is more crucial to the understanding of Southern Baptists than the Lordship of Christ. Southern Baptist views of salvation, the authority of the Scriptures, congregational church government, religious liberty and church and state relations, confessional theology, and missions and ministry are all predicated by the belief that all believers, all organizations, and all institutions are responsible to the living Lord in matters of commitment, belief, and practice. In the end every Baptist, every church, and every cooperative organization must stand under the authority of Jesus Christ whose Lordship is acknowledged and accepted through faith.

Such an understanding results in a broad definition of faith. Faith is a response of obedience and trust in the living Lord in several aspects of the Christian life. Believers express their faith in worship, both individually and corporately. Believers express their faith in theology. They "confess" their convictions by affirming "This we believe." They express their faith by service and ministry to others, again individually and corporately. And, they communicate their faith ethically in the way they conduct their lives and call for ethical living.

A Free People

Southern Baptists are a free people. Faith in the Lordship of Christ sets every believer free. This is not freedom to do as one pleases. It is not freedom to believe anything and everything that one chooses. It is freedom to be accountable to the living Christ in all matters of faith and practice. There is no greater freedom or more responsible liberty.

No human authority or organization can usurp this freedom. Neither pastor, director of missions, state or national convention presidents, nor politician can stand between the believer and Christ. Vote of the majority can never replace responsibility to the Lord. The Apostle Paul wrote, "For freedom Christ has set us free; stand firm therefore, and do not submit again to a yoke of slavery" (Gal. 5:1 ESV). Faith in Christ frees the believer to answer to him.

Faith also frees each congregation to respond to the authority of the living Lord. No association, convention, or committee can coerce, intimidate, or mandate conformity of belief or practice. Although Baptists and Southern Baptists collectively have recognized the autonomy under Christ of each congregation, at the same time they voluntarily have found ways to organize and cooperate in missions, ministry, educational enterprises, and social concerns.

A Servant People

Southern Baptists are a servant people. The basis for cooperation and unity was expressed in the Preamble of the Constitution of the newly-formed Southern Baptist Convention in 1845. It called for a plan for "eliciting, combining, and directing the energies of the whole denomination in one sacred effort, for the propagation of the gospel."[2]

At the associational, state, and national levels, Southern Baptists have done evangelistic work, performed missionary activities, established educational institutions, created social organizations, informed themselves, and responded to a changing world by creating new structures to carry out the Great Commission given by Christ and making it relative to each generation.

A Diverse People

Southern Baptists are a diverse people. Baptists are rooted in diversity. Baptist historian Bill J. Leonard stated that Baptists are the only denomination that has roots in both Arminianism (the English General Baptists) and Calvinism (the English Particular Baptists).[3] Southern Baptists, because of their ecclesiology which allows the local congregation to determine, or "call," its ministers, have as pastors both highly-educated ministers and those with no education at all. Most churches have only male deacons, but several have ordained women. A small number have even called women as pastors, much to the chagrin of many Southern Baptists.

Some churches prefer high church worship services while others embrace tendencies that are charismatic, to say the least. Some churches are comfortable with the old, standard hymns and organ and piano accompaniment. Others use everything from orchestras to guitars and drums, recorded accompaniments, and choruses as a staple form of music. Some churches, especially from rural areas, express the gospel in terms of evangelism, and others from urban areas concentrate on social ministries.

With no centralized authority passing down guidelines for acceptable and unacceptable worship, with a confessional rather than a creedal approach to theology, and with the local congregation having the responsibility to choose and define its ministry, it is no wonder that Southern Baptists have naturally expressed themselves with great diversity. Historically, this has proven to be a strength, not a weakness.

A Confessional People

As reflected in the title of the book, Baptists and Southern Baptists throughout their history have been a "confessional" people. Faith is rooted in the personal confession that Jesus is Lord. Baptists express their faith through verbal testimony and through the beautiful symbolic confession of baptism. Baptists express this faith in individual and corporate worship. Baptists confess their faith theologically, affirming "This we believe," rather than "This you must believe." Therefore, Baptist theology is a result of faith rather than a test of faith. Baptists confess their faith in mission and ministry. Baptists confess their faith ethically, again both individually and corporately. To understand Baptists is to understand that they are a confessional people in principle and practice. As they live and proclaim their faith, they confess that Jesus is Lord in all they say and do.

A People of Conflict and Controversy

Southern Baptists are also a people who have been shaped by crisis and controversy. Walter Shurden's *Not a Silent People* tells the story of a people who have demonstrated that they are free, alive, and well, if by nothing more than their inherent ability to be embroiled in controversy.[4] Southern Baptists have fought over slavery, polity, missions, methodologies for missions, religion and science, theology, the working of the Spirit, methods of financial cooperation, the Bible, educational institutions, ethical issues, sexual issues, abortion, ordination, Disney, and whether or not wives ought "graciously submit" to their husbands.

In most instances Southern Baptists became stronger, more clearly-focused, and more dedicated to the central task of the churches to take the gospel to the whole world in "one sacred effort."[5] In fact, the commitment to missions and ministry often held the denomination together in the midst of strife and conflict. Historically, no greater challenge to the unity of the denomination has surpassed the "Controversy," which will be discussed in Chapter 3. The conflict did not destroy the Baptist identity but has significantly reshaped its meaning. It has resulted in new commitment and new creativity on the part of those who call themselves "Southern Baptists" to make clear the distinctions and qualities of an established heritage in ways that will be relevant in the new century.

Conclusion

The twenty-first century will determine whether in the end Southern Baptists will be more unified, splintered, or irreparably divided. As new patterns of cooperation, service, and ministry develop, those identified with the Southern Baptist heritage may find a way to focus not within and upon internal problems and debates but on the needs of the outside world and culture. If Southern Baptists remain relevant, their historical foundations suggest that a commitment to the local church, to cooperative ventures in missions and ministry, and to educational excellence will ensure their place in a rapidly changing world.

Discussion Questions

Each chapter in this book contains important study questions to be answered by the reader or by group discussions with other participants in the course. Besides answering the questions participants will be asked to reflect upon many of the issues raised in the questions. Questions will include brief essay answers, identification questions, and reflections. The questions enable participants not only to understand but to apply what they learned to the contemporary environment of the participants, their church, and the Baptist and Southern Baptist movements.

1. After reading the opening paragraphs to the introduction, why are you reading this book on Southern Baptists?
2. Do you see your role as a Southern Baptist as a history maker or simply a history apologist?
3. In the list of topics that identify Baptists and Southern Baptists, list in order of importance to you the four topics and give a brief reason for your choices.

≡ 1 ≡

A Historical Heritage
Foundations, Beginnings, and Developments

Southern Baptists enjoy a rich historical heritage rooted in the Baptist movement in general. They were shaped by the rise and development of both English and American Baptists before their beginnings in 1845. Baptists have been influenced by the events occurring around them and have often exerted their own influence upon those events. An understanding of Baptist history is essential in defining who Southern Baptists are today and in determining where they are heading in the future. This chapter briefly examines the question of Baptist origins, the heritage of English Baptists, the heritage of Baptists in America, and the rise and development of Southern Baptists.

Baptist Beginnings: Four Theories

The first historical question to be answered concerning Southern Baptists is "Where did the Baptists begin?" Leon McBeth delineated four theories on the origin of Baptists.[1]

Continuation of Biblical Teachings

One theory traces a "continuation" of the Baptist-like faith and practice in "biblical teachings" back through the centuries, a kind of "spiritual successionism." Thomas Crosby in his four-volume *History of English Baptists* (1738–1740) emphasized a continuity of concepts. He traced Baptist principles both to the New Testament and through various groups prior to the rise of Baptists in the seventeenth century. Joseph Ivimey issued his four-volume *History of the English Baptists* from 1812 to 1830. He considered English Baptists as descendants of earlier groups that baptized believers, such as the Waldenses, but did not conclude that they were Baptists.

Other supporters of this view include David Benedict, *A General History of the Baptist Denomination in America and Other Parts of the World* (1813) and Thomas Armitage, *A History of the Baptists* (1887). Proponents of this view dismiss the idea of the need for an unbroken historical succession.[2]

Successionism

Another theory traces an unbroken "succession of Baptist churches" back to the time of Christ. The Southern Baptist expression of this view is the Landmark movement, led by J.R. Graves and J.M. Pendleton. It began in the mid-nineteenth century. It is sometimes referred to as the JJJ theory—Jesus, Jordan, John (the Baptist). Graves and Pendleton drew their views from Adam Taylor's *A History of the English General Baptists* (1818) and G.H. Orchard's *A Concise History of the Baptists* (1838), then popularized it for the American frontier.

Three premises underline this theory. First, Baptist churches are the only true churches; all others are merely religious societies. Second, in Matthew 16:18, Jesus guaranteed the perpetuity of his church. The third premise, based upon these two assumptions, concludes that Baptist churches must have had a continuous historical succession since the establishment of the church by Jesus Christ. From this foundation, the history of Christianity was studied to find other "Baptist churches" (i.e., those churches which practiced believer's baptism by immersion), whether they used the name of Baptist or not.

The successionist position became orthodoxy for most Southern Baptists by the end of the nineteenth century. The first major challenge to this interpretation was made by W.H. Whitsitt, president and professor of the Southern Baptist Theological Seminary in Louisville, Kentucky.[3] In the 1880s and the 1890s, Whitsitt authored several articles which rejected the view that Baptists could trace their history back to the time of Christ. He held the position that the Baptists as a denomination began in seventeenth-century England. A major controversy ensued, and Whitsitt was forced to resign on July 13, 1898.

In 1969, W. Morgan Patterson, church history professor at Southern Seminary, published *Baptist Successionism: A Critical View.*[4] He examined the historical development of the successionist theory from the seventeenth through nineteenth centuries, the successionist's methodology, and the factors contributing to a Baptist position of successionism. Patterson concluded that the successionist theory failed to meet the demands of logical consistency and critical examination of available sources. In other words, many of the movements considered to be Baptist by the successionists, while practicing believer's baptism, held views and practices inconsistent with the Baptist tradition. Hence, they could not be considered Baptist. Although many Baptists continue to hold to the successionist theory, the fact that Patterson supported Whitsitt's view without fear of having to resign is indicative of the rejection of successionism by most contemporary Baptist historians.[5]

Anabaptist Influence

The third theory concerning the origin of Baptists is the "Anabaptist influence" theory. Early proponents of this position, such as A.H. Newman and Walter Rauschenbusch, emphasized a spiritual relationship between Baptists and the many Anabaptist sects that arose before or during the Protestant Reformation. The word "Anabaptist" is a translation of the German word *wiedertaüfer* which means to "baptize again." During the Reformation, the term was applied to "re-baptizers" by their enemies because the Anabaptist practice of believer's baptism seemed to be an additional baptism to their previous baptism as infants. Many Anabaptist groups held to beliefs and practices similar to those of Baptists, such as baptism for the regenerate, the authority of the Bible, especially the New Testament, a disciplined church, and religious liberty/ separation of church and state.

Most Baptist scholars conclude that no historical continuity can be traced between the Baptists and the Anabaptists. Glen Harold Stassen, however, provided evidence of the influence of Menno Simons's *Foundation-Book* in the 1644 First London Confession of Particular Baptists. In two articles in *Baptist History and Heritage*, Stassen traced the origin of the English Particular (Calvinistic) Baptist to the Reformed tradition and to the Mennonite heritage, which he refers to as both the "mother" and "father" of these Baptists.[6]

At the same time, no direct historical continuity has been traced between Baptist and Anabaptist churches. Furthermore, some of the Anabaptists, such as the Mennonites, have held to principles which most Baptists have not practiced, such as pacifism, nonparticipation in civil government, and an unwillingness to take oaths. Because of these factors and in spite of the common ground they share, this theory does not adequately answer all of the questions of Baptist beginnings. Stassen's interpretation, however, provides evidence of a significant theological influence.

Outgrowth of English Separatism

The "outgrowth of English Separatism" is the last theory on the origin of Baptists. Early proponents of this theory included Whitsitt, Augustus H. Strong, John Shakespeare, and Henry C. Vedder. Today, the overwhelming majority of Baptist historians favor this viewpoint of Baptist origins. This theory proposed that Baptists originated out of the English Separatist movement of the late-sixteenth and early-seventeenth centuries. The Separatists arose out of the Puritan phase of the English Reformation during the reign of Elizabeth I. Most Puritans held to presbyterial church polity, but the Separatists practiced congregational polity. They also considered the Church of England—her congregations, her worship, and her ministry—to be false according to New Testament standards.

Although there are examples of earlier "separate" congregations in England, the movement traditionally begins with the establishment of a Separatist church at Norwich in 1581 by Robert Browne. This congregation was forced into exile in Holland, where in 1582 Browne wrote three Separatist tracts, including his famous *Reformation without tarrying for anie...*, which rejected the idea that civil officials could or should reform the English churches. Other Separatist congregations soon appeared, including one in London under the pastoral leadership of Francis Johnson. They also went into exile in Holland after the executions in 1593 of leaders Henry Barrowe, John Greenwood, and John Penry.

GENERAL BAPTISTS

Another Separatist congregation arose at Gainsborough in 1602. It divided in 1606 with one part of the church meeting at Scrooby Manor, which later sent forth from Holland the Plymouth Colony Pilgrims. In 1606, John Smyth became a Separatist and joined the Gainsborough congregation, where he was chosen pastor and was ordained. The congregation emigrated from England to Amsterdam, Holland, in 1608.

Later that year or early in 1609, Smyth rejected infant baptism. He formed a new church, not on the basis of a mutual covenant between the members, but on the basis of believer's baptism. He baptized himself by affusion (pouring), and then baptized the rest of the congregation of about forty persons. This constituted the first English Baptist Church, a General Baptist church.[7] The General Baptists were Arminian in theology, believing like Jacob Arminius (1560–1609) in a general atonement in which Christ died for all, not just the elect. Smyth held that God foreknew who would accept Christ, but did not predestinate any to destruction, and did not decree the choice that any would make.

In 1610, Smyth became dissatisfied over the question of whether or not he had the authority to baptize himself. Along with others in his group, Smyth petitioned a group of Amsterdam Mennonites for church membership. The remainder of the Baptist church came under the leadership of Thomas Helwys, a wealthy merchant who had financed the Gainsborough congregation's immigration to Amsterdam. Helwys and others disagreed with Smyth's decision to join the Mennonites. They excommunicated Smyth, declaring themselves to be the true church.[8] In 1611, Helwys led the church back to England and established the first Baptist church on English soil at Spitalfields, just outside of London. Helwys was imprisoned, and languished there until he died around 1614. However, the church and the General Baptist movement continued.[9]

PARTICULAR BAPTISTS

The English Separatist movement also gave birth to the Particular Baptists.[10] These folks were Calvinistic in theology and held to a "particular" atonement in which Christ died for the elect or predestined. The origin of the Particular Baptists is closely identified with the Independent church established in 1616 by Henry Jacob at Southwark, England, across the Thames River from London. Jacob was a Puritan. After discussions in 1596 with Francis Johnson, who was imprisoned in the Clink in London, Jacob adopted congregational polity. However, he did not become a Separatist at this time, but sought to convince James I, and other high officials, of the need to reform the Church of England on a congregational pattern of church government. Jacob was also driven into exile in Holland and eventually settled in Leyden. There between 1610 to 1616 he held numerous conversations with John Robinson, who was now pastoring the Scrooby Manor exiles.

Robinson, while moderating his Separatism, apparently convinced

Jacob of the futility of his efforts to reform the churches in England. As a result, in 1616 Jacob returned to England and established a congregation that became the mother church of English Independency. Jacob had not accepted all the tenets of Separatism, especially its harsh attitude toward the churches and ministers of the Church of England, but he did adopt Separatism's congregational ecclesiology and its practice of withdrawal from membership in the established church.

Jacob's church was pastored later by John Lathrop and then Henry Jessey, and became known as the Jacob-Lathrop-Jessey church, or the J-L-J church. Out of this church arose the Particular Baptist movement, which developed in several stages. First, in 1633 seventeen members led by Samuel Eaton, Richard Spilsbury, and Richard Blunt, dismissed themselves from membership. They desired "further baptism," and apparently rejected the validity of their baptism in the Anglican churches. The issue was thus the administrator of baptism.

The second stage resulted in the formation of what most Baptist historians consider to be the first Particular Baptist church. In this case the issue was the subject of baptism. In 1638, six members of the Southwark church became convinced that the New Testament taught that baptism was for professed believers, not infants. They requested and were granted dismissal from the Southwark congregation in order to join John Spilsbury in forming a new church established on the foundation of believer's baptism.

The third stage was concerned with the question of the mode or method of baptism. Affusion was being practiced by the Particular Baptists at this time. In 1640, Richard Blunt along with some members of the Spilsbury congregation, and perhaps several members of the Southwark church now being pastored by Henry Jessey, became convinced that immersion was the mode taught in the New Testament. No one in England practiced immersion. Thus, Blunt was sent to Holland for instructions from a group of conservative Mennonites called the Rhynsburgers or Collegiants who practiced immersion. He then returned to England, and in 1641 immersion was adopted as the mode of baptism by the Particular Baptists.[11]

In 1643, Hanserd Knollys withdrew from the Southwark church to form a Particular Baptist church. Two years later, Jessey adopted believer's baptism by immersion. Gradually, other members of his church accepted Particular Baptist views, and in 1645 the J-L-J congregation ceased to be an Independent church and became Particular Baptist.

In retrospect, English Baptists were influenced in three areas by the English Separatist movement. First, they found their source of authority for faith and practice in the Bible. Second, the Baptists continued the practice of congregational polity, which for them meant that the local church was under the Lordship of Christ and not any civil or ecclesiastical leaders or bodies. Third, the Baptists accepted the Separatists' call for toleration of Christians and expanded it to a plea and principle of complete liberty of conscience in religious matters for all. For example, in 1612 Helwys published *A Short Declaration of the Mystery of Iniquity*, which is considered to be the first demand in England for universal religious liberty. Helwys famously defended religious freedom not only for Baptists but for "heretics, Turks, Jews, or whatsoever."[12]

"Where did the Baptists begin?" is certainly an important question. One can believe the successionist theory, but the available evidence must be manipulated to prove it. The continuation of biblical teachings roots Baptist principles in the Bible. Stassen's interpretation of the influence of Menno Simons's *Foundation-Book* provides evidence to support an Anabaptist theological influence. The English Separatist descent theory, however, meets the criteria of honest and critical scholarship based upon available sources. Historically, the English Baptists arose out of the English Separatist movement by Christians deeply rooted in scriptural teachings with evidence of an Anabaptist influence in spirit and thought blended with a moderate Calvinism.

Two points must be made. First, in all four theories the origin of the Baptists really begins with the New Testament movement begun by Jesus. The Bible provides the foundation for who we are regardless of one's theory of origins.[13] Second, the primary issue for Baptists today and always must be not who we were, which is certainly important, but who we are. Do Baptists find their identity consistent with the principles and practices of the beginnings of Jesus' church as taught in the New Testament as they attempt to be God's people today?

The Heritage of English Baptists

The seventeenth century was an extremely creative and momentous period in the history of the English people. Politically, the century saw the Tudor reign come to an end with the death of Elizabeth I and the rise of the Stuart house beginning with James I in 1603, the English Civil War (1642–1649), the rise of Oliver Cromwell and the Commonwealth (1649–1660), the Restoration of the Stuart house (1660–1688), and the Glorious Revolution under William and Mary (1688–1702).

Religiously, the period was characterized by the appearance of the *King James Version* of the Bible, suppression of nonconformists under William Laud during the reigns of James I and Charles I, increased nonconformity during the Commonwealth, persecution of dissenters during the Restoration period, and the passage of the Act of Toleration in 1689. During the seventeenth century, English Baptists appeared, struggled, and developed as a significant movement in English religious life. The Baptists spread to Wales, Ireland, America, and would eventually appear in other areas of British influence, in Scotland, and in countries on the European continent.[14]

Associationalism

Several developments occurred among English Baptists which contributed to the character of the Baptist movement in general.[15] The development of associationalism was a very important process for the future of Baptists. According to W.T. Whitley, an English Baptist historian, and supported by American Baptist historian Robert G. Torbet, Baptist associations were patterned after Oliver Cromwell's New-Model Army during the English Civil War. The army was organized into "associations" from the counties to raise money and troops. This plan, according to Torbet, was transferred to church organization in 1653 in Ireland by Baptists who had been in Cromwell's army.[16]

This view, however, must be rejected. Following B.R. White, it is better to trace the origin of associationalism to Henry Jacob, founder of the Southwark congregation in 1616.[17] The idea of voluntary associationalism was certainly present in the writings of Jacob and included in his church's Confession in 1616. Furthermore, a non-authoritative classis (a Reformed Tradition term) of Separatist and Independent ministers was established in the 1620s in Holland on a pattern of voluntary associationalism. Included among the participants were a number of "Jacobites," followers of Henry Jacob. Also included among the individuals was John Davenport, who had close association with the Southwark church. Thus, not only was a theory of associationalism present in the thought of Jacob, but a sectarian model also existed through the efforts by exiled Englishmen practicing his theory. Moreover, seven churches voluntarily cooperated in producing the First London Confession in 1644.[18]

Baptists began to meet for fellowship, evangelistic cooperation, and clarification of Baptist belief and practice as early as 1624. By 1655, "association" was a common term among both General and Particular Baptists. General Baptist associations were more representative and stronger. They had a national organization by 1660. The Particular Baptists held their first general associational meeting in 1689. Finally, after a number of controversies and modifications, a group of General Baptists united with Particular Baptists in 1891.[19]

Confessions of Faith

Theologically, Baptists published confessions of faith from their beginnings. John Smyth drew up a confession in 1609, and Thomas Helwys followed with one in 1611. The first Particular Baptist confession was drawn up in 1644 by representatives from seven churches in the London area and became known as the First London Confession. The very influential Second London Confession of Particular Baptists was written in 1677. It was based on the Presbyterians' Westminster Confession and was signed by representatives of 107 churches. For Baptists, confessions were not binding creeds, but positive expressions of what Baptists did and did not believe and practice. This topic will be expanded upon in Chapter 5.[20]

Religious Liberty

The struggle for religious liberty was one of the major areas of contribution for Baptists in the seventeenth century. As nonconformists, they faced opposition from the state church prior to the English Civil War. The monarchy was restored in 1660 and with it came a renewed persecution of Baptists. Between 1661 and 1665, a series of acts called the Clarendon Code were passed. These acts made it difficult for nonconformists to the Established Church to hold public or state church positions, oppressed nonconformist worship, and limited the activity of nonconformist ministers. John Bunyan, author of the famous *Pilgrim's Progress*, spent twelve years in prison rather than yield to such coercive measures. Finally, after the advent of William and Mary,

Parliament passed the Act of Toleration in 1689, which brought for Baptists and most other nonconformists a degree of religious freedom.[21]

Revival, Missions, and Social Reform

Following the passage of the Act of Toleration, Baptists experienced a period of stagnation, as did other dissenters. The struggle for religious liberty may have exhausted its proponents. Another suggestion is that religious fervor and persecution went hand in hand. When one ceased, the other also disappeared. However, the eighteenth century was characterized by four major developments for Baptists: a new era of evangelistic concern, the rise of the modem mission movement, the appearance of outstanding ministerial leadership, and an increased concern for social reform.[22]

The Wesleyan revival that swept England in the mid-eighteenth century flowed into the Baptist movement. A key figure was Dan Taylor, a convert during the revival who became a General Baptist. He became the life and soul of the New Connexion Baptists or the Six-Principle Baptists. Many General Baptists had absorbed the weaker Christology of Anabaptists such as Melchior Hoffman. Taylor gave the New Connexion Baptists a strong evangelistic and corporate identity through his preaching and organizational skills and through his position as editor of the *General Baptist*.[23]

The Particular Baptists also became more evangelistic. A prime reason for this was a modification of Baptist theology. Pastors such as John Brine, John Skepp, and especially John Gill directed Particular Baptists toward hyper-Calvinism, an expression that questioned exhortations to sinners and public calls to profess Christ.[24] Andrew Fuller was instrumental in leading a change from hyper-Calvinism to a more moderate and evangelistic theological approach. Fullerism eventually won over the vast majority of Particular Baptist ministers and churches.[25]

The birth of the modem mission movement is often equated with the name of William Carey. As a shoe cobbler and minister, he developed a deep concern for the heathen. He overcame numerous obstacles and eventually led in establishing the Baptist Missionary Society on October 2, 1792. On January 9, 1793, Carey and John Thomas, a British surgeon, were appointed as missionaries to India. Carey has been given the title of "Father of Modern Missions."[26]

Baptists profited from strong leadership during the nineteenth century. Among the outstanding ministers were Robert Hall, Charles Haddon Spurgeon, Alexander Maclaren, and John Clifford. These men excelled as pulpiteers and contributed in a variety of ways to the intellectual, social, and ministry achievements of Baptists.

Baptists also became active in several areas of social concern in the nineteenth century. Robert Hall led Baptists to call for Parliamentary reform which enabled commoners to serve. Joseph Ivimey and William Knibb were leaders who called for the abolition of slave trade. John Howard studied prison conditions throughout Europe and Britain and aroused the public to call for improvement. Charles Stovel led the charge for temperance. In education, Baptists were influenced by William Fox in the Sunday School movement. Baptists were also active in providing schools to train ministers and in safeguarding the public schools against sectarianism. They continued to insist upon religious freedom. Through their efforts, combined with those of other dissenters, a more liberal Toleration Act was passed in 1812.[27]

The formation of the Baptist Union occurred in 1813. It became the first national organization for Baptists. Nevertheless, the Baptist Missionary Society overshadowed it for years. The Baptist Union reorganized in 1873 and moderated some of its Particular Baptist emphases in order for General Baptists to join. But some Particular Baptists, such as Spurgeon, were dissatisfied with these changes that weakened Reformed doctrines. This precipitated the Down Grade Controversy which hastened Spurgeon's departure from the Baptist Union.[28] Spurgeon lamented universalist interpretations of the Bible which some General Baptists espoused as well as doctrinal decay among all Baptists. Not all English Baptists agreed with his assessments, and General Baptists and Particular Baptists united with the Bible Union in 1891.[29]

The twentieth century witnessed a steady numerical decline among English Baptists. British Baptists have analyzed these statistics, explained it, mounted campaigns against it, yet it continues into the twenty-first century. Factors included theological polarization, ecumenism, the charismatic movement, and a mindset that expects decline. Nevertheless, their heritage is significant. Their ancestors were the first in England to stand for complete liberty of conscience. These Baptists displayed a deep love for self-government. They developed a zeal and enthusiasm for evangelism and missions both at home and abroad. Standing on the authority of the Scriptures, practicing congregational polity and associational cooperation, and holding to confessionalism in theology, British Baptists exerted a strong influence upon other Baptists, and upon sectarian developments wherever they found themselves.

The Heritage of Baptists in America

In America, Baptists were few, scattered, and showed little promise until the arrival of the Great Awakening. Most Baptists established themselves in the North with far less settling in the middle and southern colonies. Most Baptists came from a British background. Yet they must not be regarded as an extension of England. Baptists in America held a considerable variety of beliefs. These included General, Particular, Seventh Day, Six Principle, and Free Will Baptists, among others. They eventually formed along a sociological fault into Regular and Separate Baptists. This section highlights significant personalities, places, and events that led to the rise of Southern Baptists.[30]

Roger Williams and John Clarke

The origin of Baptists in America is traced to Roger Williams, an English Separatist who came to Boston in 1631. He found the Congregational Puritans of Massachusetts Bay no more tolerant than the Anglicans in England. In 1636, after being banished from the colony, Williams founded a settlement at what is now Providence, Rhode Island, on Narragansett Bay. In 1639, Williams led a group of dissenters in organizing at Providence the first Baptist church in America. He remained a Baptist for only a few months before becoming a "Seeker." Yet he had an enormous influence upon Baptists because of his devotion to religious liberty and by his establishment of a place (Rhode Island) in which the Baptist witness could exist free from persecution.[31] A second Baptist church was founded by John Clarke at Newport, Rhode Island, in 1644. The church was second in date (after Williams), but first in devotion to Baptist principles. Many contemporary historians consider Clarke—not Williams—as the true founder of Baptists in America.[32]

Persecution

Baptists were victims of persecution in New England during the middle of the seventeenth century. Obadiah Holmes, for example, was publicly whipped for conducting services in Lynn, Massachusetts, an event described in Clarke's *III Newes from New England*. Henry Dunster, who served as president of Harvard for twelve years, was forced to resign in 1653 after becoming convinced that baptism was for believers and not infants. However, Baptists continued to experience a gradual growth. John Myles, founder of the first Baptist church in Wales, immigrated to America in 1663 and organized a church in Rehoboth. In 1665, Thomas Gould established the first Baptist church in Boston. In Kittery, Maine, on the Piscataqua River, William Screven established a Baptist church in 1682. This congregation resettled in Charleston, South Carolina, in 1696. Nevertheless, by 1700 only ten churches, with no more than 300 total members, could be found in New England. The majority of these members were General Baptists.

Middle Colonies

The Middle Colonies became the major center for Baptist growth during the colonial period. In the late-seventeenth and early-eighteenth centuries, several churches were established in the vicinity of Philadelphia. The Pennepek Church was founded in 1688 by Elias Keach, the son of Benjamin Keach, the well-known London pastor who introduced the practice of congregational hymn singing. Out of this church came several others in New Jersey and Pennsylvania. On July 27, 1707, five of these churches united to form the Philadelphia Association, the first Baptist association in America. In 1742, the association adopted, with a few revisions, the 1689 version of the Second London Confession of Particular Baptists. This identification with Calvinistic theology gave direction to American Baptists theologically.[33]

Morgan Edwards, pastor of the Philadelphia Church, was one of the most important ministers of the association. He was the first historian of Baptists in America. He visited Baptist churches from New Hampshire to Georgia and compiled and published four volumes of a projected twelve-volume history of Baptists in America. He also proposed a national organization and suggested the establishment of Rhode Island College (1764), the first Baptist college in America.[34]

Prior to the Great Awakening most Baptists resided in the North. Some scattered congregations existed in Virginia and the Carolinas and possibly after 1733 in Georgia. The most important church in the South was the congregation which emigrated under the leadership of William

Screven from Kittery, Maine, to Charleston, South Carolina, in 1696. This church became one of the key churches in the Southern Baptist Convention after its establishment in 1845.

Great Awakening

Baptist growth was generally slow in the colonies until the Great Awakening. This movement began in the Middle Colonies about 1726 with the preaching of Theodore Frelinghuysen, a Dutch Reformed minister, and Gilbert Tennent, a Presbyterian minister. The arrival of George Whitefield, the English evangelist who was a leader of the Wesleyan revival, resulted in a high tide of revival in the Middle Colonies. The revival spread to New England through the preaching of Jonathan Edwards, pastor of the Congregational church at Northampton, Massachusetts, and America's first important theologian.

The peak of the New England revival was in 1740 and 1741. The revival also spread to the South, led by Samuel Davies, a Presbyterian, and Devereux Jarratt, a Methodist. The Great Awakening resulted in increased church membership, in a strong interest in missions, education, social and humanitarian concerns, and in divisions among the Presbyterians and Congregationalists.[35]

"New Lights"

The division among the Congregationalists into the "Old Lights" and the "New Lights" (the evangelistic party) benefited the Baptists. Many of the New Lights became Separate Congregationalists, forming new congregations. Many of these churches, because of an emphasis on a regenerate membership, adopted believer's baptism and became Separate Baptists. One church, led by Shubal Stearns and his brother-in-law, Daniel Marshall, left Connecticut and eventually settled in 1755 in Sandy Creek, North Carolina. The church grew from sixteen to 606 members in a short time.

During the next seventeen years, forty-two other Separate Baptist churches and 125 preachers found their roots in the Sandy Creek congregation. In 1758, the Sandy Creek Association was established with churches in North Carolina, South Carolina, and Virginia. Many of the Separate churches would become a part of the Southern Baptist Convention, bringing with them an unparalleled evangelistic fervor.[36]

Religious Liberty

Between the American Revolution and the establishment of the first national Baptist organization in 1814, Baptists were characterized by their struggle for religious liberty and by incessant evangelism. As the new nation arose, Baptists demanded religious freedom. The struggle for such freedom was fought on two levels, state and national. On the state level, one of the major struggles was fought in Virginia where the Episcopal Church was established. Through the efforts of John Leland, the leading Baptist advocate for religious freedom, and James Madison and Thomas Jefferson, disestablishment finally arrived in 1797.[37]

The other major struggle on the state level came in Massachusetts. Isaac Backus, an evangelist and historian, was the key figure. In 1772, he became the agent for the Warren Association to promote religious liberty. In 1774, Backus presented Baptist grievances to the Continental Congress. For more than a decade, he called for religious freedom through pamphlets, newspapers, sermons, and petitions. He published *History of New England*, which was actually a polemic against religious intolerance and a plea for liberty. Backus died before Congregationalism was disestablished in 1833, but he is chiefly responsible for laying the ax to the roots.[38]

On the national level, Baptists led a sectarian group calling for guarantees for religious freedom. They were the only prominent sect not represented at the Constitutional Convention. Still, Backus was sent to Philadelphia to request constitutional guarantees for religious freedom. Furthermore, Leland exerted a strong influence on James Madison, who became the principal author of the Bill of Rights. The First Amendment to the Constitution of the United States (1791) holds a strong Baptist ring to it as it begins with the statement "Congress shall make no law respecting an establishment of religion, or prohibiting the free exercise thereof." Future struggles would involve the preservation of the ideals stated therein.

Frontier Evangelism

The period from 1776 to 1814 was also a time of increased evangelism. Baptists, including some entire congregations, began to migrate beyond the Alleghenies. They were well-suited for the frontier. Their democratic polity allowed them to form churches without hierarchical red tape. Their ministers, whose only requirement was a call from God, were a part of the people. They were farmers or artisans during the week and preachers on Sunday. Baptist doctrine, which had developed into a moderate Calvinism, was highly appealing to the frontier. As a result, Baptists experienced excellent growth.

The Second Awakening appeared during the latter part of the eighteenth and early nineteenth centuries. Along the Atlantic seaboard the revival was less emotional, but in Kentucky and Tennessee it was spectacular. The protracted camp meeting was the major technique used on the frontier. Methodists, Presbyterians, and Baptists benefited greatly from the awakening. Baptists saw outstanding growth in the number of churches and members, and the movement spread to Mississippi (as early as 1780), Alabama (1808), Louisiana (1812), Arkansas (1818), Florida (1821), Texas (1830), and Missouri (1840). In 1776, there were approximately ten thousand Baptists in America. That number grew to one hundred thousand by 1800, and eight hundred thousand by 1848.[39] Baptists were well on their way to becoming a significant religious force in the United States and its territories.

The Triennial Convention and the American Baptist Home Mission Society

In 1814, Baptists in the United States organized for the first time on a national level. The reason was the rise of the modern mission movement. The story of the conversions of Adoniram and Ann Judson and Luther Rice from Congregationalism to the Baptist faith is well known. Traveling in 1812 to India, the Judsons became convinced of the Baptist position on baptism. After arriving in India, they were immersed by William Ward, the English Baptist missionary. Judson subsequently convinced Rice upon his arrival, and he too became a Baptist.[40]

Rice returned to the United States to challenge the Baptists of America to unite in the cause of world missions. In 1814, the General Missionary Convention of the Baptist Denomination in the United States for Foreign Missions was founded. Since it met every three years, it was called the Triennial Convention. A managing board was appointed to conduct the business of this first national organization of Baptists. Eventually, the American Baptist Home Mission Society was formed (1832). During this time, several state conventions were formed by Baptists in the South which quite early supported mission causes.

Among these were South Carolina (1821), Georgia (1822), and Alabama (1823).

Many Baptists west of the Alleghenies did not support the missions cause, and a movement known as "anti-missions" developed. John Taylor, Daniel Parker, and Alexander Campbell were leaders of this movement. There were several reasons for the rise of anti-missionism. They included ministerial jealousy, suspicion of missionary organizations, the issue of money, and the hyper–Calvinistic theology of many of the adherents of the movement. Yet despite a loss in their ranks, Baptists came out of this conflict more committed than ever to the mission cause.[41]

A larger problem, however, loomed on the horizon. The slavery issue was rapidly becoming a divisive factor for both the denomination and the nation. Over this issue Baptists would divide, and the Southern Baptist Convention would come into existence.

The Rise and Development of Southern Baptists

In 1845, Baptists of the South established the Southern Baptist Convention. Several reasons for the division between Baptists of the North and the South have been proffered. Baptists of the North favored a society approach, or a decentralized approach, in which individual societies were preferred over one denominational convention. Baptists of the South favored a more centralized approach, which was adopted in 1845. A second issue dividing the Baptists was the neglect of home mission work in the South and Southwest by the American Baptist Home Mission Society. It is unlikely, however, that either of these two issues would have necessitated a division.

Slavery

Slavery was the primary issue that divided Baptists.[42] Not all Baptists in the South justified slavery, but as cotton became more profitable and the base of the southern economy, and as the attacks of the abolitionists became more severe, Baptists began to polarize sectionally. The boards of both the Triennial Convention and the American Baptist Home Mission Society attempted to remain neutral on the slavery question. In 1844, however, the boards of both groups violated this principle, and a call for a new convention was issued by the Virginia Foreign Mission Society.

On May 8, 1845, at Augusta, Georgia, the Southern Baptist Convention was organized.[43] William B. Johnson was chosen president. Two boards were established—the Board of Domestic Missions at Marion, Alabama, and the Foreign Mission Board at Richmond, Virginia. Discussion of the development and ministry of all of the boards and the commissions of the convention will be presented in Chapter 2.

Baptist Traditions

What background and traditions characterized this new group of Baptists? Walter Shurden proposed four distinct traditions among Baptists of the South that blended together in the eighteenth and nineteenth centuries. They are the Charleston tradition, Sandy Creek tradition, Georgia tradition, and Tennessee tradition.[44] This section will briefly describe these traditions, along with an update from Leon McBeth, and later developments.

CHARLESTON TRADITION—ORDER

The Charleston tradition, which arose from the influential First Baptist Church of Charleston and from the Charleston Association (founded in 1751), was characterized by "order." Theological order was provided by adoption by the association in 1767 of the Philadelphia Confession of Faith, which instilled a Calvinistic perspective in Baptists in the South. Adoption of "A Summary of Church Discipline" by the association provided ecclesiological order. The independence of the local church was protected, but cooperation in associational life was encouraged. Worship was orderly and stately and, while warmly evangelistic, had the purpose of praising God rather than entertaining people. Ministerial order was developed through the establishment by the association of the first educational fund by a group of Baptists in America. Baptist colleges, such as Furman, Georgetown, Richmond, Wake Forest, and Mississippi College, as well as the establishment of Southern Seminary in 1859, were a result of this pro-educational concern.

SANDY CREEK TRADITION—ARDOR

Shurden describes the Sandy Creek tradition by the word "ardor." Separate Baptist ardor was expressed by revivalism in worship. The

1. *A Historical Heritage*

Separate Baptists' primary concern in worship was to lead sinners to an emotionally identifiable experience with Jesus. Their ministry was charismatic, in other words, called of God and primarily uneducated. Ecclesiologically, they formed associations, but local church autonomy was vigorously protected, a practice which may have provided roots for later Landmarkism. Their theology was biblicistic. As a result they were ardently opposed to confessional statements. Their unsystematic theology was probably a cross between Calvinism's sovereignty of God and Arminianism's free will of mankind. Beginning in North Carolina in 1777 and carrying over into the early nineteenth century, unions between the Charlestonian Baptists and the Separate Baptists occurred. From these unions the roots of the Southern Baptist Convention can be observed.

Georgia Tradition—Local Color

The Georgia tradition of "local color" was characterized by two locales and two persons. The first was Augusta and William B. Johnson, first president of the Southern Baptist Convention. The second was Atlanta and Isaac Taylor Tichenor, the corresponding secretary of the Home Mission Board, who overcame difficult days to create a denominational consciousness. The Augusta meeting that established the convention in 1845 was an expression of sectionalism over the issue of slavery. This heritage colored Southern Baptists not only racially, but more generally regionally. The organization of the convention was colored by cooperative denominationalism which was more connectional, more centralized, and more cooperative than any previous Baptist efforts. The model was held together not by theological uniformity, but by a cooperative effort to propagate the gospel.

Tichenor was the person primarily responsible for intensifying sectionalism and denominationalism. In 1882, he became executive secretary of the Home Mission Board, which was then moved to Atlanta, Georgia. He broke southern support for the Baptists' northern society for home missions by appealing to sectionalism. Doing this saved the Home Mission Board and probably the convention. He also persuaded Southern Baptists to work through the denominational board rather than the state convention boards, whose powers had been expanding.[45]

Tennessee Tradition—Successionism

The Tennessee tradition centered around the figure of J.R. Graves and the movement of Landmarkism. Holding to Baptist successionism and the view that Baptist churches, ministers, and ordinances were the only valid ones that God ordained, Graves and fellow Landmarkists gave Southern Baptists a long historical heritage based on unproven assumptions. Baptists felt good about themselves, especially in their polemical debates with the Campbellites, the Methodists, and the Presbyterians. Landmarkism helped build Southern Baptist loyalty and "put iron into the Baptist bloodstream."[46] At the same time, the anti-ecumenical attitude of Southern Baptists and most of their sectarianism are rooted in the Landmarkist tradition.[47]

The conclusion is that out of these four traditions emerged Southern Baptists. From Charleston came leadership and stability, a churchly tradition. Sandy Creek provided a love for freedom and an evangelistic fervor. A cultural identity of "Southerness" and a denominational identity came from the Georgia tradition. The ecclesiological identity of the Landmark tradition, even though it was expressed by a narrow sectarianism, gave Southern Baptists a sense of pride in the nineteenth century.

Texas Tradition—Conservatism, Evangelism, and Independence

Leon McBeth suggested a fifth tradition to be added to Shurden's list.[48] He called it the "Texas Tradition" or the "Southwest Tradition." It arose in the nineteenth century and continued into the twentieth century. Intense conservativism is one feature of the tradition, based upon the views of early pioneers in Texas, such as Z.N. Morrell, Daniel Parker, and R.E.B. Taylor, and perpetuated by B.H. Carroll, first president of Southwestern Seminary. Fervent evangelism was the result of leaders like L.R. Scarborough, second president of Southwestern Seminary.

McBeth also mentioned the spirit of independence among Texas Baptists. He added that controversy in the last two decades of the twentieth century was led by two Texas Baptists, Paige Patterson and Paul Pressler. Precedent was found in controversy that centered around J. Frank Norris, fundamentalist pastor of First Baptist, Fort Worth, in the 1920s. This Controversy will be examined in Chapter 3.

Twentieth-Century Developments

Shurden moreover identified several developments in the first half of the twentieth century which contributed to the Southern Baptist synthesis. The denominational structure which was more centralized and more cooperative was important. The Home Mission Board and the

Foreign Mission Board both were unifying factors. Baptist colleges and five new Baptist seminaries were very significant. The Woman's Missionary Union, which was organized in 1888, increased mission awareness enormously among the churches. The Sunday School Board (1891) did more to educate and unify Southern Baptists than any other agency. The establishment of the Executive Committee (1917), the institution of the Cooperative Program (1925), and the adoption of the first Baptist Faith and Message contributed to the denominational synthesis that held Southern Baptists together for much of the twentieth century.[49]

Challenges and Crises

Perhaps the best way to trace the history of the Southern Baptist Convention from its origin is to examine the challenges and crises facing the denomination and its responses to these. Institutional and organizational development is also important. This will be addressed in Chapter 2. Therefore, it will be mentioned only briefly in this section.

CIVIL WAR

The first major challenge to the new convention arose from the Civil War and its consequential effects.[50] The war disrupted all of the programs of the convention. The Foreign Mission Board faced the obstacles of communicating with its missionaries in China and Africa and the solicitation and distributing of funds to those missionaries. Richard Fuller, president of the convention, eventually arranged for funds to be sent by flag of truce to Baltimore, from where they were forwarded to the missionaries. The work of the Board of Domestic Missions was devastated by the war and was limited primarily to religious work among the Confederate soldiers.

Reconstruction (1865–1877) hampered the numerical strength of Southern Baptists. The establishment of the new state of West Virginia in 1863 resulted in the eventual loss of about 15,000 members and 249 churches from the General Association of Virginia. Perhaps as many as 400,000 African American Baptists left white churches to form their own congregations. Nevertheless, the Southern Baptist Convention made substantial numerical progress during this period. The northern Baptists made overtures toward reunion, but these overtures were rejected by both the southern state organizations and the Southern Baptist Convention. A major problem facing the Board of Domestic

Missions after the war was rivalry with the northern American Baptist Home Mission Society, which by 1867 had almost 100 missionaries in twelve southern states. It was not until the Tichenor's administration that comity agreements were worked out with the northerners which helped to assuage the rivalry between the two groups.

LANDMARKISM

A major crisis of the nineteenth century was the rising influence of Landmarkism upon the convention. Landmarkism, with its firm commitment to the authority of the local church, posed a major threat to the "board method" of missions of the convention on three different occasions. In 1859, at the convention's session in Richmond, Virginia, J.R. Graves claimed that churches and associations, not boards, should select, appoint, and support foreign missionaries. After a full day's debate, the board approach finally won out.

The issue resurfaced between 1885 and 1893 in the "Gospel Missions" movement, which was led by T.P. Crawford, a former missionary to China. Once again the convention's approach to foreign mission work was supported, but a number of missionaries followed Crawford and engaged in independent work. Finally, a split came in 1905 when Ben Bogard helped establish the Baptist General Association in Texarkana, Arkansas. The group was thoroughly Landmarkist, emphasizing the local church and rejecting the board method of missions. In 1924, the organization changed its name to the American Baptist Association.

Although distinct Landmark churches and denominations exist, a Landmark influence is still present today in the Southern Baptist Convention. Many Southern Baptists continue to emphasize the local and visible nature of the church, a successionist view of Baptist origins, and a negative attitude toward ministers of other denominations. In terms of the ordinances, a rejection of "alien immersion" (immersion in a non–Baptist church by a non–Baptist minister) and the practice of "close" or as some call it "'closed' communion" (the policy of admitting to the Lord's Supper only members of the local Baptist church) is also noticeable.[51]

SUNDAY SCHOOL BOARD

One of the most significant developments in the nineteenth century for Southern Baptists was the establishment of a permanent publication board in 1891. An earlier Sunday School Board existed from 1863 to 1873, but financial difficulties necessitated its consolidation with the domestic mission work. A year later the name "Home Mission Board" was adopted. Furthermore, Southern Baptists continued to contribute to and use literature published by the American Baptist Publication and Sunday School Society (established in 1824 as the Baptist General Tract Society). This situation resulted in resistance from many Southern Baptists to proposals in the 1880s for a separate Southern Baptist publication board.

Finally, and primarily through the efforts of Virginia Baptist James M. Frost, the convention established in 1891 the Sunday School Board at Nashville, Tennessee. No institution has been more significant in unifying the convention. Through its common literature, high standards, evangelistic emphasis, and promotion and financing of numerous ministries, the board has been a powerful force in fostering denominational unity in the rapidly expanding Southern Baptist Convention.[52]

EXPANSION

The convention experienced extensive geographical expansion during the twentieth century and into the twenty-first century. Forty-one state conventions are now affiliated with the SBC, and over forty-seven thousand churches are now found in all fifty states. This expansion resulted in a change from a sectional or southern identity to a national perspective. The consequence is a creative tension for the convention because of an influx of people with different outlooks and backgrounds. Ethnic minorities, northerners, and westerners have brought a cultural diversity to which the convention had to respond.[53]

FINANCIAL CRISES

The convention also experienced financial difficulties in the twentieth century. In 1919, the $75 Million Campaign was launched and by May 1920, more than $92 million had been pledged. A severe depression hit in the last half of 1920, and Southern Baptists found themselves with expanded programs based on promised funds that were never received. The result was staggering debt that by 1926 was approximately $6.5 million. This was followed by the embezzlement from the Home Mission Board of $909,461 by Clinton S. Carnes, treasurer for almost a decade, and the embezzlement of $103,000 from the Foreign Mission Board by George N. Sanders. However, through the leadership of Charles E. Maddry of the Foreign Mission Board, J.B. Lawrence of the Home Mission

Board, and the work of the Executive Committee, Southern Baptists survived the depression and completely paid all the convention's debts by 1943.[54]

THEOLOGICAL CONTROVERSIES AND OTHER CONCERNS

The convention also engaged in several theological controversies in the twentieth century. Southern Baptists were not as severely affected as other denominations by the liberal-fundamentalist controversy at the turn of the century. The most noted agitator was the fundamentalist, J. Frank Norris of Fort Worth, Texas. He attacked numerous Southern Baptist programs, institutions, and personalities before being expelled by the Baptist General Convention of Texas in 1923 and 1924. The issue of evolution was discussed by the convention for several years beginning in 1922. Out of this concern came the adoption in 1925 of the Baptist Faith and Message as a confessional statement.

Another controversy arose in the 1960s with the publication by Broadman Press of *The Message of Genesis* by Ralph H. Elliott of Midwestern Baptist Theological Seminary. This resulted in the eventual firing of Elliott for insubordination when he sought a new publisher, in suspicion of the seminaries, and in the revision and adoption by the convention in 1963 of The Baptist Faith and Message. The Sunday School Board's publication of the *Broadman Bible Commentary*, especially the first volume in October 1969, resulted in additional controversy. The commentary was withdrawn, and Clyde T. Francisco replaced G. Henton Davies as author of the Genesis commentary. Then in the last two decades of the twentieth century, the controversy over theology continued with the politicization of many aspects of convention life. This controversy has been called the Moderate-Conservative Controversy and the Inerrancy Controversy.[55]

Other controversies have arisen in the convention over social concerns and issues arising from church and state relations. The latter resulted in the establishment in 1939 of a standing committee that worked with eight other Baptist denominations through the Baptist Joint Committee on Public Affairs. The BJCPA researches church-state issues, represents affiliated Baptists in Washington, D. C., and publishes information on current public issues.[56] The BJCPA was defunded by the Southern Baptist Convention in 1991 after more than fifty years of support. Religious liberty issues were revamped as part of the Ethics and Religious Liberty Committee.

In the latter years of the twentieth century and into the twenty-first century, the denomination was characterized by several trends. Controversy arose at both the state and national levels over the teaching of religion in the colleges, universities, and seminaries. The major issue focused on the question of the Bible, especially as it appeared in the original manuscripts. This debate resulted in the surfacing of a new tradition in the convention in terms of the New Evangelicalism which cut across denominational lines, especially through the influence of the "electronic church." It also expressed itself in organized political involvement, much of which seemed to be inconsistent with previous Baptist positions on church and state issues. Other controversies and challenges facing Southern Baptists include the role of women in ministry, the rise of ethnic Southern Baptists, gifts of the Holy Spirit, and the inroads of Calvinism.

Conclusion

Despite controversies and tensions throughout its history, the denomination continued to expand. It became the largest non–Catholic denomination in the United States. Its commitment to evangelism and missions; to education at the church, college/university, and seminary levels; and to an aggressive publishing ministry enabled the denomination to respond effectively in a changing world. Visible expressions of denominational concerns would be the strengthening and establishment of Southern Baptist agencies, state conventions, and church and associational programs (Chapter 2). At the same time, growth and success would threaten the diversity of the denomination and its unity as the twentieth century came to a close (Chapter 3).

Discussion Questions

1. List the four major theories of Baptist origins. Which theory of Baptist origins sounds best to you? Why? Is it important to you to know how Baptists began? Defend your answer.
2. What difference does it make that Baptists can claim both Reformed (Particular) and Arminian (General) roots? Which group do you identify with the most? Why?

3. State briefly the contribution of each of the developments of English Baptists: associationalism, confessionalism, religious liberty, revivalism, missions, and social reform. Rate in order of importance to you and a brief reason for your choices.

4. In the section on the Heritage of Baptists in America, write a brief paragraph on the importance of the following individuals and movements:
   • Roger Williams
   • John Clarke
   • Pennepek Church and Elias Keach
   • Shubal Stearns, Daniel Marshall, and the Sandy Creek Church
   • Isaac Backus

5. In light of what you have read about Baptist beginnings in England and America, why do you think the Baptists were so successful on the American frontier during the Second Awakening?

6. Why do you think Baptists who stressed the importance of the local church developed cooperative organizations for missions and ministries?

7. Why and how did Baptists reflect their culture over the issue of slavery? How does this teach contemporary Baptists about the influence of twenty-first-century culture upon who they are today?

8. Walter Shurden lists four traditions and Leon McBeth adds a fifth that shaped the development of Southern Baptists. How many of these can you see in your own Baptist identity? Do any stand out more than the others? What do these traditions tell you about the impact of diversity upon Southern Baptists?

9. What twentieth-century developments stand out to you in shaping the Southern Baptist synthesis described by Shurden? Are there new developments in Southern Baptist life in recent years that have resulted in a different emphasis in identifying who Southern Baptists are?

10. In reviewing the Challenges and Crises of Southern Baptists at the end of this chapter do you see any continued carryover in contemporary Southern Baptists on each one: the Civil War and slavery, Landmarkism and local church influence, Sunday School Board and publishing expansion and financial crises or challenges, and theological controversies? Using your prophetic skills, do you see any crises that Southern Baptists may be facing in the near future?

⇛ 2 ⇚

An Ecclesiological Heritage
Agencies, Institutions,
and Denominational Structure

Any attempt to describe and define the people called Southern Baptists requires an examination not only of historical heritage (Chapter 1) but of ecclesiological heritage as well. An awareness and understanding of the practical and functional nature of Southern Baptists is essential if an accurate and complete description is to be presented.

Southern Baptists from the level of the local congregation to that of the national convention have been an activistic people known for the practical application of their faith. At the center of all associational cooperation by Southern Baptists is a commitment to the mission of proclaiming the gospel of Jesus Christ from the local level to the world scene that people might accept the truth of its message and live their lives in accord with its consequent demands. In fact, the primary unifying force that binds together the diverse people and churches identified as Southern Baptists may not be their common history or a consensus of theological beliefs. Rather, Southern Baptists have sought and do seek union primarily through spirit and organization in order to carry out the command of Jesus given to his disciples in the Great Commission: "Go therefore and make disciples of all nations, baptizing them in the name of the Father and of the Son and of the Holy Spirit, teaching them to observe all that I have commanded you. And behold, I am with you always, to the end of the age" (Matt. 28:19–20 ESV).[1]

With this imperative in mind, this chapter will examine the priesthood of believers, the nature and function of the local church, the area association, the state convention, and the Southern Baptist Convention.

An overview of the history and function of the Southern Baptist Convention's boards, commissions, institutions, and affiliated organizations prior to the major restructuring adopted around 1995–1997 will follow. Finally, concluding remarks will be offered concerning the contributions, influence, and future of Southern Baptists.

The Priesthood of Believers

Southern Baptists have traditionally held to a highly individualistic approach to religion. Each person stands before God with the choice of deciding whether to be in or out of fellowship with him. The priesthood of believers is one of the most important doctrines of Southern Baptists in relation to this emphasis on the individual Christian. Basically, this doctrine rests on the foundation that every Christian has direct access to God through Christ, who mediates for the believer. Thus, earthly priests in a professional sense are not necessary. Each believer has the privilege and responsibility to read and interpret the Scriptures under the guidance of the Holy Spirit, to pray directly to God through Jesus, to confess individual sins directly to God without any human mediator, and to express personal faith through ministry, worship, and theological understanding.[2]

One of the more important, yet most often neglected, responsibilities implied in the concept of the priesthood of believers is the duty of each Christian to serve as a priest in relation to others. Believers are to make intercession for others and pray for others. They are to express their priestly function through teaching, preaching, evangelism, and missions as they seek to confront and unite other people with God.

Each Christian is expected to exercise these priestly duties. Therefore, there is no distinction made between clergy and laity. Every believer is called to be a priest. From this perspective for Southern Baptists, the role of each believer functioning as a priest is not understood in the sacramental sense (where the rites such as baptism and the Lord's Supper convey the grace of God) nor the sacerdotal sense (where a professional priest is necessary to administer the sacraments) but in a functional sense. Each believer is a minister who has the practical task of serving as a mediator between God and others in order that all might know and share his love, grace, and blessings.

However, several Southern Baptists have challenged an overly individualistic nature that some attribute to this doctrine. In fact, the priesthood of believers became a significant issue of debate of the Conservative Resurgence (discussed in Chapter 3). James Leo Garrett, Jr., for example, observed that accenting the doctrine can lead to every individual Christian deciding his/her own authority in matters of belief and conduct. Priesthood, Garrett emphasized, is exercised as a part of God's called-out people. Individualism must give way to the needs of corporate Christian life.[3] Timothy George added that although the doctrine of the priesthood of believers forms a precious part of Reformation heritage and Baptist legacy, it must not be equated with modern individualism.[4]

The Controversy (see Chapter 3) swung the pendulum from an emphasis on soul competency to corporate responsibility.[5] Malcolm Yarnell divided Baptist understanding of the priesthood of believers into two categories—formative and fragmentary. Past representatives of the formative emphasis include John Smyth, Andrew Fuller, and Isaac Backus. For them, the priesthood of believers meant doing the kingly work of admonition, examination, excommunication, and absolution. The fragmentary heritage, on the other hand, is observable in the careers of Roger Williams, John Leland, and Francis Wayland. These Baptists stressed free will, the conscience, and personal unmediated access to God.[6]

In a nutshell, some Baptists emphasized individual freedom over pastoral authority while others elevated pastoral authority over individual freedom. Thus, a tension and balance should be part of the understanding of this doctrine. Walter Shurden noted two dual motifs at work in the priesthood of believers—freedom-responsibility and individual-community. "The priesthood of believers is a two-handed doctrine, and distortion results from a one-handed approach."[7] Both ideas, therefore, should be emphasized—individual freedom and corporate responsibility.

The Local Southern Baptist Church

The concept of the priesthood of believers finds its initial corporate expression in the fellowship of the local church, the basic unit of all Baptist life and ministry. Southern Baptists consistently believe that it was the intention of Jesus to establish the church in order to continue his redemptive mission and ministry on earth. Other functions of the church found in the New Testament include worship, Christian fellowship, the proclamation of and witness to the gospel, and the education and nurturing of believers.

The Greek word *ekklesia*, which is usually translated "church," is used over one hundred times in the New Testament. Even though it is used in some instances in a general sense for the redeemed of all ages, *ekklesia* is normally reserved to describe a particular local congregation. Southern Baptists, while recognizing the general nature of the church, have traditionally placed their greatest emphasis on the local church. This emphasis can be traced to our English Baptist heritage and was accentuated by the influence of Landmarkism. The local congregation, as an independent and self-governing body under the Lordship of Jesus Christ, is the highest human, corporate authority in Baptist life. Although Southern Baptist churches unite together in local, state, and national associations, the local congregation ideally never relinquishes its authority to any of these bodies.[8]

The local Southern Baptist church can be characterized in two ways. First, the church is a spiritual fellowship of redeemed persons. It is the body of Christ, composed of baptized believers who voluntarily unite together through mutual faith in obedience and allegiance to Jesus Christ and his will and purpose. Second, the church is a functioning institution, ordained of God to proclaim his message of redemption and its ethical implications for humanity. The local congregation organizes with the election of officers, and by the development of programs and plans in order to effectively and efficiently fulfill its spiritual imperatives.[9]

As such, the typical Southern Baptist church is characterized by a practical commitment to mission and ministry. The local Southern Baptist church, of which there are over 47,000,[10] has among its responsibilities the task of fulfilling the Great Commission in the community where it is located. This task includes ministry to the believers through opportunities for worship, education, nurture, fellowship, and service. The task also includes witness to and proclamation of the gospel to the lost in the community; social, benevolent, and ethical ministries that flow out of the imperatives of the gospel at the local level; and a commitment to participate with other Southern Baptist churches in cooperative missions and ministries.

Southern Baptist Associations

The oldest Baptist organization beyond the local church is the association.[11] Baptists cherished their independence yet soon realized the value of interdependence. Baptists in England began to cooperate together during the mid–1600s. In the 1700s, Baptists in America formed associations in Pennsylvania, Rhode Island, Virginia, and North and South Carolina. At the close of the twentieth century, there were over 1,200 Southern Baptist associations.[12] These associations are composed of messengers elected by cooperating churches to attend annual meetings and to participate in the business of the association. Because messengers are not official delegates of the churches, the churches do not exercise control over the association nor does the association have authority over the churches.

Associations began many ministries, such as hospitals, children's homes, and schools, which were not conducted by state conventions. Evangelism and missions were included among the early important functions of the associations. This included ministries to Native Americans and African Americans, the sending of preachers into frontier regions, and the distribution of Bibles. On the contemporary scene, the association serves as promoter of denominational agencies and programs. It also provides a means of communication between the local congregation and the denomination. In all of these aforementioned capacities, the area association is a vital link in the practical enterprise of Southern Baptists.[13]

Associations, however, have undergone changes in their traditional roles. A recent noticeable trend is the merging of associations. In the Northwest Baptist Convention, for example, seventeen associations were reconfigured into five regions.[14] This is one reason the SBC has witnessed a reduction of 1,200 associations in 2000 down to 1,126.[15] Ed Stetzer explained that associations are being challenged to clarify their roles. Many SBC churches maintain multiple layers of partnerships. As they network, they often choose what to support and focus upon. Associations must also become involved in those networks and partnerships. "In some ways," Stetzer claims, "networks are replacing associations."[16] Thus, the role of associations is changing and must be ready to change. Nevertheless, as Josh Ellis surmised, "Purposes may change, strategies may shift, populations will diversify, but associations that strive to fill relevant niches will not only endure, but thrive. There are reasons to believe the future is bright."[17]

Southern Baptist State Conventions

Southern Baptists practice their faith beyond the levels of the local church and the association through the programs of state conventions. South Carolina Baptists established in 1821 the first state convention in the South, which was followed in 1822 by Georgia Baptists.[18] By 2020, there were forty-one state conventions serving Southern Baptists.[19] The state convention, like the area association, operates on the Baptist principle of voluntary cooperation. It operates institutions and conducts programs and ministries which demand greater support than what can be provided by the local congregation or the area association.

Organizationally, state conventions are composed of elected messengers from cooperative churches who meet annually to evaluate past work and plan future action, and to elect officers, committees, boards of directors, and trustees. The state convention's ongoing work is then carried out by institutions, agencies, and the convention staff under the direction of an executive director-treasurer.

State conventions provide numerous services and ministries for its constituents. Through the Cooperative Program, a board of directors of the convention usually oversees a variety of programs, such as annuity and ministerial services, publication of a state paper, and Baptist student work on college and university campuses in respective states. State conventions often operate camps and assemblies for conferences.

Chaplaincy and retirement centers are concerned with the chaplaincy programs at numerous hospitals and medical centers and with retirement centers in some states. Child care is another ministry which helps children and families in crisis. Child care ministries often include group care, foster homes, adoptive care, counseling ministry, unwed mother care, and family aid service. State conventions cooperate with associations and provide assistance in church music, cooperative missions, evangelism, the Woman's Missionary Union, and religious education.

Some state conventions operate or support foundations, colleges and universities, and seminaries. Some conventions support a Baptist historical organization, as well as associational and area assemblies. Such provisions demonstrate that Southern Baptists on the state level are actively involved in ministering to churches, associations, and individuals and groups with special needs through organizations and personnel that evangelize, educate, care, inform, and lead in benevolent and mission enterprises.

The Southern Baptist Convention

The establishment and history of the Southern Baptist Convention demonstrates effectively the willingness and dedication of more than 14 million Southern Baptists in over 47,000 local and independent churches to cooperate and minister together to carry out the Great Commission. From its origin in 1845, the Southern Baptist Convention has been characterized primarily by a commitment to mission and ministry in the name of Jesus Christ. Its nature, purpose, and structure have consistently emphasized the practical and functional in scope, rather than ecclesiastical or theological.

At the organizational meeting of the Southern Baptist Convention held May 8–12, 1845, in Augusta, Georgia, it was stated that the convention was established "for the purpose of carrying into effect the benevolent intentions of our constituents, by organizing a plan for eliciting, combining and directing the energies of the whole denomination in one sacred effort, for the propagation of the gospel."[20] The purpose of the convention was Christian benevolence and the propagation of the gospel of Jesus Christ. Membership was based upon contributions.

The plan was to establish as many boards as necessary to carry out the purpose of the new convention. Requirements for service included membership in a regular cooperating church. Missionaries of the convention were to give evidence of genuine piety, zeal for the cause of Christ, and talents necessary to fulfill their calling.[21] Interestingly, no confessional statement was adopted. A statement by William B. Johnson, first president of the convention, reflects this position: "We have constructed for our basis no new creed; acting in this matter upon a Baptist aversion for all creeds but the Bible.... Our objects, then, are the extension of the Messiah's kingdom, and the glory of our God."[22]

In other words, Southern Baptists united around their commitment to mission and benevolent concerns, not rigid theological conformity. The convention's primary action was not the publication of a statement on Southern Baptist beliefs. It was the establishment of boards centering around benevolent service, the Foreign Mission Board, and the Board for Domestic Missions.[23] The unifying factor was voluntary cooperation for the cause of Christ. At the same time, full respect was constitutionally guaranteed for "the independence and equal rights of the Churches."[24] Obviously, the Southern Baptist Convention was founded by Christians who individually and corporately stood for freedom and independency of conscience, belief, and practice. Yet they voluntarily joined together to use their talents and resources to minister for the cause of the gospel of Jesus Christ.

Organizationally, the Southern Baptist Convention is composed of messengers from cooperating churches who meet annually each summer. Before 1931, messengers and voting were based on financial contributions. However, the rapid growth of the convention and its programs made it obvious that the loudest complaint or the largest church were first in line to receive what they wanted. At the 1931 annual meeting, E.C. Routh made a substitute motion that was adopted—one messenger per church plus one additional messenger for every $250 given up to three messengers. Later, that was changed to up to ten messengers. Then in 2014, it was changed to one additional messenger for each $6,000 the church contributes, up to twelve messengers. The convention messengers elect a president, two vice presidents, a recording secretary, and a registration secretary. The president presides at the following year's annual session, serves on the convention's Executive Committee, and is an ex-officio member on the convention's boards. The president, in consultation with the vice presidents, names the Committee on Resolutions and the Committee on Committees. The latter appoints the Committee on Boards, which nominates trustees to oversee the policy of each Southern Baptist Convention agency.

When the convention is not in session, the Executive Committee is authorized and commissioned to act for it.[25] This committee formulates recommendations concerning programs, budgets, and the coordination of the work of the boards, commissions, and institutions. Generally, it promotes and publicizes Southern Baptist work. Prior to the restructuring of the Southern Baptist Convention (1995–1997), there were four boards of the Convention: Home Mission Board, Foreign Mission Board, Sunday School Board, and Annuity Board. Seven commissions served Southern Baptists: Brotherhood Commission, Christian Life Commission, Education Commission, American Baptist Theological Seminary Commission, Historical Commission, Radio and Television Commission, and Stewardship Commission. The convention operates six seminaries: Southern

Baptist Theological Seminary, Southwestern Baptist Theological Seminary, New Orleans Baptist Theological Seminary, Golden Gate (now Gateway) Seminary, Southeastern Baptist Theological Seminary, and Midwestern Baptist Theological Seminary. The Southern Baptist Foundation was a separate organization which administered gifts and bequests to denominational causes. Southern Baptists through the Public Affairs Committee cooperated with eight other Baptist denominations through the Baptist Joint Committee on Public Affairs until 1991.

The Woman's Missionary Union is an auxiliary to the convention. It cooperates with the convention but is not controlled by it. Until 2004, Southern Baptists voluntarily worked and fellowshipped together with the Baptist World Alliance, which links together more than 47 million Baptists from 239 conventions and unions in 125 nations.[26] The above entities and their subsequent changes will be discussed below. With this general information as background, a more complete examination of the history and purpose of each Southern Baptist agency will be presented. In this chapter denominational agencies will be discussed historically and organizationally from their beginning until about 1997 or so, when the convention was restructured. After discussing the Controversy in Chapter 3, the subsequent restructuring and updates of the Southern Baptist Convention will be the topic of Chapter 4.

The Cooperative Program

Before reviewing the ministry and history of each Southern Baptist Convention agency, it is important to understand how the Convention's work is supported. In 1845, the work of the Board of Domestic Missions and the Foreign Mission Board was supported through contributions from churches, associations, state conventions, and individuals. Each board had to solicit funds. The Foreign Mission Board, for example, employed "agents" to provide information on its work and to seek financial contributions.

From 1919 to 1924, the convention conducted the $75 Million Campaign. This was an effort to raise contributions and pledges over a five-year period. Pledges totaled more than $92 million. But a depression and defalcations at the Home Mission Board and the Foreign Mission Board left the convention and its agencies in debt. Only $58 million was received, and budgets were based upon an anticipated $75 million. This resulted in a severe financial crisis.

The $75 Million Campaign, however, showed Southern Baptists what they could do when they cooperated and prioritized their giving. In 1925, the Cooperative Program was established to provide support for both the state conventions and the Southern Baptist Convention.[27] Through the Cooperative Program, churches send contributions to the state convention, which then forwards a designated percentage to the Southern Baptist Convention. The Executive Committee receives the funds and distributes the contributions to the agencies and institutions based upon percentages approved by the messengers to the convention in the previous year. Convention agencies and institutions are prohibited from making direct appeals but can count upon consistent support from the churches.[28]

The Home Mission Board

The Board of Domestic Missions was one of two boards established in 1845 and was located at Marion, Alabama, where it remained for thirty-seven years.[29] After J.L. Reynolds declined the position as corresponding secretary and Daniel P. Bestor resigned after serving only a few months, Russell Holman accepted the position. During the first year of the board's existence, six missionaries were employed: two in Texas and one each in Florida, Virginia, Alabama, and Louisiana. By the time of Holman's resignation in 1851, the board grew to fifty missionaries and averaged $ 1,000 per month in receipts. Its objectives were twofold: to assist weak churches in the South and the Southwest; and to provide the gospel where there were no churches.

Following Thomas F. Curtis's uneventful term as corresponding secretary (1852–1853), Joseph Walker held the position from 1853 to 1856. Work was begun among the Chinese in California. In addition, in 1855 the work of the American Indian Mission Association, with its liabilities of $12,000 and income of $6,000 was transferred to the board, which was renamed the Domestic and Indian Mission Board. Holman succeeded Walker and served a second term which ended in January 1862.

The period beginning with the Civil War and continuing until 1882 saw the near collapse of the board. The war led to a shortage of funds and a reduction of the number of missionaries, which declined from 159 in 1860 to 32 only three years later. During the administration of Martin T. Sumner (1862–1875), indebtedness continued to be a problem. Issues included a war-time economy, the loss of value of Confederate money, financial depression in the early 1870s, and the absorption of the work and indebtedness of the first Sunday School Board in 1873 by the board, whose name was changed to the Home Mission Board a year later. By the end of the administration of William H. McIntosh (1875–1882), funds reached the lowest level since the Civil War, and missionaries were serving in a total of eight states. The future of the board was in grave jeopardy.

Enter Isaac Taylor Tichenor. He served from 1882 to 1889 as secretary of the board, which was moved to Atlanta, Georgia. Tichenor steered every state organization in the South to cooperate with the board. This led the convention in the development of a denominational consciousness. Tichenor is credited with saving not only the struggling board but perhaps the Southern Baptist Convention as well.[30]

After the administrations of Franklin H. Kerfoot (1889–1901) and Fernando C. McConnell (1901–1903), Baron Dekalb Gray (1903–1928) was chosen as corresponding secretary. The board experienced sustained growth and expansion during Gray's administration. He led in the establishment of Southern Baptist Hospital and New Orleans Seminary, built a system of mountain schools, created various church building loan funds, and established a program of organized evangelism. However, a depression in the early 1920s led to heavy indebtedness because many of the pledges to the $75 Million Campaign were not paid. Furthermore, Clinton S. Carnes, the board's treasurer since 1919, was discovered in 1928 to have embezzled $909,461. The board was saved only through aggressive action by the Executive Committee of the convention, the reorganization of the board, and competent leadership by acting secretary Arch C. Cree.

Through the leadership of J.B. Lawrence (1929–1953), the financial crisis was overcome, and by 1943 all debts had been paid. Jesse Fletcher observed that under Lawrence, "the climb back was to be resolute if uneven."[31] Through the remainder of the administration of Lawrence and his successor, S. Courts Redford (1954–1965), expansion continued in new mission fields and programs. Redford oversaw missionary growth from 936 to 2,353.[32]

Arthur B. Rutledge served as secretary from 1965 to 1976. Twelve new programs were approved, and the board continued to expand the number of missionaries. Rutledge was remembered for his work with national Baptists, social ministries, and his progressive spirit in Civil Rights battles.[33] In 1977, William Tanner succeeded Rutledge. Tanner was in charge of the HMB when the Controversy erupted. He was a loyal denominationalist who grew frustrated by the rising division within the convention. He left the board in 1986 to become executive secretary of the Baptist General Convention of Oklahoma.[34]

Tanner was succeeded by Larry Lewis, but not without controversy. The original search committee was asked to resign and a new, more conservative search committee was installed.[35] Lewis was a stalwart conservative and was rewarded by fellow conservatives with his election as the new president of HMB. Yet Lewis attempted to steer the HMB away from political controversies. As president, he expanded on what Rutledge and Tanner stressed, particularly in ministry to African Americans and Hispanics. Moreover, he assisted churches in establishing crisis pregnancy centers.[36] By 1992, the HMB supported 1,825 missionaries among 102 ethnic groups, using 98 languages.[37] Lewis served from 1987 to 1997. By 1999, the full number of home missionaries of the board totaled over 4,800.[38]

The Foreign Mission Board

In 1845, the Foreign Mission Board was also established by the new convention and was located at Richmond, Virginia.[39] James B. Taylor was elected as the first corresponding secretary and served from 1846 to 1871. J. Lewis Shuck and I.J. Roberts, Triennial Convention missionaries, were appointed to China. The first two missionaries commissioned by the board were Samuel C. Clopton and George Pearcy, who also were appointed to China. A second field, Africa, was entered in 1850. It was not until 1870 that a third field, Italy, was established when William H. Cote, a minister and medical doctor, was charged with establishing a mission field in Europe.

During the administration of Taylor, several problems were faced and overcome. One was the securing, sending, and supporting of competent missionaries to foreign fields. I.J. Roberts, for example, proved to be an unwise missionary choice. "Agents" were appointed to make churches, associations, and state conventions aware of the board's program and to enlist support. The first agent was William B. Johnson, the first president of the Southern Baptist Convention. The anti-missions movement also made the young board's task difficult. Furthermore, a crisis occurred in 1859 at the annual convention when Landmarkists, led by J.R. Graves, claimed that churches and associations, not boards, should select, appoint, and support foreign missionaries. The board won by maintaining that the continuity of a mission and avoidance of duplication of effort could best be preserved through their approach. Finally, the Civil War and the federal naval blockade made it necessary for permission to be obtained from the Secretary of State in Washington, D. C., to forward funds under a flag of truce to Baltimore, from which they were forwarded to the mission field. Nevertheless, during Taylor's administration, more than $600,000 was raised and eighty-one missionaries were appointed.[40]

During the administration of Henry Allen Tupper (1872–1893), mission work was initiated in Mexico, Brazil, and Japan. Tupper promoted the work of women missionaries.[41] The work of the board was threatened in the late 1880s and early 1890s by the Gospel Missions Controversy which was led by T.P. Crawford. Gospel Missions was essentially an offshoot of the Landmark movement. It claimed that no schools should be conducted by the missions and that the missionaries should live in terms of housing, dress, and food like the people whom they served. Many missionaries became independent, and a Landmark association was eventually founded in 1905. It was also during Tupper's administration that the first Christmas offering was taken. This would be named in 1918 after Lottie Moon, a missionary to China whose appeal for help had resulted in the first offering.

During the administration of Robert Josiah Willingham (1893–1914), Argentina and Uruguay were entered as mission fields. Willingham traveled extensively on behalf of the FMB, and was known for his expressive challenges to Southern Baptists to bear the financial burdens of missions. The number of missionaries rose from 94 to 300 during his tenure. Willingham especially emphasized the building of educational institutions. Over $1,000,000 was raised for missions in the Judson Centennial Campaign.

J. Franklin Love served as secretary from 1915 to 1928. New fields were entered, bringing the total to 489 missionaries in fifteen countries. However, the crisis of the $75 Million Campaign severely hampered the work of the board, as did the embezzlement in 1927 of $103,772.38

by George N. Sanders, treasurer of the board. Love was succeeded by T.B. Ray, whose administration from 1928 to 1932 was characterized by retrenchment. Southern Baptists joined the rest of America in suffering through the Great Depression. No new mission fields were entered. Although eighty-two missionaries resigned and nine died, only twelve new missionaries were appointed.[42]

Charles E. Maddry served as executive secretary from 1933 to 1944. He led the board toward financial stability. Maddry's contributions instilled a new "faith, courage, vision, and hope" upon the Foreign Mission Board.[43] In 1938, publication of *The Commission* was launched. World War II hampered but did not defeat missionary work. Five hundred and two missionaries were under appointment at the time of his retirement. M. Theron Rankin, former teacher, dean, and president of Graves Theological Seminary in South China, and secretary for the Orient since 1935, succeeded Maddry in 1945. Rankin served through 1952. A total of 640 missionaries were appointed during his administration, raising the overall number to 913 missionaries in thirty-three countries. Rankin's major project was the Advance Program, which called for 1,750 missionaries and an annual budget of $10 million.

Baker James Cauthen (1954–1979), former missionary to China and secretary for the Orient, succeeded Rankin. Cauthen sought innovative ways to enhance the Advance Program initiated by Rankin. This included Jubilee Advance (1959–1964) and Bold Mission Thrust (1976–2000). In addition, short term missionary service was introduced as well as a new accent on volunteers. Cauthen's tenure was remarkable. The board expanded from 913 missionaries in thirty-three countries to 2,981 missionaries in ninety-four countries. Receipts leaped from $16 million to $70 million.[44]

R. Keith Parks, missionary to Indonesia and secretary of Southeast Asia, succeeded Cauthen in 1980. The momentum for Bold Mission Thrust was financially stymied once the Controversy started. In response to financial shortfalls, Parks reorganized the board for streamlining purposes. Parks was also remembered for his stress on the need for intercessory prayer, partnership missions, and the dedication of the Missionary Learning Center in Rockville, Virginia. However, the now majority of conservative trustees defunded the seminary in Rüschlikon, Switzerland, over charges of less than conservative theology and financial costs. Several European missionaries resigned in protest. Parks himself concluded that the trustees were not affirming his leadership.

He retired in 1992. The missionary force stood at 3,918, scattered in 126 countries.[45]

Career missionary Jerry Rankin became president in 1993. He initiated new directions toward World A with realignment in missionary deployment toward unreached people groups. By 1998, the board was supporting almost 4,000 missionaries who were working with 4.4 million Baptists in over 40,000 local churches.[46]

The primary purpose of the mission board is to be a means for Southern Baptists to confront all people of the world with the message of Jesus Christ. The missionaries of the board then seek to involve new converts in Christian growth and service as members of indigenous churches. The board also seeks to train national leaders for future self-supporting conventions. The missionaries engage in many types of work, such as evangelism and preaching; theological education; student and youth work; religious education; women's leadership training; music; home and church; elementary and secondary education; college and graduate teaching; adult education; medicine, dentistry, nursing, and paramedical professions; social ministries; business management; publications; and mass media.

The Foreign Mission Board customarily receives over 50 percent of the Cooperative Program funds sent to the convention. Of the $177 million that Southern Baptists channeled through the board in 1998, almost $77 million came through the Cooperative Program. Through such support the Southern Baptist Convention developed the largest and most productive mission enterprise of any American denomination in the twentieth century.

Baptist Sunday School Board

From the beginning of the Southern Baptist Convention in 1845, a division existed concerning the need for a publication organization.[47] Baptists of the South had been active in the establishment and operation of the Baptist Tract Society established in 1824, which later became the American Baptist Publication Society. It was not affected by the separation of Baptists in the North and South, and continued to draw much support from Southern Baptists.

Another force that made it difficult to form a publishing arm of the convention was J.R. Graves, the Landmarkist. In addition to his role as editor of the *Tennessee Baptist*, Graves organized a tract society and a publishing firm, and published Sunday School literature promoting his views. Moreover, limited finances caused many to draw back from entering the publication competition.

A resolution was proposed in 1846 by Thomas Starks of Georgia to appoint a committee to consider organizing a publication enterprise. However, the committee was unsuccessful in leading the convention to proceed in that direction. In 1847, some dissenting messengers organized the Southern Baptist Publication Society with headquarters in Charleston, South Carolina. Many Southern Baptist organizations began to use their materials. The society ceased publications by early 1864, primarily because of the Civil War.

In 1863, Basil Manly, Jr., and John A. Broadus led the convention to organize the first Sunday School Board. It published hymnals, catechisms, teachers' books, and question books. Under C.C. Bitting (1866–1869), the board published *Kind Words*, which became the forerunner of the Sunday School quarterly. In 1873, the board was consolidated with the Domestic and Indian Mission Board. During this time under the auspices of the Home Mission Board (renamed in 1874), the publication enterprise overcame financial difficulties and, led by I.T. Tichenor, began to show signs of vitality.[48]

In February 1890, James M. Frost, pastor of the Leigh Street Baptist Church in Richmond, Virginia, published an article in the *Religious Herald* proposing the establishment of a separate Sunday School Board. A committee was established at the 1890 convention which recommended in 1891 that a Sunday School Board be created. The report carried, and Nashville, Tennessee, was chosen as the location of the board. Among its tasks the board was authorized to publish and publicize the Sunday School series, to assume the Sunday School interests in the territory of the convention, and to aid mission Sunday Schools by providing literature and money. Frost was elected as the first corresponding secretary. He served less than two years but was successful in launching the enterprise on a firm financial footing.

Theodore R. Bell served as secretary from 1893 to 1896. Despite a severe financial situation, the board's receipts increased annually. During Bell's administration the foundations of Training Union began with the establishment in 1895 of the Baptist Young People's Union. It was initially an independent body.

After Bell's resignation following his purchase of the *Christian*

Index, Frost was selected as secretary for a second term (1896–1916). The number of church members enrolled in Sunday School grew from 38 percent to 65 percent during this time as the board provided leadership in developing a graded Sunday School, standards for measurement of quality, training for teachers, the integration of the program into denominational life, improved methodology for laymen, and better lessons. The BYPU made great strides, and new enterprises included the publication of books (the first being Charles E. Taylor's *The Story of Yates the Missionary* in 1879), Bible and tract distribution, establishment of the Home Department, plans for the establishment of a Baptist assembly in North Carolina (operation of Ridgecrest Baptist Assembly by the Sunday School Board began in 1929), assistance in church architecture, and a developing concern in student work.[49]

Before 1900, the Baptist Sunday School Board was strictly a publishing house. Bernard W. Spilman changed that when he aggressively started Sunday Schools in as many Southern Baptist churches as possible. Then Arthur Flake's influential book *Building a Standard Sunday School* (1922) was published. Before 1900, the Sunday School was also thought of strictly as a children's movement. Southern Baptists introduced the idea of age groups, including adults, and began to publish Sunday School literature for all ages, along with specialized literature and teacher training information.[50]

Isaac J. Van Ness served as corresponding secretary from 1917 to 1935. His administration was characterized by continual reorganization, financial stability, and steady growth. By 1919, five new departments had been organized: Editorial, Church Architecture, Organized Class, Baptist Young People's Union, and Missionary Publications. From 1919 to 1924, five additional departments were created: Elementary; Sunday School Administration; Survey, Statistics, and Information; Book Publishing; and Vacation Bible School. During this time Southern Baptists and the board experienced phenomenal growth in terms of membership in a variety of programs, receipts, and the publication, circulation, and quality of books. The board did not depend upon Cooperative Program funds and was able to provide assistance to the other agencies during the financial crisis of the $75 Million Campaign. From 1924 to 1928, three new departments were added: Intermediate, Church Administration, and Student Work. In 1930, the name Broadman Press, after John A. Broadus and Basil Manly, Jr., became the official imprint of the board's general book publishing. In the words of Robert Baker, "Any evaluation of Van Ness and his service to the denomination through the Board must be expressed in superlative language."[51]

T. Luther Holcomb was executive secretary from 1935 to 1953. Holcomb developed a highly successful Five-Year Campaign in which the district association would lead in promoting all phases of Sunday School and Training Union work. *The Broadman Hymnal* was published in 1940 and was edited by B.B. McKinney. He became secretary of the Department of Church Music, which was established in 1941. In 1950, plans were approved for the construction of Glorieta Baptist Assembly in New Mexico. In 1953, the Dargan-Carver Library resulted from the combination of the collections of the board and the Historical Commission, which was serving as "custodian" of the library of the Southern Baptist Historical Society. By the end of Holcomb's tenure, forty-four Baptist Book Stores were in operation. The Sunday School Board had become a "giant" in Southern Baptist life.[52]

James L. Sullivan was secretary from 1953 to 1975. During this time, more new programs were established, such as a Church Administration Department (1958) and a program for study and leadership relative to church-related vocations (1958). In 1962, the Church Recreation Service was given departmental status. The rapid growth of church music publishing was a highlight.[53] Sullivan led in a program to coordinate the work of the board within and with other convention agencies, to reorganize organizational structure, and to enlarge the board's physical properties. Among the many publishing enterprises during Sullivan's administration were the creation of the Life and Work Curriculum, the Broadman Readers Plan, and the *Broadman Bible Commentary*. Several problems developed, including a slowdown in enrollment gains of the church program organizations. There also appeared a decrease in circulation of church literature, and tax problems on board property and operations in Tennessee and New Mexico. Furthermore, it was during Sullivan's administration that conservatives began to flex their muscles. Broadman Press published Ralph Elliott's *The Message of Genesis* in 1961. Then in 1969, conservatives reacted to the Genesis volume of the *Broadman Bible Commentary*. Jerry Sutton declared that the Sunday School Board "was known as a bastion of moderate influence."[54]

Sullivan's leadership resulted in a smooth transition to the administration of Grady C. Cothen (1975–1983). Cothen gave priority to four areas: in-depth Bible study for the masses, equipping believers for the work of ministry, support and enrichment of family life, and aid and encouragement for pastors and church staff members.[55] Among significant developments during Cothen's term were *Centrifuge* (a week-long, fourteen-hour-day camping program; 1979), purchase of the Holman Bible Publishing Company (1979), and the establishment and funding at each of the six seminaries for a chair of religious education or denominational relations. It was during Cothen's service that the Conservative Resurgence began. Cothen recalled that during his tenure, "there were no serious theological incidents that caused national concern."[56] Yet conservatives grew unsatisfied with the traditional approach of unity within diversity. They perceived in the Sunday School Board more loyalty for moderate causes and resentment toward conservatives.

Lloyd Elder was elected to succeed Cothen beginning in 1984. He would become one of the first casualties of the Controversy. The turnover of trustees for the BSSB shifted to a conservative majority by 1988. Elder attempted his best to please the new trustees. He committed to publishing an inerrantist commentary series (New American Bible Commentary) as well as producing anti-abortion programs and materials. These actions were not enough. Elder's support of the Baptist Joint Committee on Public Affairs was part of the desire to have him fired. The catalyst that led to his forced resignation, however, was the attempted publication of Leon McBeth's centennial history of the Sunday School Board, titled *Celebrating Heritage and Hope*. Thus, the battle for control over the agency, which did more to shape the minds of Southern Baptists at the local church level than any other organization, had roots in the Elliott and the *Broadman Bible Commentary* controversies. It reached its climax with the opposition against Elder. Once again, a publication was a precipitating influence of the conflict. Trustees accused McBeth of a bias against the Conservative Resurgence and characterized the manuscript as unbalanced. McBeth defended his work as being consistent with his assignment to write an interpretive history. In August 1990, the board voted not to publish McBeth's book. Elder was blamed for the controversy and resigned at a special meeting of the trustees on January 17, 1991.[57]

Elder was succeeded by James E. "Jimmy" Draper. He would serve from 1991 to 2006. Draper laid out four dimensions to his new role, a vision that emphasizes the spiritual, business, organization, and people leadership. His restructuring focused on the needs of the church and people, improving product quality, and promoting greater flexibility. To accomplish this, downsizing was in order. More than 80 percent of employees that were eligible for retirement accepted it. The Baptist Book Store was overhauled. Broadman Press was redirected from being more of a vanity press to seeking out major authors.[58]

Annuity Board

Prior to the establishment in 1918 of the Relief and Annuity Board by the Southern Baptist Convention, provisions for the economic security of church vocational workers were made by the states. South Carolina (1813), Tennessee (late 1860s), Virginia (1872), and Maryland (1893) were among the early leaders in this ministry.[59]

Convention-wide interest was initiated in 1916 at a pastors' conference in Nashville. The key figure at this meeting was William Lunsford, pastor of the Edgefield Baptist church, Nashville, Tennessee. With tremendous passion, Lunsford convinced his fellow pastors of the plight of Baptist ministers and their families who faced suffering, hardship, and physical needs in their old age. Several of these ministers, including Lunsford, served on the Sunday School Board. This issue was mentioned informally at the next board meeting, and a fund of $100,000 was established for ministerial relief. At the next Southern Baptist Convention meeting, upon the suggestion of the board, a commission was established to gather information and materials to be used to formulate a relief program.

At the 1918 convention meeting, the report of the commission to establish a relief board was adopted with one change: Birmingham, Alabama, was recommended as the site, but Dallas, Texas, was chosen. The plan called for a relief department which would be financed from church contributions, endowment, and denominational budget assistance. The fund contained provisions for ministers, widows, minor children, and disability benefits.

On July 10, 1918, at the first meeting of the Relief and Annuity Board in Dallas, Lunsford was selected as executive secretary. By 1925, every state convention had turned its relief work over to the board. Lunsford was aggressive in securing endowment funds, including gifts from John D. Rockefeller which eventually totaled a million dollars.

Lunsford died on May 24, 1927. He was succeeded by Thomas J. Watts, who served as executive secretary from 1927 to 1947. During his administration eleven retirement plans were inaugurated or in operation, including: the Special Annuity Plan (a lump annuity), the Savings Annuity Plan (designed to aid ministers, missionaries, and salaried denomination employees in conserving savings), the Service Annuity Plan, the Foreign Mission Board Plan, the Institutional Employees Retirement Plan (for orphanages), the Age Security Plan (revised in 1940 for non-ministerial church employees), the Baptist Boards Employees Retirement Plan, the Institutional Employees Retirement Plan (for colleges and seminaries), the Special Deferred Annuity Plan, the Ministers Retirement Plan, and the Widows Supplemental Annuity Plan.

Walter R. Alexander succeeded Watts in 1947 and served through 1954. During his administration liberalization of the major retirement plans began. Assets increased from more than $12 million in 1947 to more than $35 million in 1954. New Programs included the Ministers Security Plan and the Southern Baptist Protection Plan.

In March 1955, R. Alton Reed was elected to replace Alexander, who died in December 1954. He had been responsible for recommending the Southern Baptist Protection Plan, which unlike other plans appealed to young ministers. Because some older plans had allowed age benefits for years of service rendered when no dues were paid, the board faced an actuarial liability in 1958 of over $250,000. Through the leadership of Reed, this liability was wiped out in less than a decade.

In 1960, the board offered the first variable plan by a denominational pension agency built around common stocks. In 1964, the Life Benefit Plan (term insurance) was offered. In 1965, the Health Benefit Plan began, which provided hospital-surgical-major medical benefits. The name of the agency was changed in 1960 to the Southern Baptist Annuity Board. Then in 1970, the board was reorganized, a new business system was installed, and a change in staff titles was made, including the title of president to replace the title of executive secretary. Reed retired in 1972 with the board's assets totaling more than $292 million.

Darold H. Morgan became president of the board in 1972. During his first year, the payment of a thirteenth check for participants began and a health benefit plan for church employees was developed. The board experienced continued growth and in 1978 began the Southern Baptist Retirement Program. This program offered participants a choice of investment funds, plus high earnings, and flexible benefits. By the early 1980s, the board's assets totaled approximately $2.38 billion. The Annuity Board provided not only for churches and their staffs. Notably, colleges and universities, seminaries, children's homes, retirement homes, hospitals, SBC agencies, and thirty-three state conventions also received help. Fletcher remarked, "In the troubling years that followed the breakup of the uneasy consensus, pastors were heard to say more than half seriously, 'I go with the side that gets the Annuity Board.'"[60]

The Annuity Board, therefore, proved to be the least controversial SBC agency during the Controversy. Cothen related President Morgan's warning that controversy over the Annuity Board might cause a "run on the bank" had its effect.[61] Paul W. Powell was chosen in 1990 to replace Morgan and maintain equilibrium. Nevertheless, Powell was identified as a moderate. Fletcher noted that conservative activism was limited to a call for shareholder action against "a large American retailer in support of anti-pornography initiatives," and added that there was a small effort among some moderates "to offer an alternative annuity arrangement."[62]

O. S. Hawkins became president in 1997. His contributions will be mentioned in Chapter 4.

Brotherhood Commission

McBeth related that the "success of the Woman's Missionary Union in channeling the energies and efforts of Southern Baptist women led to a desire for a similar agency for Baptist men."[63] In 1907, at the convention's annual meeting, an organization called the Laymen's Missionary Movement was established.[64] From 1927 to 1950, it was called the Baptist Brotherhood of the South. In 1950, the name was changed to the Brotherhood Commission of the Southern Baptist Convention. Often it was simply called Baptist Men.

J. T. Henderson was elected in 1908 as the first executive secretary. Henderson led in the establishment of Baptist men's organizations in every state convention but two. He educated the constituency concerning the work and inspired and enlisted men to unite in the task. In 1927, with the first name change, the movement expanded its concern from missions to the entire denominational program. In 1936, headquarters were established in Memphis, Tennessee.

In 1938, Lawson H. Cooke became executive secretary, serving until 1951. George W. Schroeder served from 1951 to 1970. The Royal Ambassadors movement, which had been established by the Woman's Missionary Union in 1908, was transferred beginning in 1954 to the Brotherhood Commission. In 1967, the term "Brotherhood" was used to describe the complete missionary education and mission involvement tasks in the churches. The work was divided into three divisions: Royal Ambassadors, Baptist Young Men, and Baptist Men. James H. Smith was elected executive director in 1979. In 1988, a new program called High School Baptist Young Men began. The first annual rally of the organization drew 450 high school students. Jim Williams began service as the last executive director of the commission in 1991. The commission found new opportunities through a program of volunteerism. Disaster relief work and building new church buildings was a major outlet of ministry. By utilizing a new way of reporting that included more than 75,000 volunteers, the commission claimed that volunteers gave time worth $67 million in almost 9,000 projects.[65]

Christian Life Commission

The Southern Baptist Convention slowly found its voice on social and moral issues. By the turn of the twentieth century, a standing committee was created on the issue of temperance. The Christian Life Commission was established in 1913 under the name of the Social Service Commission.[66] In 1914, it was combined with the standing committee on temperance. The Temperance and Social Service Commission was adopted as the new name for the agency. Under Arthur James Barton, the primary emphasis during those first years of the commission's existence was temperance, and the agency led an aggressive campaign against the manufacture, sale, and use of alcohol.

Jesse B. Weatherspoon became chairman of the commission in 1942 after the death of Barton. He enlarged the scope of social concerns of the commission, especially in the area of race issues. The agency became funded for the first time in 1947. Since that time, there have been five executive secretaries. One of Hugh A. Brimm's (1947–1952) major accomplishments was the establishment in 1948 of *Light*, the commission's official publication.

During A.C. Miller's administration (1953–1960), the headquarters of the commission was moved from Louisville to Nashville. In 1954, the agency's name was changed to the Christian Life Commission. Miller spoke out forcefully on race issues, as well as other moral concerns, even though Southern Baptists were slow in response to and support of the commission's stances.

Southern Baptists

Foy Valentine served from 1960 to 1986. The commission printed and distributed innumerable pamphlets, held annual workshops, and sponsored special programs. The commission in 1961 issued a program statement, which provided direction during Valentine's administration. It stated that the commission:

> shall assist Southern Baptists in the propagation of the gospel by (1) helping Southern Baptists to become more aware of the ethical implications of the gospel with regard to such aspects as family life, human relations, moral issues, economic life and daily work, citizenship, and related fields; and by (2) helping them create with God's leadership and by His grace the kind of moral and social climate in which the Southern Baptist witness for Christ will be most effective.[67]

Nevertheless, as the commission expanded its work, it stirred renewed opposition. Racial equality was still a radical concept for many Southern Baptists in the 1960s. The commission's stands on world peace, world hunger, capital punishment, and especially abortion also alienated conservatives.[68] The efforts to restrict or abolish the commission reached a crescendo during the Controversy.

Valentine announced his retirement in 1986. Conservatives were intent on replacing this agency with a more conservative voice but they did not have a majority of conservative trustees in place yet. Larry Baker, professor of ethics at Midwestern Seminary, was selected to replace Valentine in 1987. His tenure lasted thirteen months. Baker was elected by a secret ballot of 16 to 13. Paul Pressler advised Baker that he needed to look for another job before the next trustees' meeting since conservative trustees would be in the majority. Baker resigned in the summer of 1988.[69]

Richard Land, academic vice president at Criswell Bible College, was selected to replace Baker. He would serve from 1989 to 2013. The new leader opposed abortion, favored the death penalty, and possessed political acumen.[70] It was with this commission and during this time that Southern Baptist political affinities began to crystalize. Conservative leadership supported the Republican party. In 1992, even though the Democratic party nominated two Southern Baptists (Bill Clinton and Al Gore), the SBC supported a George Bush and Dan Quayle ticket.[71] Moreover, in the early 1990s, the SBC became more and more disgruntled with the direction of Baptist Joint Committee on Public Affairs. A Baptist lobby in Washington, D. C., it was jointly funded by many Baptist groups in the USA to monitor national legislative matters affecting the churches. The BJCPA was adamant about total separation of church and state as the "classic Baptist conviction." But during the Conservative Resurgence, many Southern Baptists began to feel more accommodating on church-state issues. This was especially made evident when a national "voucher" plan surfaced in Washington which might allow private, including Christian (Baptist) schools to receive public tax funds for their operations. In 1991, the SBC dropped its support of BJCPA.

Education Commission

The purpose of the Education Commission was to serve the educational interests of the SBC.[72] A temporary agency on education was established in 1915 which became permanent in 1916. The organization led in the planning for a $15 million drive. The SBC adopted the idea and it became the $75 Million Campaign. It was raised to board status in 1919, but the Great Depression led to its abolishment in 1928. Then it was restored again to commission status in 1931. Until 1951, Charles D. Johnson led the work on a voluntary basis.

In 1951, a central office was established in Nashville, and Richard O. Cornett became the first executive secretary. Their charter was to serve the educational interests of the convention. Subsequent executive secretaries since Cornett were Rabun L. Brantley (1959–1970), Ben C. Fisher (1970–1978), and Arthur L. Walker (1978–1993). Stephen Carleton was elected to head the commission in 1993 and served until its dissolution on December 31, 1996.

In 1972, the commission summarized its work through five functions: Christian education leadership and coordination, school and college studies and services, teacher-personnel recruitment and placement services, student recruitment, and convention relations.[73] It worked closely with the Association of Southern Baptist Colleges and Schools, which began in 1948 and was chartered in 1952 as the Southern Association of Baptist Colleges and Schools.[74]

American Baptist Seminary Commission

The American Baptist Theological Seminary is an educational institution for African American ministers and religious workers.[75] The seminary was established in 1924 in Nashville. It was jointly owned by the Southern Baptist Convention and the National Baptist Convention, Inc. The SBC helped with promotion, funding, and scholarships. Rabun L. Brantley, the executive secretary of the Education Commission, also served as the secretary of the American Baptist Seminary Commission. The school enrolled approximately one hundred students. But the convention severed official ties in 1996, pointing to waning attendance and theological differences for its defunding of the school.

Historical Commission

In 1921, the convention appointed a committee to preserve Baptist history.[76] It lasted until the death of its chairman, A.H. Holt, in 1933. In 1936, a similar committee was established with William O. Carver as its chairman. In 1938, the Southern Baptist Historical Society was organized. Its main purpose was to give direction to the preparation of historical writings for the convention's centennial in 1945. In 1947, the work of the committee was transferred to the Historical Society, which then served as the convention's history agency until 1951.

In 1951, the Historical Commission was chartered, and the society became its auxiliary. Norman W. Cox was chosen as the first executive secretary, serving from 1951 to 1959. He was followed by Davis C. Woolley (1959–1971), Lynn E. May, Jr. (1971–1995), and Slayden A. Yarbrough (1995–1997). The commission's responsibility was to record, procure, and preserve Baptist historical materials and to utilize historical materials in serving the history needs of Southern Baptists. Among the major achievements of the commission were the publication of the quarterly periodical, *Baptist History and Heritage* (begun in 1965); publication of the four-volume *Encyclopedia of Southern Baptists* (1958, 1971, 1982); publication of four brochure series: "The Baptist Heritage Series," "Shapers of Southern Baptist Heritage," "Understanding Southern Baptists," and "Foundations of Baptist Heritage"; and production of three six-tape video series: "Meet Southern Baptists," "Making History," and "Baptists in America." The commission was committed to serving Southern Baptists:

> by (1) intensifying and expanding its role as interpreter of Southern Baptist heritage and life; (2) developing a library containing all necessary materials and adequate physical facilities to become a world center for Baptist studies;

and (3) continuing to produce and distribute materials for the study of Baptist heritage and life.[77]

The commission was originally funded about $5,000 per year. By 1982, Cooperative Program receipts had grown to $282,060.

Radio and Television Commission

In 1938, Samuel F. Lowe petitioned the convention at its meeting in Richmond, Virginia, to investigate the field of radio broadcasting as a potential means of communicating the Baptist message. Lowe was appointed chairman of a radio committee, and in 1941, a thirteen-week series of half-hour evangelistic programs called *The Baptist Hour* began. In 1946, the committee became the Radio Commission.[78]

Lowe died in 1952, and Paul M. Stevens was elected director. On his recommendation, the agency was renamed the Radio and Television Commission. Stevens retired in 1979. Under his direction the commission became the world's largest producer of religious programs for broadcast on free air time. Jimmy R. Allen, president of the commission beginning in 1980, resigned in 1989. Jack Johnson became president in 1990 and served until the commission merged into the North American Mission Board in 1997.

The commission was located in Fort Worth, Texas. A number of major radio programs and television productions were broadcast on as many as 3,000 radio and television stations. Among the many successful programs of the commission were radio programs such as *The Baptist Hour, Master Control, Power Line*, and *Country Crossroads*, and television programs such as *Jot, The Human Dimension*, and *At Home with the Bible*.

Stewardship Commission

The task of promoting Christian stewardship was committed first to a Conservation Committee and then in 1929 to the fledgling Executive Committee.[79] The Stewardship Commission was established in 1960 with Merrill D. Moore elected as executive director-treasurer. After a brief two-year administration of James V. Lackey, A.R. Fagan was elected to lead the commission in 1974. The commission led in the development of church members as good stewards of possessions and assisted the convention and related organizations in raising funds to finance the Cooperative Program. The commission also operated a program of endowment and capital giving and provided a supportive role to the work of the foundations of the convention. In 1994, Ronald E. Chandler was elected as the last executive director of the commission, which was dissolved in 1997. Its work was reassigned to the Executive Committee and LifeWay.

Other Institutions of the Southern Baptist Convention

The convention operates six seminaries, plus the Seminary Extension Department, located in Nashville, Tennessee. The discussion on seminaries is found in Chapter 4. The Southern Baptist Foundation was chartered in 1947 and is also located in Nashville. In 1977, Hollis E. Johnson III became president of the foundation. Its work was placed under the Executive Committee of the Southern Baptist Convention in 1997. It handles bequests and endowments given to the convention, manages such funds, and provides informational and consultative services.[80]

Standing Committees and Associated Organizations

In 1948, the Calendar Committee began projecting the calendar of the convention to inform constituents of Southern Baptist programs and ministries. It projects the denominational calendar five years beyond the present year. Its name was changed to the Great Commission Committee in 1998.

The Baptist Joint Committee on Public Affairs, located in Washington, D. C., was a cooperative effort of nine Baptist denominations to act in the area of public affairs on issues related to the denominations, including church-state relations and public affairs information. This committee represented Baptists' longstanding concern for safeguarding religious liberty.[81] The convention ceased support of the BJCPA in 1991.

The Woman's Missionary Union is an auxiliary organization to the convention. Organized in 1888, the Woman's Missionary Union has a long and distinguished history of mission concern, involvement, and support. Among the basic activities of the organization are mission study, stewardship, community missions, and prayer. In 1999, over 100,000 women were enrolled in the work of the organization. Dellanna O'Brien served from 1989 to 1999 as the executive director of the WMU, which is located in Birmingham, Alabama.[82]

Southern Baptists also voluntarily cooperated with the Baptist World Alliance and the American Bible Society. The Baptist World Alliance had almost 41 million members in over 150,000 churches and meeting places in 1998.[83] Southern Baptists provided more than $425,000 in annual budget support to the American Bible Society in 1998.[84]

Conclusion

This chapter briefly described Southern Baptist agencies from their inception up to the late 1990s.[85] In 1995, a committee recommended a major restructuring of the Southern Baptist Convention. Some agencies were dissolved or merged. Others were expanded. Some remained without change. The Controversy, however, altered how all the agencies worked, and it will be the subject of the next chapter. After discussing the Controversy, an update on how the agencies were restructured and how they adjusted under more conservative leadership will be attempted.

Discussion Questions

1. In terms of defining Baptists how do you understand the relationship of the local church with the structures of Southern Baptists? Do you see the various organizations as cooperative or authoritative or a combination of both?
2. Write your own definition of the priesthood of believers. What does this concept mean to you and your faith as a Baptist?
3. Evaluate your local church: do you see it expressing itself in terms of helping the various affiliations from the associational, state, and national level to understand what your church sees as important

in terms of beliefs, practices, and needs? Or do you see your local church as a group of believers who follow the direction of the larger bodies from the national down to the associational levels? What are the strengths and weaknesses of these two viewpoints?

4. Briefly define in your understanding the purpose of the association, the state convention, and the national convention.

5. When the SBC was organized in Augusta, Georgia, in 1845, its stated purpose was to "carry into effect the benevolent intentions of our constituents, by organizing a plan for eliciting, combining and directing the energies of the whole denomination in one sacred effort, for the propagation of the gospel." How is this purpose consistent with the denomination today?

6. A statement by William B. Johnson, first president of the convention, stated: "We have constructed for our basis no new creed; acting in this matter upon a Baptist aversion for all creeds but the Bible.... Our objects, then, are the extension of the Messiah's kingdom, and the glory of our God." Is this still relevant for Southern Baptists in the twenty-first century? Explain your answer.

7. Write a paragraph summarizing cooperative support of churches through the Cooperative Program. What percent does your church give annually?

8. Does the history of each of the boards and commissions prior to the restructuring of the SBC in 1995–1996 help you to better understand more comprehensively the cooperative work of the SBC? List five contributions during the combined history of the agencies that impressed you. How does the ministries of your local church contribute to the larger denominational ministry of the SBC?

9. Why is the Woman's Missionary Union called a society instead of an agency? Do you think its work would be stronger or weaker as an agency rather than an independent society?

10. Do you think that the huge size of the SBC and its various agencies is a plus or a minus in terms of its effectiveness? List strengths and weaknesses for being such a large organization.

⇒ 3 ⇐

A Heritage of Conflict

The Controversy

Southern Baptist history (Chapter 1) and ecclesiology (Chapter 2) assist in understanding Southern Baptist theology. Chapters 3 through 5 are largely theological in nature. The Controversy described here in Chapter 3 fashioned the restructuring, changes, and updates that are detailed in Chapters 4 and 5. The issues, major players, and results of the Controversy are addressed in this chapter.

The Controversy: An Introduction

Baptists, and especially Southern Baptists, have weathered their fair share of controversy. The denomination was birthed in the slavery controversy that would soon become the Civil War. Landmarkism and anti-missionism in the late nineteenth century gave way to the fundamentalist-modernist controversy of the early twentieth century. The last two decades of the twentieth century, however, witnessed an intense struggle for control of the resources and the theological and ideological direction of the Southern Baptist Convention. This resulted in a dramatic transformation of the denomination. The struggle was termed by many Southern Baptists simply as the "Controversy." Most settled on the title of the Moderate-Conservative Controversy or the Inerrancy Controversy. Other titles include Conservative Resurgence, Conservative Reformation, and Conservative Renaissance from the point of view of conservatives, and the Fundamentalist Takeover from the perspective of moderates. This chapter will use the single-capped term, Controversy. Although the major public battles ceased in the 1990s, the fallout and consequences continue to reverberate throughout the convention into the twenty-first century.

The Controversy embroiled Southern Baptist life in a way never experienced in previous conflicts within the convention. It officially began with the election of Adrian Rogers as president of the convention in 1979 in Houston, Texas. It continued unabated in the years that followed. The conflict took on several dimensions, including theological, political, and methodological. Cooperation was threatened by a loss of trust, and harmony was replaced with adversarial attitudes that resulted in monumental changes within the denomination and in the rise of new organizations. Ironically, during the convention in 1979, fifty thousand Southern Baptists filled the Astrodome in Houston to initiate a major evangelistic effort called Bold Mission Thrust, which was soon forgotten in the wake of the battle for control.[1]

By the end of the twentieth century, Southern Baptists had undergone the most significant restructuring in their history. It changed not only the denominational shape of doing ministry and missions but also the relationships between the Southern Baptist Convention and state Baptist conventions, associations, churches, and individual Baptists. The new conservative leadership dissolved some national organizations, which were replaced by associations and societies committed to carrying on their respective ministries and services. The work of some agencies was absorbed into other Southern Baptist Convention entities. Some ministries and relationships disappeared altogether. Name changes began to appear at a rapid pace, reflecting new emphases and new realities.

Those displeased with the new direction of the Southern Baptist Convention, who were known as moderates, revitalized older organizations or created new ones. Some focused on the national level. Some established groups centered at the state level. Some groups disappeared. Others moved away from the national organization. Others sought to remain within the Southern Baptist Convention but to provide viable options.

State conventions examined their relationship to the Southern Baptist Convention. Some were pleased with the new directions at the national level. Some took a wait-and-see attitude. Others took a more independent approach and moved away from traditional cooperative relationships with the Southern Baptist Convention. In two states (Virginia and Texas) new conservative conventions arose, organized by those who were disappointed in their failure to redirect older state conventions along the new Southern Baptist Convention pattern.

Associations and churches also felt the tension created by the Controversy and the changes taking place at the national level. Some churches separated all official ties with the Southern Baptist Convention. Some churches distanced themselves from the Southern Baptist Convention and in some cases even from state conventions. They sought new alliances while at the same time attempting to remain Southern Baptist. Numerous churches experienced no change, and many applauded the new directions in denominational life. Others saw their congregations divided over future directions and alignment.

As Southern Baptists moved into a new century following two decades of conflict, the shape of the denomination was becoming clearer. The national convention was becoming much more conservative. State conventions were taking on a renewed importance and asserting their independency. And churches were rediscovering the significance of congregational polity in response to the changes that had taken place.

A primary issue in understanding the Controversy is who speaks the truth? For example, if readers absorb only reports and articles from the moderate perspective, then similar to the Whitsitt Controversy, ignorant Southern Baptists were taken over by extreme fundamentalists. On the other hand, if readers study only histories from the conservative point of view, then God saved the SBC before a modern Down Grade Controversy occurred. A modern analogy would be, "Do you receive your news from CNN and MSNBC or FOX and Newsmax?" Therefore, it is crucial that both sides be heard from their own perspectives. Bias is not necessarily wrong so long as one recognizes his or her own. Those blinded by their bias are hard-pressed to hear why likeminded people disagree with them. Moderate historians who documented the era include Walter Shurden, Bill Leonard, Grady Cothen, Robison James, David Morgan, and Barry Hankins.[2] Conservative histories that were written include those by Jerry Sutton, James Hefley, Paige Patterson, Paul Pressler, Roger Richards, Anthony Chute, Nathan Finn, and Michael Haykin.[3] Jesse Fletcher and Leo Garrett attempted brief, evenhanded studies.[4]

The Controversy: The Strategy

The Controversy was rooted as far back as the Texas Baptist conflict with J. Frank Norris, the notorious fundamentalist pastor of First Baptist Church, Fort Worth. In the 1920s, Norris began to attack Baptist leaders and institutions so vociferously that he was eventually banned from the Texas state convention for life. Southern Baptists, however, were not permanently damaged by the Norris assault, and his brand of fundamentalism was rejected by the denomination. Foundations for the Controversy are also noted in the previous conflicts over the Sunday School Board's publication of Ralph Elliott's *Message of Genesis* (1961) and Volume 1 of the *Broadman Bible Commentary* (1969).[5]

From the conservatives' perspective, however, the foundations reach farther back in time even than Norris. For example, Gregory Wills traces problems back to the Toy Controversy of 1879. C.H. Toy, an Old Testament professor at Southern Seminary, embraced modernist views. Toy resigned, but modernist views remained among the Southern Baptist ranks. According to Wills, progressive theology took hold of the convention, saturating all agencies by the 1950s.[6]

The unofficial beginning of the Controversy in the Southern Baptist Convention took place during the annual meeting held in Houston, Texas, in 1979. During the Pastors' Conference prior to this meeting, supporters led by Paige Patterson, president of Criswell College, and Paul Pressler, an appellate court judge from Houston, Texas, initiated a strategy of electing the president of the convention who would commit to carrying out the agenda of the developing movement.[7]

Conservatives were concerned with what they considered to be doctrinal deviations in the institutions and agencies of the Southern Baptist Convention. Progressive and liberal theology had taken hold particularly in the seminaries. If the seminaries did not right themselves then the convention would divide.[8]

In the early days of the Controversy, conservative leaders called for "parity" in trustee appointments and also called for "designated giving."[9] In the end, they achieved much more than they asked for. The strategy for changing the convention was simple: control the presidency and its appointive powers and the control of the convention is eventually assured. Pressler had studied the constitution of the convention and concluded that the president in conference with the vice presidents of the convention has the authority to appoint the Committee on

Committees. This committee in turn appoints the Committee on Boards (known during the early years of the Controversy as the Committee on Nominations).

The Committee on Boards nominates trustees for the agencies and institutions during the annual meeting of the convention. The messengers usually elect the trustees without dissension, although nominations can be received from the floor. The trustees then serve as the legal authority for their respective agencies. They approve the chief executive officer of the agency to which they were appointed. The executive often called the president, executive secretary, or executive director, administers the agency according to the charter of the respective agency and the policies approved by the trustees. Each agency or institution is a separate, legal entity controlled by its trustees and not by the convention. Pressler concluded that if the president appointed to the Committee on Committees only persons committed to the agenda of the conservatives, and that this committee in turn appointed only the same kind of persons to the Committee on Boards, who then would nominate for trustees only those committed to the cause, then control of the convention and its agencies could be achieved.[10]

Throughout their history Southern Baptists opposed any hierarchical system that placed too much authority in an individual or a small group of individuals. Yet in the system being advocated, the president of the Southern Baptist Convention could theoretically exercise such authority. In order to serve through any of the agencies or institutions of the convention, a person must not only be conservative in theology, he or she must agree with the agenda and positions of the president. For conservatives, this was an unfortunately necessary tactic to gain control and stop the creeping theological liberalism in the convention. Moderates, however, considered such political machinations and power grabs outrageous and unchristian.

In the Southern Baptist system, trustees are elected to four-year terms. A trustee can be reelected for a second term. Most trustees serve for eight years. If a trustee completes an unexpired term of no more than two years, that trustee can serve a total of ten consecutive years before being required to rotate off the particular board. The strategy of the conservatives was to control the presidency for a ten-year period, during which time the entire body of trustees of the agencies would be replaced by those committed to the agenda of the group. The ongoing successful implementation of the conservative strategy resulted in what became known simply as the Controversy.

The Controversy: The Players

It is difficult to organize a discussion of the Controversy. The contributions and personalities of the key players on both sides were important factors.[11] The issues dividing the convention were important. The key developments in the two-decades battle were essential, especially as they related to specific agencies. In fact, a number of agencies experienced small battles with the same intensity and consequences of the convention-wide struggle.

A number of individuals played key roles. Always identified with the movement was W.A. Criswell, the influential, patriarchal pastor of First Baptist, Dallas, Texas. He authored *Why I Preach That the Bible Is Literally True* in response to the *Broadman Bible Commentary*.[12] For many conservatives Criswell was the ideological leader of the movement.[13]

For conservatives, the specific starting point was the roles played by Paul Pressler and Paige Patterson. Pressler is credited with studying the Southern Baptist Convention constitution to determine that real power rested in the office of the president of the convention, if he chose to use it. Pressler also led in developing the strategy revolving around appointments.[14]

Pressler played a major role in enlisting supporters for the cause and in getting out the vote by visiting potential supporters. Sympathetic pastors would lead their respective churches to elect the maximum number of messengers to attend the annual meeting of the convention. Churches and collections of churches could simply "bus in" messengers for the election of the president. The messengers could then return home after the vote. During the early years of the Controversy, some of the largest Southern Baptist Convention annual meetings were held, including the record-establishing Dallas Convention in 1985 that saw 45,531 registered messengers. Pressler would also become a key trustee of the powerful Executive Committee. Following this tenure, he was elected as a trustee of the Foreign Mission Board.

Paige Patterson championed the cause of the movement through his position as president of Criswell College. Sutton stated that if

Criswell was the ideological godfather and Pressler was the organizer and strategist, then Patterson was the apologist for the Conservative Resurgence.[15] Following the success of the Controversy, Patterson was elected president of Southeastern Seminary, Wake Forest, North Carolina, in 1992. In 1998, Patterson was elected president of the Southern Baptist Convention. He was the first seminary-related leader elected president of the convention since 1942. Then in 2003, Patterson was elected president of Southwestern Seminary, Fort Worth, Texas.

Adrian Rogers was the pastor of Bellevue Baptist Church in Memphis, Tennessee. At the Houston meeting in 1979 he was the first president elected by the conservative movement. He became a powerful figure in the movement. Some viewed him as the key figure in the resurgence. He was also elected president in 1987 and 1988. Among the pastors elected president during the years of the Controversy were Bailey Smith, Del City, Oklahoma; Charles Stanley, First Baptist, Atlanta, Georgia; Jerry Vines, First Baptist, Jacksonville, Florida; and Morris Chapman, First Baptist, Wichita Falls, Texas.

Those who opposed the conservatives became known as moderates. Among the early leaders of the yet-to-be-organized movement were Abner McCall, president of Baylor University; Kenneth Chafin of Southern Seminary; Roy Honeycutt, who served as president of Southern Seminary; Cecil Sherman, pastor of First Baptist, Asheville, North Carolina, and his brother Bill Sherman, pastor of Woodmont Baptist, Nashville, Tennessee.

Others who served in leadership roles early in the Controversy joined the fray. These included Randall Lolley, president of Southeastern Seminary, Wake Forest, North Carolina, and Lloyd Elder, former Southwestern Seminary professor and administrator who became president of the Sunday School Board. Dan Vestal, pastor of First Baptist, Midland, Texas, and later Dunwoody Baptist, Atlanta, Georgia, and Winfred Moore, pastor of First Baptist, Amarillo, Texas, were two conservative pastors who rejected the agenda and approach of the conservative leadership and sided with the moderates. John Baugh, a Texas Baptist layman, was a wealthy Houston businessman who organized a laity movement called Baptists Committed in Texas.

Many others would join the battle on both sides. The intensity of the polemic was illustrated in the statement of Pressler describing the conservatives as "going for the jugular"[16] and Roy Honeycutt's convocation sermon at Southern Seminary often referred to as his "Holy War" address.[17] The war and its aftermath consumed Southern Baptist energies and resources for two decades. Battles were fought over a number of issues that reflected not only Baptist life and theology but the cultural and political wars being waged in the nation. Many casualties and losses were sustained. Even after the conservatives gained victory at the national level, conflict did not cease. In the end the Southern Baptist Convention would never be the same as it was prior to the Controversy.

The Controversy: Efforts at Peace

As the Controversy developed, many people, including denominational and institutional leaders, tried to remain above the battle or assume a neutral or conciliatory position. Perhaps the most well-known figure was Herschel H. Hobbs, retired pastor of First Baptist Church, Oklahoma City, Oklahoma, former president of the Southern Baptist Convention, and architect of the 1963 Baptist Faith and Message (BFM). During the 1981 convention in Los Angeles, Hobbs presented a motion reaffirming the 1963 BFM and its article on the Bible, which was approved by standing vote.[18] This unified vote was a highlight of that year's convention. Little room, however, was given for statesmanship in the long-term, and the Controversy continued unabated in the years that followed.

Efforts at resolving the Controversy were attempted. During the 1985 convention in Dallas, Texas, a motion was passed to establish a "Peace Committee." The committee included representatives from both sides of the Controversy, as well as non-aligned denominational leaders. The committee was instructed to determine the sources of conflict and to present its findings and make recommendations to resolve disagreements.[19]

The Peace Committee issued a progress report to the 1986 convention in Atlanta, Georgia. On October 22 of that year, the presidents of the six Southern Baptist seminaries in an attempt to contribute to the cause of peace issued what was called "The Glorieta Statement." It stated that the Bible "is fully inspired" and that its books "are not errant in any area of reality." The presidents expressed a commitment to fairness, respect, and peace. They also announced the scheduling of three conferences: Conference on Biblical Inerrancy (1987), Conference on Biblical Interpretation (1988), and Conference on Biblical Imperatives (1989).[20]

The first two conferences were held as scheduled. The third was canceled due to a lack of interest.

Following the Glorieta Statement, moderate Cecil Sherman resigned as a member of the Peace Committee, which had voted to affirm the efforts of the seminary presidents. He concluded that their statement was a victory for the conservatives. He also expressed his concerns that suggestions to the Peace Committee to reduce tension, such as providing balanced representation at the Pastor's Conference, by establishing both a moderate and a conservative track in theological education and Sunday School literature, and by fair representation in appointments in the denomination had been given little consideration.[21] On the other hand, Paul Pressler approved of the Glorieta Statement. "I'm extremely grateful for the seminary presidents finally admitting the legitimacy of the concern we have been expressing these eight years."[22] The Glorieta Statement, however, became another example of the two sides interpreting the peace effort for their own causes. Some of the seminary presidents did not define "inerrancy" the same way that conservatives did.[23]

The Peace Committee finally presented its report to the convention in St. Louis, Missouri, in 1987. The report identified the sources of the Controversy to be theological and political. It recognized theological diversity within the denomination and provided examples in its report. The committee stated that most rank-and-file Southern Baptists took a more conservative view on issues of interpretation but recognized that in the convention and even on the committee there were differing opinions. On political activity, the committee called upon present and future presidents, the Committee on Committees, and the Committee on Boards of the Southern Baptist Convention to nominate persons "who endorse the Baptist Faith and Message statement and are drawn in balanced fashion from the broad spectrum of loyal, cooperative Southern Baptists, representative of the diversity of our denomination." Unfortunately, the "balanced fashion" was essentially ignored by future leaders. The report also called for a cessation of organized political activity and polemical language, which was likewise ignored by both sides.[24]

The Peace Committee, therefore, was not successful. Even though it passed, its report primarily affirmed the issues of the conservative element. The failure of the presidents to follow the call for fairness and balance in the nomination process all but assured the effort for reconciliation was doomed. The battle would continue.[25]

The Controversy: The Issues

Southern Baptists have been theologically conservative in comparison to other religious groups. Yet within their conservatism, some Southern Baptists are more conservative and some more liberal than others. Herschel Hobbs believed that 90 percent of Southern Baptists were centrist like himself, with 5 percent to the right and 5 percent to the left.[26] Nancy Ammerman, a sociologist appealed to by both sides of the Controversy, placed percentages on no less than five groups.

- Self-identified fundamentalists (11 percent)—super-church pastors and much of the leadership of the Conservative Resurgence can be placed here. Inerrancy of Scripture, premillennialism, narrow roles for women in ministry, and a literal interpretation of Scripture were some of their keystone issues.
- Fundamentalist conservatives (22 percent)—these Baptists held to the same beliefs as above but chose to describe themselves as conservatives, not fundamentalists. Richard Jackson and Winfred Moore, who both ran for president during the Controversy, may belong here. They were inerrantists in theology but strongly identified with the old guard in the denomination.
- Conservatives (50 percent)—conservative beliefs and theology, but not in full agreement with strictness of fundamentalists nor the openness of moderates. They fully identified with the convention. Herschel Hobbs is an example.
- Moderate conservatives (8 percent)—members of this group rejected the fundamentalist way of understanding Scripture yet were still conservative in theology. Much of the old Southern Baptist establishment could be placed here—theologically conservative but progressively open.
- Self-identified moderates (9 percent)—these people rejected literalist interpretations of the Bible, premillennialism, inerrancy, and everything the fundamentalists did. Cecil Sherman and Roy Honeycutt exemplify this position. They did not hesitate to say fundamentalists were wrong in their thinking and their actions.[27]

The Controversy was in large measure a conflict between the first-second and fourth-fifth groups, both vying mightily to sway the majority middle group to the rightness and the truth of their respective sides. With the failure of attempts at achieving a compromise, the battle for control of the convention moved from early concerns over inerrancy to a number of other issues.

The Bible

Throughout their history Baptists have expressed a love for the Scriptures. This conviction is rooted in the Protestant Reformation's teaching of *sola scriptura* on matters of faith and practice. During times when persons or groups attacked the Bible, the Baptists were more than eager to come to its defense. In the Controversy both conservatives and moderates held to a high view of the Scriptures but often varied on the terms used and the scope of their usage.

For conservatives, the issue at stake in this battle was crystal clear—the truth of the Bible. Those not believing the Bible is true should not be teaching in Southern Baptist schools or writing Southern Baptist literature or serving any denominational leadership role. Fully 95 percent of conservatives agreed that "doctrinal soundness" was the number one criterion for SBC leadership and "doctrinal soundness" meant believing the Bible. For them, the Bible is either completely accurate or it is completely untrustworthy. Without the Bible all other doctrines will slip away. The issue at stake was the Bible and addressing those who do not believe it. Thus, conservative leadership early in the conflict used the Bible as the unifying issue justifying their actions. They defined the debate over the nature of the Scriptures rather than interpretation of the Scriptures. They championed the word "inerrancy" and the phrase "the Bible is inerrant in the original autographs."[28] Conservatives essentially rejected approaches such as higher criticism, which included literary criticism and historical criticism. They usually identified persons who used such approaches as "progressives" or "liberals," even though such persons may have held very conservative theological views.[29]

Moderates described the conservative approach on the Scriptures as frustrating and misleading rhetoric. For them the issue was not whether the Bible was true or not—it was. Rather, it was how one interprets the Bible that is the issue. The very term inerrancy was defined differently by different conservatives. In other words, the issue for

79

moderates was not inerrancy, but hermeneutics. Moderates stated that ultimate commitment should be placed upon the person, Jesus Christ, not upon a book. For moderates, the Bible was true and authoritative, but the theories on how it was true were open to debate. Moderates were more comfortable with terms such as "reliable" and "authoritative" when speaking of the Bible, although many also had no problem using "inerrancy" or "infallibility." They likewise stressed the issue of faith and practice when speaking of the Bible but were not as concerned with questions related to history and science as they were with matters of religion. Most moderates had an appreciation for developments in biblical criticism but for the most part maintained a conservative theological stance in their interpretations.[30]

The issue over the Bible and these descriptive terms focused upon the original manuscripts or autographs. Patterson affirmed this position stating that there are "transcribal inadvertencies or whatever you want to call them" in contemporary Bibles, and added that "we can now arrive at a 98 percent accurate text." He believed that the remaining two percent were "scribal problems that could be worked out gradually."[31] In such a debate it is important to remember that no original manuscripts are known to exist. Only handwritten copies from later periods are available. All copies differ from each other because of scribal mistakes that arose during the centuries of the transmission of the text. The majority of biblical scholars, conservative and moderate, agree upon these facts.

Therefore, the question of the originals is a question of faith, not of fact. Neither side can prove that its respective interpretation is correct unless texts of the original autographs are discovered. This is not likely to happen. Yet Southern Baptists argued fervently over what they did not have, and in so doing the largest non–Catholic denomination in the United States was divided irreparably. The winner was determined through the election of the president by majority vote of a very small percentage of the membership in the convention churches. Even more tragic was that solid biblical teachings were ignored in the heat of battle, as name-calling, slander, and viciousness ruled the day.

Church and State

Perhaps no issue was more evident in terms of changes than the issue of church and state relations. Traditionally, Baptists and Southern

3. A Heritage of Conflict

Baptists more than any other denomination championed not only the cause of religious liberty but also the separation of church and state. The Controversy resulted in shifts which had consequences beyond the denomination.

One reason for the changes was the political climate in the United States in the 1980s. The majority of Southern Baptists had long been identified with the Democratic Party into the administration of President Jimmy Carter (1977–1981), a dedicated Southern Baptist layman who continued teaching his Sunday School class in Plains, Georgia, during his administration. Although Carter was supported by a strong majority of Southern Baptists during his quest for the presidency, his liberal views on several social issues alienated many Baptists who were moving further to the right.

During the Carter years, the nation was changing. Denominational identity began to be replaced with a new kind of ecumenism that saw evangelicalism and fundamentalism more closely aligned with the Republican Party. This shift became noticeable during the election and administration of President Ronald Reagan (1981–1989). The lines between church and state were blurred as conservative Christianity began to express political power. Debates over prayer in public schools, religious practices in the marketplace and the public arena, and sharply-drawn lines on ethical issues, such as abortion and euthanasia, resulted in tensions among Southern Baptists that were not considered a few years earlier.

As late as 1981, the convention adopted a strong resolution in support of separation of church and state and the Baptist Joint Committee on Public Affairs (BJCPA).[32] The conservatives' developing conflict with the BJCPA, however, illustrated the changes sweeping the convention. Included in the battle were the struggles between James Dunn, executive director of the BJCPA, and Paul Pressler. Dunn and Pressler clashed on more than one occasion. Although it took several years and five votes to accomplish, by 1991 the Southern Baptist Convention eliminated all funding for the BJCPA. Of all the issues debated in the Controversy, the separation of church and state was exemplified in the struggle with the BJCPA. It was the hardest battle for the conservatives to win.[33]

Thus, conservatives were more likely to be Republican, in favor of prayer in schools, strongly pro-life and pro-family, against the ERA, against evolution, and especially against abortion and homosexuality. The encroachment of modernism and the giving in to culture must be stopped and can be stopped at the voting polls.[34] Many moderates aligned with these same issues. Percentage wise, however, more moderates supported ERA, the rights (but not necessarily the beliefs) of gays, and options on abortion and evolutionary teachings. Prayer in schools, however, was a more widely divergent issue. Moderates felt school prayer infringed upon the doctrine of separation of church and state. Conservatives felt that since America was founded upon Christian principles, then Christians should be allowed to introduce laws that reflect that history in public schools.[35]

Thus, some Southern Baptists softened the historic ideals of separation of church and state and adopted a more accommodationist approach. This allowed greater religious involvement in the public sectors of government and education. This was evidenced in the changing positions adopted by the Christian Life Commission, which became the Ethics and Religious Liberty Commission as a result of the restructuring of the convention in 1995–1997. The BJCPA continued with the support of other Baptist denominations as well as individual Southern Baptist state conventions, associations, and churches who opposed the new directions in the convention.

Women in Ministry

No issue stirred the passions of Southern Baptists more than the role of women in the churches. Especially explosive was the issue of the ordination of women as ministers and deacons. Women in ministry has been debated not only since the inception of the Southern Baptist Convention in 1845, but from the very beginnings of Baptists in the 1600s.[36] Early Southern Baptists such as R.B.C. Howell, J.R. Graves, and B.H. Carroll all agreed the New Testament allowed for women deacons.[37] A limited number of churches had recognized women as deacons. For example, the First Baptist Church, Waco, Texas, had "appointed" deaconesses as early as 1877. The Wake Forest Church in North Carolina used women deacons since 1924. According to *The Deacon*, two to three hundred Southern Baptists churches had women as deacons by 1973. The 1980s experienced a blossoming of women deacons.[38] Even conservative leaders such as W.A. Criswell allowed for the churches themselves to decide whether deaconesses were acceptable.[39] Whether women could preach, pastor, or be ordained proved to be more controversial.

In August of 1964, the Watts Avenue Baptist Church of Durham,

North Carolina, went a step further. The church ordained Addie Davis as a minister of the gospel, a young Virginia woman and a 1963 graduate of Southern Seminary. She was the first Southern Baptist woman recognized for ministry since the beginnings of the denomination.[40] By 1988, over 500 women had been ordained by Southern Baptist churches. A dozen were serving as senior pastors, with the rest serving other staff positions, and as campus ministers, chaplains, or counselors.[41]

Once the Conservative Resurgence settled in, several Southern Baptist churches experienced divisions, some associations sought to disfellowship wayward congregations, and resolutions and motions spiced the developing polemic at the state and national levels. Active leaders for an increased role of women in the church included Molly Marshall, professor at Southern Seminary, and Nancy Sehested, one of the first woman pastors of a Southern Baptist church during the Controversy.

In 1983, the convention met in Pittsburgh, Pennsylvania. Sehested was a leader in the organization of Southern Baptist Women in Ministry. James Hefley took note that 175 ordained "clergywomen" formed part of the denomination, adding that as a result of their organizing, "women's ordination led all other controversies in the fall state conventions."[42] During the summer of 1984, the Center for Women in Ministry was organized and began publication of *Folio*, a newspaper-type publication. Conservatives responded to these developments at the 1984 convention in Kansas City, Missouri. Carl F.H. Henry, former editor of *Christianity Today*, introduced a resolution which 58 percent of the messengers supported, based upon 1 Timothy 2:12–15. The resolution effectively excluded women from pastoral leadership in order "to preserve a submission God requires because the man was created first in creation and a woman was first in the Edenic fall."[43] Opponents of the resolution claimed that it violated the autonomy of the local church.[44]

In 1987, Sehested was called as pastor of the Prescott Memorial Baptist Church in Memphis, Tennessee. The church was quickly "disfellowshipped" by the Shelby Association.[45] This event symbolized the division in the convention over the role of women in the church. In 1988, the division was on display in two point-counterpoint articles in the journal *Baptist History and Heritage*. Jann Aldredge Clanton and Dorothy Kelley Patterson were the authors. Clanton supported women in leadership positions based on biblical witness, Baptist history, and the giftedness bestowed by the Holy Spirit. Patterson countered that the Spirit's gifts must be exercised within the natural order of God's creation. Biblical authority prohibited ordaining women.[46]

By 1990, the lines of polarization were set. Sociologist Ammerman noted that for conservatives, the Bible stated that the pastor is the "husband of one wife" which plainly ruled women out of the pastoral position. No matter how a woman felt about this, the Bible clearly stated that she could not genuinely be called by God to be a pastor. Women deacons are also unbiblical, and ordination is out of the question for women pastors and deaconesses. Fully 95 percent of conservative leadership stated that women should not be ordained, and conservative laity came in at 77 percent. Another 78 percent said that schools or agencies that did so should be censured and 59 percent added that churches should be disfellowshipped if the ordination of women occurred.[47]

By contrast, moderates were defenders of women in ministry. A total of 87 percent believed women could be ordained as pastors and 96 percent supported women deacons. Moreover, those moderates who disagreed stated they would never censure a church for ordaining a woman because of the autonomy of the local church. Biblical injunctions against women in ministry are only apparent and needed contextual interpretation, especially since other biblical passages seemed to affirm women in ministry.[48] Thus, the struggle over women in ministry made its presence felt from the local church to the national convention as a major issue of the Controversy.

Abortion, Homosexuality, and Culture

Several issues are interrelated. One's view on the Bible and on modern culture compels decisions on women at home and in the ministry, on abortion, and on homosexuality. Moderates were not as strict on abortion as conservatives were. Ammerman's percentages on "allow abortion never or only to save mother" produced ranges of 13 percent for self-identified moderates, 27 percent for moderate conservatives, 39 percent for conservatives, 55 percent for fundamentalist conservatives, and 63 percent for self-identified fundamentalists. Moreover, one-third of fundamentalists would never allow abortion over any circumstances.[49] Southern Baptists began producing yearly resolutions on abortion starting in 1971. Once conservatives were able to gain control of the Christian Life Commission, only the stricter viewpoints on abortion were promoted. Albert Mohler stated, "I think moderates, to their dying day, are going to underestimate that issue. They just don't get it."[50]

Another volatile issue was homosexuality. For conservatives, such a lifestyle was an "egregious violation of biblical morality in society today."[51] Only 2 percent of all of Ammerman's respondents, regardless of theological position, agreed or strongly agreed that homosexuality was a "viable Christian alternative." However, more moderates were willing to add that they were unsure (11 percent) and more conservatives were more likely to say they "*strongly* disagreed" (56 percent).[52]

Many conservatives emphasized the evils of an encroaching modernist culture upon Christianity. Baptists needed to be separate from the world and its worldly practices and entertainments as a part of one's lifestyle and witness toward unbelievers. Thus, 98 percent of conservatives were against swearing; 97 percent against drinking; 80 percent against smoking; 72 percent against social dancing; 67 percent against going to movies; and 65 percent against card playing. Moderates were also against such worldly practices, but there was wide variation in which practices were condemned. For moderates, 83 percent were against swearing; 75 percent against drinking; 44 percent against smoking; but only 12 percent against social dancing; 15 percent against going to movies; and 10 percent against card playing.[53]

Confessionalism and Creedalism

The place of theology and denominational doctrine comprised an important part of the Controversy. Baptists and Southern Baptists have a reputation as a confessional people. In actuality, Southern Baptists were slow to accept confessional statements. A basic consensus of conservative theology, a fear of confessions becoming creeds, and a respect for the right of believers and churches to "confess" their faith were reasons for this hesitation. Southern Baptists had no confession for the first eighty years until concerns over evolution caused the convention to adopt the first Baptist Faith and Message in 1925. E.Y. Mullins was the leader in forming the statement. It was introduced with denials that it was in any form a step toward creedalism.[54] Nevertheless, as early as 1934, historian W.W. Barnes warned that the 1925 statement was the first step toward creedalism.[55]

The Elliott Controversy was the catalyst for the revision of the Baptist Faith and Message, which was adopted in 1963. It was essentially the same confession with minor variations. Herschel Hobbs chaired the committee for the revision. Once again, this iteration stressed that these were confessional guidelines. Conservatives went along with the 1963 revision, but felt some denominational employees took the phrase "truth, without any mixture of error" too loosely.[56] They desired a stricter interpretation of the confession.

The Controversy once again raised concerns that the Baptist Faith and Message might be used in a more creedal sense. Conservatives denied that the denomination was becoming creedalistic, but issues related to the Bible seemed to place greater emphasis not only on the article on the Scriptures but also correct interpretation of the article. This concern appeared in the earliest stages of the Controversy. At the 1979 convention meeting in Houston, Larry Lewis proposed a resolution that included a call for agency trustees to affirm "the inerrancy of the Original Manuscripts." Hobbs and Wayne Dehoney (another former convention president) were then pressed to clarify the meaning of the 1963 Baptist Faith and Message article on Scripture. Their response reassured conservatives, and Lewis withdrew his motion.[57] However, *Baptist Press* did not publicize the incident. Pressler appealed to this lack of reporting as an evidence of liberal bias.[58]

In 1980, the convention meeting was held in St. Louis, Missouri. Conservatives produced an even stronger resolution on doctrinal integrity that exhorted agency trustees to "faithfully discharge their responsibility to carefully preserve the doctrinal integrity of our institutions," and to employ only those who believe in "the infallibility of the original manuscripts."[59] Hobbs responded to the resolution on the point of personal privilege to caution the convention against an encroaching creedalism. Nevertheless, the resolution passed overwhelmingly, paving the way for the Conservative Resurgence. What moderates recall, however, was that Hobbs, perhaps the most distinguished Southern Baptist statesman of the day, was drowned out in a chorus of boos from the audience. Bill Leonard interpreted the episode as "a collapse of the old methods of denominational compromise."[60]

Further evidence of a growing creedalism was provided in Slayden Yarbrough's article in 1983 in *Baptist History and Heritage* entitled "Is Creedalism a Threat to Southern Baptists?" He documented contemporary developments in light of the historical, theological, and missional heritage of Baptists.[61] Conservatives, however, reiterated the need for the convention to adopt stronger guidelines. In November of

1983, newly-elected president, Jimmy Draper, suggested guidelines that detail what Baptists should believe. Draper stated that the convention's confession of faith is "creedal in a sense." He listed four bedrock doctrines—full humanity and deity of Christ, substitutionary atonement, justification by faith, and bodily resurrection of Christ. He left out a statement on inerrancy since it would create controversy over its definitions. If leaders and teachers cannot accept these four things, Draper asserted, "they ought to leave. Anyone who cannot accept them is not a true Southern Baptist and ought to have the integrity to leave."[62] Draper's proposal, however, was too simplistic for some and not enough for others. Grady Cothen, outgoing president of the Sunday School Board, warned "Any Baptist who thinks he knows what another Baptist ought to be is in danger of not being a Baptist.... 'Believe or depart' is not the prerogative of any single Baptist or group of Baptists."[63]

Thus, lines were drawn over the Baptist Faith and Message. Conservatives believed the confessional guidelines should be followed more strictly. If agency employees could not agree to the confession, they should not be working for the convention. Moderates, on the other hand, sensed a departure from historic Baptist principles and an avenue toward creedalism.

Despite ongoing debate, the convention avoided making any changes to the Baptist Faith and Message until 1998. In Salt Lake City, Utah, a new article on the family was approved. A part of that article called for the wife to "submit herself graciously" to her husband.[64] This action set off more heated debate. The decision to require acceptance of this article by the faculty at Southwestern Seminary resulted in a major public disputation and was at least in part among the reasons for the resignation or retirement of some professors.[65]

In 1999, several state conventions adopted diverse positions related to Article 18 on "The Family." The Baptist Convention of New Mexico voted to instruct its executive board to study the language of its bylaws in order to require acceptance of the revised Baptist Faith and Message in order for a church to be in "good standing" with the state convention. Baptists in Oklahoma voted to affirm the 1963 confession, including the 1998 revision. Virginia and Texas Baptists voted to endorse only the 1963 Baptist Faith and Message without the revised article on the family.[66]

During the 1999 convention in Atlanta, Georgia, T.C. Pickney, a conservative from Virginia, made a motion calling upon the appointment of a committee to review the Baptist Faith and Message.[67] President Paige Patterson, while expressing his opinion that he did not anticipate a rewrite of the statement, appointed a fifteen-member review committee that included several key players in the Controversy, such as Adrian Rogers, Albert Mohler, Jerry Vines, Richard Land, and Pickney.[68] The committee issued its recommendations, which will be discussed in Chapter 5, at the SBC meeting in June 2000 at Orlando, Florida.

These actions confirmed that many Southern Baptists wanted a more restrictive confession consistent with the interpretations of those who had paved the way for the conservatives. Conversely, the actions in 1999 of the state conventions in Virginia and Texas to affirm only the 1963 Baptist Faith and Message was interpreted as a preemptive move. They anticipated a narrower document, especially in terms of the Scriptures.

Evangelism and Cooperative Giving

Conservative pastors were more aggressively evangelistic when compared to their moderate counterparts. Their churches baptized more. They held to a strict conversionist model of faith—a person is either saved or not saved. Everyone must make an individual, life-changing, once-for-all decision for Christ. Conservative churches were committed to soul winning and personal evangelism. Therefore, it made no sense to conservatives to talk to moderates about cooperating on missions. Moderates showed neither the missionary zeal nor the commitment to Scripture to succeed.

Moderates, on the other hand, characteristically pointed to the high percentage of rebaptisms at conservative churches that sometime inflated statistics. Moderates were more likely to view faith as a nurturing, developmental process. This development would change and grow through various stages of life and thus rebaptism to recognize those changes was irrelevant. The moderate approach to evangelism was more ambivalent. Some were uncomfortable with the rhetoric of winning souls. They practiced a more gradual and nurturing approach, especially with children. Moderates were more than willing, therefore, to cooperate ecumenically with other groups on the missionary endeavor. Common goals, common enterprises, and the pooling of resources for greater effectiveness were the important things for moderates.[69]

3. A Heritage of Conflict

Ironically, attitudes toward the Cooperative Program and what became known as "designated giving" underwent changes. In the early stages of the Controversy, Paige Patterson defended the conservatives' practice of "designated giving." He concluded that persons should not be expected to give financial support to causes in which they did not believe. He received support from Adrian Rogers, who referred to the Cooperative Program in 1982 as a "golden calf." Rogers concluded that it is "not only illogical, it is immoral to ask a man to support with his money and with his influence ... things that are theologically repugnant to him."[70] Moderates who held convention control at the time criticized this approach and defended the Cooperative Program.

As leadership shifted to the conservatives, it was moderates who became critical of the Cooperative Program. Decisions by the Executive Committee to recommend reductions and then defund the Baptist Joint Committee on Public Affairs and significant increases for the Christian Life Commission, which was adopting more right-wing positions on ethical issues, resulted in many moderates withholding contributions. With the development of the moderate-driven Cooperative Baptist Fellowship, individuals and churches began to designate contributions through a variety of options.[71]

Executive Committee leadership responded by surveying the trustees of Southern Baptist agencies on whether or not to continue accepting designated Cooperative Baptist Fellowship gifts. Not all agencies were prepared to give up CBF contributions. During the 1995 convention meeting in Orlando, Florida, a motion passed which instructed all convention agencies to no longer accept CBF gifts.[72] No plan was put forth to replace the lost income, especially to the smaller agencies.

Such developments resulted in some state conventions redefining "Cooperative Program." Texas Baptists adopted five different acceptable options. These actions resulted in the organization of the Texas Southern Baptist Convention, a conservative organization in competition with the Baptist General Convention of Texas. The Baptist General Association of Virginia also provided options for their churches to choose the traditional track of Cooperative Program giving or have their Cooperative Program percentage channeled to the CBF. In 1996, 115 churches founded the Southern Baptist Convention of Virginia. In 1999, 253 churches were members, with 200 uniquely aligned and 53 dually aligned with the SBCV and the BGCV.[73]

Education and Publications

A major battle during the Controversy focused on the mind. The conflict appeared in two major arenas: educational institutions and news services publications. In fact, the conservatives established three institutions prior to the beginning of the Controversy. They were Criswell Bible Institute (now College) in Dallas, Texas; Mid–America Baptist Theological Seminary, initially located in Little Rock, Arkansas, but later moved to Memphis, Tennessee; and Luther Rice Seminary, a correspondence school located in Jacksonville, Florida.

Southern Baptist seminaries had been sources of contention especially since the Elliott and *Broadman Bible Commentary* controversies in the 1960s. Suspicions and attacks on seminary professors, their views, and their publications became constant during the Controversy. During the Pastors' Conference prior to the 1979 convention in Houston, Texas, evangelist James Robison delivered a sermon which set the stage for the conservatives' strategy related to higher education. He stated that "we need to elect a president who is totally committed to the removal from this denomination of any teacher or any educator who does not believe the Bible is the inerrant, infallible Word of the living God."[74] Robison's statement allowed no room for compromise, diversity, or discussions over terminology. The direction was set for future battles at Southern Baptist seminaries.

Major conflicts and power struggles took place at Southeastern Seminary in Wake Forest, North Carolina, Southern Seminary in Louisville, Kentucky, and Southwestern Seminary in Fort Worth, Texas. Conservatives understood the power of the trustee appointments, and succeeded in making controversial changes to carry out their goals. A fuller discussion of the seminaries will be a topic for Chapter 4.

At the university and college level, a number of battles took place. These struggles were complicated by the fact that the controversies were fought at the state level rather than the national level and because the relationships between the educational and state conventions were less clearly defined from institution to institution. An attack upon David Moore of William Jewell College in the early 1970s signaled what was to come. Soon other schools felt the assaults and the accusations from the right, with professors of religion being the most visible targets at schools such as Southwest Baptist College in Bolivar, Missouri, and Oklahoma Baptist University in Shawnee.[75]

3. A Heritage of Conflict

The most visible response was the surprise action by the trustees in 1990 to change the charter of Baylor University to prevent a possible conservative takeover of its board. Joel Gregory, who was in the process of becoming the pastor of First Baptist, Dallas, Texas, led the outcry against Baylor and became a leading spokesman for the conservative movement. Furman University, Greenville, South Carolina, followed Baylor's action less than a month later.[76] Other schools, such as Samford University in Birmingham, Alabama, and Carson-Newman College in Jefferson City, Tennessee, risked defunding by their respective state conventions by following Baylor's example. The surprise announcement in late 1999 that Jerry Falwell's Liberty University had become a Southern Baptist school brought mixed reactions.

The Controversy also resulted in the organization of a number of new seminaries and divinity schools. Some, like the Baptist Theological Seminary in Richmond (Virginia), were the direct result of moderate initiatives. Others were closely tied with universities, such as Truett Seminary at Baylor University, Logsdon School of Theology at Hardin-Simmons University, Campbell University Divinity School, Gardner-Webb Divinity School, Wake Forest Divinity School, and McAfee School of Theology of Mercer University.[77]

The Controversy was also felt by Baptist state newspapers. Reporting on developments related to the conflict resulted in countless letters to editors, accusations of favoritism, and demands that would have violated the journalists' responsibility to inform the people. Conservatives understood the power of the press and became experts at using the media to enhance their positions. They were convinced that Baptist news media was slanted toward moderates. Nashville disseminated information to state newspapers which spread only moderate perspectives. An important goal for conservatives was to gain ground on the dissemination of their views. Letters to the editor, quick responses to accusations, and counterattacks were used effectively to put forth their views.[78]

The most controversial event related to news publishing was the firing of two of the writers for *Baptist Press*, the official news agency of the convention. Dan Martin and Al Shackleford were dismissed during a meeting of the Executive Committee. Many Southern Baptists were appalled when armed security guards were brought into the Southern Baptist Convention Building in Nashville during the session of the Executive Committee where the firings took place. An interesting fact is that

Shackleford was theologically conservative. The firings of Shackleford and Martin resulted in the organization by a number of Baptist editors of the *Associated Baptist Press*, which began receiving support from the Cooperative Baptist Fellowship (CBF).[79]

Freedom and Toleration and Pastoral Authority

Albert Mohler divided conservatives and moderates into the "Truth Party" and the "Liberty Party." The Truth Party insisted on the affirmation of biblical truth, a clear understanding of revealed truth that demanded certain doctrinal essentials. The Liberty Party, on the other hand, asserted individual rights to interpretation, theological formulation, and experience.[80] The Truth Party emphasized the necessity of pastoral authority to maintain their doctrinal essentials. The Liberty Party stressed freedom and toleration of views through the historic doctrine of priesthood of the believers.

Conservatives argued that at some point lines must be drawn on several issues. Baptists must not bow to the pressures of modern culture. True, Baptists have individual freedom and should tolerate differing opinions. But there are specific restrictions on what toleration might be. For example, Baptist teachers may think anything they like, but they must not teach anything they like if they want to be paid by Southern Baptists. Anyone teaching or writing Southern Baptist literature must be held accountable.

Moderates viewed freedom and toleration as the primary issue at stake in the Controversy. Individual freedom versus strict codes of belief and conduct was their take on the battle. For them, the priesthood of believers meant limits on pastoral authority and on the ability of one Baptist to impose and enforce his interpretation upon another Baptist. Just as conservatives pointed to an error-free Bible as the main issue, moderates pointed to "soul competency" as the main issue. Moderates believed that toleration was a defining point of what it meant to be Baptist. Diversity was important. Restrictions upon and enforcement of what a Baptist was to believe were considered creedal, not confessional.[81]

Important battles were fought over the issue of individual freedom and pastoral authority. Conservatives preferred a more authoritarian model for pastors whereas moderates appealed to a persuasive model.[82] Individual congregations preferred one model over the other but both models were found in the convention.[83] A major conflict over the rising support for pastoral authority in opposition to individual freedom erupted during the 1988 convention meeting in San Antonio, Texas. The messengers elected by 692 votes Jerry Vines, pastor of First Baptist Church, Jacksonville, Florida, over Richard Jackson, pastor of the North Phoenix Baptist Church in Arizona. Interestingly, Jackson was a conservative theologically and an avowed inerrantist. But he rejected the political agenda of convention leadership.[84] During the convention messengers adopted SBC Resolution No. 5 on the "Priesthood of All Believers." The resolution presented a weakened concept of the priesthood of believers.[85] It also stated that the doctrine "in no way contradicts the biblical understanding of the role, responsibility, and authority of the pastor which is seen in the command of the local church on Hebrews 13:17, 'Obey your leaders, and submit to them; for they keep watch over the souls, as those who will give you an account.'"[86] Paige Patterson offered that church members must "mimic, obey and submit" to the pastor. The congregation like sheep must "voluntarily and willingly follow the shepherd of the sheep. They are following the leadership role of the pastor."[87] A number of messengers marched to the Alamo and burned their ballots on the resolution in symbolic protest.[88]

The Controversy: The Results

The first signal that change was on the horizon occurred when Adrian Rogers was elected by a narrow margin over several other candidates during the 1979 Houston convention. Since that time the convention has elected a conservative as president in every convention.

The Changing of the Guard

As predicted by Pressler, the shape of the Southern Baptist Convention began to change radically. The Executive Committee of the convention began to assume more power, as well as a greater percentage of the budget allocations (which it recommended to the messengers of the convention for approval). Conflict arose in a number of the agencies. Trustees developed an adversarial relationship with each other during the early years of the Controversy. As the boards switched from moderate trustees to conservative trustees, conflict continued in terms of relationships between the executives and agency staffs and the trustees. The result often was removal by early retirement, forced resignation, or firing of staff members.

Perhaps no change was more significant than the makeup of the Executive Committee. The Executive Committee began in 1917. Its purpose was to coordinate the annual meeting and serve in an advisory capacity for the convention. It also developed the responsibility to make sure that the programs of the agencies did not conflict with nor overlap each other. It was originally not intended to become a super agency with potential authority over the agencies of the convention. But that is what happened during the Controversy.

Pressler understood the power of the Executive Committee, especially through the assignment of recommending to the messengers of the annual conventions budget appropriations for the various agencies. Any agency that came into conflict with the Executive Committee ran the risk of having cuts in its Cooperative Program allocation. The use of such power was evident in the efforts to reduce and then defund Cooperative Program allocations to the Baptist Joint Committee on Public Affairs.[89]

Convention Agency Battles

Control of the convention required control of the agencies. As the new trustees of each agency took conservative control, conflicts arose. By the time the restructuring of the convention was announced in February 1995, each of the four boards of the denomination had elected conservative chief executives. Some changes (Foreign Mission Board, Sunday School Board) were the result of struggle and conflict. Others were accomplished more smoothly (Home Mission Board, Annuity Board).

Transition to conservative leadership took place smoothly at the Home Mission Board. William Tanner resigned. The new president, Larry Lewis, was conservative but tried to represent all Southern Baptists and openly recognized that moderate voices were needed. Under his leadership, however, the Home Mission Board refused to financially support women pastors and enforced policies preventing the appointment of divorced persons and charismatics as missionaries.[90]

The Foreign Mission Board felt the effects of the Controversy in

October 1991. Conservative trustees reversed a funding agreement recommended by the administration with the Baptist Theological Seminary in Rüschlikon, Switzerland. This action resulted in tensions between the trustees and President Keith Parks, and he announced his retirement.[91] He was later appointed to lead the global mission program of the Cooperative Baptist Fellowship.

The key event at the Sunday School Board was the forced retirement of Lloyd Elder. The board received criticism for the Elliott and the *Broadman Bible Commentary* controversies. It reached its climax with the opposition against Elder. Again, a publication precipitated the conflict. Leon McBeth's centennial history of the board, *Celebrating Heritage and Hope*, was rejected by conservative trustees. Elder, among other ongoing issues, was blamed for the controversy and resigned at a special meeting of the trustees on January 17, 1991.[92]

All of the commissions underwent a change of leadership with the exception of the Historical Commission, where Lynn E. May Jr., would complete twenty-four years as executive director and over thirty-nine years as a staff member. Most of the changes in leadership at the other commissions were accomplished without major tension and with little concern over the theological divisions within the convention.

However, the Christian Life Commission did receive the effects of the Controversy. When Larry Baker replaced Foy Valentine in 1987, the election was by a narrow margin. Conservative trustees disagreed with Baker's stances on abortion, capital punishment, and women in ministry. When it became known that Baker would be fired once a majority on the trustees was reached by the conservatives, he resigned. He was replaced by Richard Land. The CLC quickly prepared new materials that condemned abortion and euthanasia.[93]

Each of the seminaries saw a change in the chief executive officer. The transitions at Southeastern, Southern, Southwestern, and Midwestern represented the deep division within the convention. The resignation of Randall Lolley at Southeastern, the retirements of Roy Honeycutt at Southern and Milton Ferguson at Midwestern, and the firing of Dilday at Southwestern were results of the struggle for power over these institutions. These actions signaled a new direction for seminary education more attuned to the conservative theology.

The Woman's Missionary Union was also a source of contention in the Controversy. From its beginning, the organization has been a society. It elects its own officers and trustees without convention action and receives no financial support through the Cooperative Program. In 1988, the Woman's Missionary Union celebrated its centennial anniversary. A year later Dellanna O'Brien, former missionary along with her husband to Indonesia from 1963 to 1971, became executive director. O'Brien was considered sympathetic toward moderates. Thus, when the Woman's Missionary Union provided support for some mission projects of the Cooperative Baptist Fellowship, conservative opposition developed. Talk of an implied competition in women's work through the Sunday School Board increased the pressure for the Woman's Missionary Union to conform to the Conservative Resurgence agenda. The Woman's Missionary Union continued to identify its purpose as missions and not politics but felt the pressure of trying to maintain a neutral posture in light of the struggle in denominational life.[94]

Conclusion

Moderates underestimated, misunderstood, and miscalculated the Conservative Resurgence. For them, the Controversy erupted into a fundamentalist political takeover in a reaction to modern cultural encroachments. For example, Southern Seminary president Roy Honeycutt declared in the heat of the battle, "The crisis facing Southern Baptists is neither biblical nor theological. It is political. However much [Paige Patterson] and his political party may use biblical and theological smokescreens, this is the issue: our convention is being wrenched apart by an unprecedented political crisis engineered by Dr. Patterson and Judge Pressler."[95]

Yet conservatives were successful in interpreting the Controversy as primarily theological. For example, Tom Nettles stated, "We speak out on abortion and homosexuality because these are the very points where our culture denies scriptural truth" and "we believe our denomination and churches will be stronger if they adhere to the scriptural mandate that limits the preaching office to men."[96]

Was the Controversy a reaction to culture or was it a theological issue? Perhaps Barry Hankins hits the target when he explains that it was not either/or but rather both/and. Theological concerns did not solely drive the cultural wars nor did modern culture alone produce a theological backlash. They were both closely related and not oppositional. Hankins concludes, "Finally, as to the question of whether culture drives theology or theology drives cultural engagement, my answer is still 'Yes!'"[97]

Discussion Questions

1. Southern Baptists have experienced numerous controversies throughout their history. What are the positives and negatives of major controversial conflict?
2. The Controversy took place starting in 1979 and continued to the end of the twentieth century. Briefly evaluate how it affected the SBC, state conventions and associations, and local churches. What do you see as the positive and the negative results from the Controversy?
3. Describe in a paragraph the basic strategy of those wishing to change the SBC in terms of achieving control of the convention's agencies. How effective was this strategy?
4. After reading about the strategy of those seeking to control the SBC and the personalities involved on both sides, what do you think was the major issue or issues in the conflict?
5. Why do you think that efforts at peace failed?
6. List the major issues in the Controversy and write a brief statement defining the positions of each side. Was the battle over these issues successful, or do they continue to exist in the SBC today?
7. Among the issues fought over, list what you view as the three most important. Write a brief paragraph explaining your choices.
8. In terms of the results of the Controversy the power of the Executive Committee was greatly enhanced. What are the strengths and weaknesses of this enhanced power?

≋ 4 ≋

A Heritage of Change

The Restructuring of the Southern Baptist Convention

The Controversy resulted in the most significant reorganization in the history of the denomination. This chapter relates what Southern Baptist agencies looked like after the Controversy and restructuring occurred. The one exception is that this chapter will also discuss the six Southern Baptist seminaries from their inception to 2021. One reason for consigning their story to this chapter is that the restructuring did not affect them like it did all the other agencies. On the other hand, the Controversy upended most of the seminaries. The Conservative Resurgence coveted the seminaries. Steering future generations of educated ministers toward conservative theology was a central goal of the resurgence.

The Program and Structure Study Committee

In June 1993, during the meeting of the Southern Baptist Convention in Los Angeles, California, C.B. Hogue, a messenger from California, made a motion calling for the president of the convention to appoint a committee to review the structure and agencies of the SBC. The motion was referred to the Executive Committee for consideration.

In September 1993, the chairman of the Executive Committee appointed the Program and Structure Study Committee (PSSC), a seven-man committee chaired by Mark Brister, pastor of Broadmoor Baptist, Shreveport, Louisiana. It is important to understand that the committee was appointed by the Executive Committee. Upon completion of its work, it would report to the Executive Committee, who had the responsibility to decide whether or not to take the report to the convention.

During the February 1995 meeting of the Executive Committee, the PSSC issued its report. It entitled its recommendation "A Covenant for a New Century." The report called for a radical restructuring of the Southern Baptist Convention by reducing the structure of the denomination to five entities and by recommending the dissolution of the Brotherhood Commission, Education Commission, American Baptist Theological Seminary Commission, Historical Commission, Radio-TV Commission, and Stewardship Commission, and the placement of the Southern Baptist Foundation under the Executive Committee.

The Executive Committee adopted the PSSC report and recommended it for approval by the Southern Baptist Convention. One hundred and fifty years following the organization of the Convention in Augusta, Georgia, in June 1995, in Atlanta, Georgia, messengers adopted the "Covenant" with hastily agreed upon changes related to the Woman's Missionary Union and the Home Mission Board. It also voted to change the convention's Bylaw 15, which names the agencies of the denomination. This change required and received a vote of approval at two consecutive conventions.

In September 1995, the Executive Committee appointed the Implementation Task Force (ITF), chaired by Robert Reccord, pastor from Norfolk, Virginia. The ITF was assigned the responsibility of carrying out the changes recommended in the PSSC Report. In June 1997, the convention in Dallas, Texas, adopted necessary charter changes for the affected agencies and the "Covenant" became a reality.

Not all supported the reorganization.[1] Several procedural concerns were expressed. First, the PSSC included a member who, perceived or real, had a conflict of interest. Albert Mohler was president of Southern Seminary. The dissolution of agencies resulted in financial savings which could be divided among surviving entities. Including a person on the PSSC whose institution could financially benefit from the closing of other agencies was considered inappropriate.

Second, one of the most important concerns related to the fact that the PSSC was a committee appointed by the Executive Committee of the SBC, serving under its authority, and submitting its final report for consideration to the Executive Committee. Failure of the PSSC and the Executive Committee to involve the trustees of the convention agencies prior to the release of the PSSC Report was inconsistent with Bylaw

20, section (I) of the SBC, which states that the Executive Committee is "to maintain open channels of communication between the Executive Committee and the trustees of the agencies of the Convention."[2] Not communicating with nor involving the trustees of affected agencies during the study phase and prior to the vote of the Executive Committee on restructuring violated not only the legal foundations of the convention but also the spirit of the relationship between the Executive Committee and the respective agency trustees.

Third, the failure to have a second vote on the PSSC Report in New Orleans in 1996 violated the action of the SBC messengers in Atlanta in 1995 in adopting the PSSC Report for the first time. Legally, the convention only had to express itself one time on the issue of restructuring. The PSSC Report, which was amended in relation to the Woman's Missionary Union and the Home Mission Board prior to the first vote in Atlanta, however, stated clearly in the "Implementation" section that "upon final approval of the Report by the Southern Baptist Convention (June 1996), the Executive Committee will implement the changes required by the Report on behalf of the Convention."[3] If the SBC was not going to vote a second time, then the Report should have been amended in Atlanta before final approval. The PSSC, the Executive Committee, and legal counsel for the convention failed to recognize what the messengers approved.

A fourth concern was the failure to provide adequate time to discuss the "Covenant," which recommended the most comprehensive and radical restructuring in the history of the convention. Repeatedly, prior to the SBC meeting in Atlanta in 1995, Southern Baptists were told that the discussion of the report would be given all of the time needed. A review of the video of the business session when the report was discussed confirmed that with an extension of five minutes a total of sixty-five minutes was given to the report. Approximately forty minutes were spent explaining and promoting the report of the PSSC, including a well-prepared video presentation and efforts on the platform to accommodate concerns related to the Home Mission Board and the Woman's Missionary Union. When the recommendation finally reached the floor for discussion, most of the remaining time was spent on parliamentary and procedural questions. Only four and one-half minutes were spent discussing the agencies affected by the report. A motion to save the Historical Commission (three minutes) and the response by a member of the PSSC (one and one-half minutes) comprised the only discussion on the content of the PSSC Report other than the prearranged com-promises with the Woman's Missionary Union and the Home Mission Board. Messengers attempting to address concerns related to other agencies were left standing at microphones waiting to be heard when debate was concluded.

A fifth concern was the careful control that prevented agency trustees, administrators, supporters, and friends from having mean-ingful communication with the PSSC and/or the Executive Commit-tee. After adoption of the report by the Executive Committee trustees, PSSC members offered to meet with trustees of the affected agencies and explain the report. But there was no opportunity given to nego-tiate. The PSSC stated unequivocally that the report would stand as presented with no changes and would be accepted or rejected by the vote of the messengers. Some opponents of the restructuring con-cluded that the negotiations with the Woman's Missionary Union and the Home Mission Board were unfair. The smaller agencies with fewer supporters were not given any opportunity to negotiate, even though some requested to appear before the Executive Committee prior to the convention.

The only hope for changing the report was on the convention floor during the debate on the PSSC's "Covenant for a New Century." That did not happen. Only the Historical Commission was able to take its case before the messengers but failed in revising the "Covenant." Two years later, the restructuring was completed.

The Restructured Southern Baptist Convention

The restructuring organized the Southern Baptist Convention into five new categories. "Missions" included the International Mission Board, formerly known as the Foreign Mission Board, and the North American Mission Board, which was comprised of the Home Mission Board, the Brotherhood Commission, and the Radio-Television Com-mission. A Great Commission Council comprising fourteen members was established for communication between the two mission boards. The council, however, was given no authority over the two mission boards.[4]

"Theological Education" included the six Southern Baptist sem-inaries. The seminary presidents became the Council of Seminary

Presidents. This organization was given responsibility for operating the Seminary Extension program. The council also was assigned the operation of the Southern Baptist Historical Library and Archives, which previously the Historical Commission administered.[5]

The Christian Life Commission became the Christian Ethics and Religious Liberty Commission. It was the only commission to remain intact in the restructuring. It was also given the assignment to be the denominational agency to represent the convention on religious liberty and church and state matters. It received a 50 percent increase in its Cooperative Program allocation.

"Church Enrichment Ministries" characterized the assignment to the Sunday School Board. Besides its former program assignments, the board was given responsibility for promoting stewardship education, which had previously been a ministry of the Stewardship Commission. The board was also assigned the task of publishing Baptist history curricula materials, although this was not included in the program statement for the board in the PSSC report, nor would it be included in the program statement when the name of the agency was changed to Life-Way Christian Resources in 1999.

"Facilitating Ministries" was established to support the convention and the churches. The Executive Committee was assigned additional responsibilities of the remaining work of the Stewardship Commission. Moreover, the Southern Baptist Foundation was placed under the Executive Committee. The Annuity Board was included in this category as well.

The Woman's Missionary Union continued as an auxiliary of the convention. As an auxiliary the Woman's Missionary Union elected its own board and officers. It received no funding from the convention, yet had a traditional historic role in missions education and support, especially in terms of the two annual missions offerings. The independency of the organization resulted in some anxious and tense moments in the months leading up to the vote on restructuring. Thus, at the last minute, the PSSC report was changed to clarify the work and relationship of the Woman's Missionary Union with the convention.

Upon final approval of the "Covenant for a New Century," six commissions were dissolved and their work was either eliminated or assigned to other agencies: Brotherhood Commission, Education Commission, American Baptist Theological Seminary Commission, Historical Commission, Radio-TV Commission, and Stewardship Commission.

The Southern Baptist Foundation no longer was a separate entity. Eventually, the names of three of the four boards would be changed, as well as the one surviving commission. In 1998, two motions recommending a name change for the convention itself were made, but these efforts failed at the 1999 convention held in Atlanta, Georgia.

The Return to the Society Method

One of the consequences of the restructuring of the convention was a return to the society approach which was practiced during the early history of Baptists in both England and America. In the society method individual organizations exist as voluntary entities who determine their membership and ministry. Each society elects its own board which gives oversight to the organization. Each society is free to solicit support without the restrictions of the denomination. The Woman's Missionary Union is the only organization related to the Southern Baptist Convention which has always practiced the society method.

The restructuring and the dissolution of several commissions contributed to the reappearance of the society method. Two organizations provide examples. First, the Historical Commission (1951–1997) was dissolved with the Southern Baptist Historical Library and Archives being placed under the newly-formed Council of Seminary Presidents. The Southern Baptist Historical Society (SBHS), which was organized in 1938 and which became an auxiliary of the Historical Commission in 1953, reverted to an independent status. After a brief tenure by Albert W. Wardin Jr. (1995–1996), Slayden Yarbrough, professor of religion at Oklahoma Baptist University, Shawnee, Oklahoma, was chosen as the executive director in 1996. The work was relocated to the campus of the university in 1997. The SBHS voluntarily assumed the Historical Commission's ministries not reassigned in the restructuring. These included publishing and distributing historical products and the journal *Baptist History and Heritage, Baptist History and Heritage Update*, sponsoring an annual meeting, and working with historical organizations of state conventions, associations, churches, and other Baptist enterprises. Charles Deweese became fulltime executive director in June 1999. The society moved to the Tennessee Baptist Convention in Brentwood, Tennessee. In 2001, its name was changed to the Baptist History and Heritage Society. Several books and booklets were produced during this time period. Deweese served until 2009. Bruce Gourley was selected as the next director, and served from 2010 to 2017. He effected the move from Mercer University in Atlanta to a dual office in Macon, Georgia, and Bozeman, Montana. John Finley has served as the executive director since 2017. His tenure has emphasized the discovery of new donors and a solid financial future. The offices are in Macon and Savannah, Georgia.[6]

Second, the Education Commission dissolved on December 31, 1996. Its ministry continued through the Association of Southern Baptist Colleges and Schools (ASBCS). In 1998, the association chose Bob R. Agee, past president of Oklahoma Baptist University, as its executive officer. The ASBCS located in Nashville, Tennessee, although the office of the executive director was located in Jackson, Tennessee. In 1999, the ASBCS had a membership of forty-eight colleges and universities, three Bible colleges, and three academies. The six Southern Baptist seminaries, acting in concert, withdrew from the organization in the same year. The association coordinates relations and services among the institutions and publishes *The Southern Baptist Educator*. Agee also was elected executive director of the Consortium on Global Education, which was previously known as the Cooperative Services International Education Consortium.[7]

As societies these organizations had no official connection with the Southern Baptist Convention. Yet they continued to serve Southern Baptist constituents, churches, organizations, and institutions. Because they were societies, they were free to solicit support from state conventions, associations, and churches. Organizations which recognized the importance of the ministries of these groups provide some financial resources which previously had been available through Cooperative Program distributions to the affiliated but now dissolved commissions.

An Update on Southern Baptist State Conventions and Associations

State conventions and associations must address contemporary challenges in order to thrive in the future. Some state conventions are large and easily sustainable. Other state conventions are small and need more help. Ed Stetzer encourages state conventions, especially smaller ones, to staff toward the mission (mission advance and mission strengthening strategies), staff with player/coaches (doers over teachers), staff according to need, and staff according to population (smaller conventions of necessity have smaller staffs). Stetzer suggests that state conventions should be organized and structured in a way that the local leadership would take responsibility. "State conventions, therefore, should reflect their member churches more than the national structure. And, smaller conventions should reflect their states and churches more than larger church conventions."[8]

Michael Day addresses the situation more strongly. He noted several syndromes in which Southern Baptists have painted themselves into corners concerning state conventions and associations. His list includes duplicated-effort syndrome, institution-first syndrome, autonomous-hierarchy syndrome, thinly spread missions dollar syndrome, and the lost-influence syndrome.[9] Day offers several ways forward for the future of state conventions and associations. These include church-driven, priority-based, resource-focused, institutionally free, strategically managed, regionally located but not geographically bound, denominationally connected but not traditionally bound, and kingdom-conscious.[10] His conclusion is that state conventions and associations must address these issues now because "the clock is ticking and the pressure is on."[11]

An Update on Southern Baptist Convention Agencies and Entities

As Southern Baptists moved into the twenty-first century, the Southern Baptist Convention was firmly in the hands of conservative leadership committed to the agenda set into motion during the annual meeting in 1979 in Houston, Texas. The "old guard" had been removed, and the convention had gone through an extensive restructuring. The Executive Committee had expanded its influence and power in a way not anticipated in 1917. Numerous name changes characterized the agencies. Many had been dissolved or absorbed into other agencies. For the most part, the outside world listened to the voices of those in convention leadership roles for a characterization of the denomination. A brief updated synopsis of agencies and entities follows. Readers may want to review Chapter 2 before proceeding.

The Cooperative Program

Despite the Controversy, the Cooperative Program (CP) for funding mission, education, and ministry remains a marvel of modern Christianity. For example, Southern Baptist churches through the Cooperative Program pay for 40–55 percent of the cost of the seminary education for their students at SBC seminaries. The Executive Committee continues to recommend the percentage allotments to the SBC at the annual meeting. The budget for 2018–2019 was $194 million. The distribution of these CP gifts rarely moves percentage-wise from the following:

- 50.41 percent to the International Mission Board
- 22.79 percent to the North American Mission Board
- 22.16 percent to theological education
- 1.65 percent to the Ethics and Religious Liberty Commission
- 2.99 percent to the Executive Committee and SBC operating budget

Each state convention votes a set of percentages by which it determines what CP gifts from the churches are reinvested within the state and which are forwarded to the SBC. Smaller state conventions cannot give as much to the CP. Thus, allotments run similar to New England's 85/15 and Montana's 75/25 split with the larger percentage staying in state. Larger state convention examples are Alabama's and Nevada's 50/50 split between state and SBC.[12]

The benefits of the Cooperative Program are threefold. First, it is economical. Only a fraction of funds funnel toward administrative overhead. Second, it is balanced. All ministries receive their due, not simply the most outspoken or more glamorous. Third, it offers perspective. Churches are helping all Southern Baptist work, not just a portion.[13]

There are, however, drawbacks and challenges for the Cooperative Program. First of all, there remains ignorance among many Southern Baptists on what the Cooperative Program actually does. Indeed, the majority of Southern Baptists continue to be uninformed on how the Cooperative Program works or how the money that they give to their local church is distributed between agencies and institutions at state and national levels. Convention leadership continues to be frustrated over the large number of churches that do not give to the Cooperative Program at all (almost 40 percent). Total receipts and total dollar amounts continue to decline, but only slightly.[14] A perpetual challenge in the convention is to educate rank and file Southern Baptists on the value and necessity of the Cooperative Program.

Another drawback is the continuing tension between state conventions and the Southern Baptist Convention. Ideally, a 50/50 split between state missions and SBC missions takes place. Most state conventions cannot do that. The average split is closer to 65–35 percent, the larger portion being kept for work within the state and the smaller portion forwarded for national/international SBC agencies. If leaders of a state convention, however, do not approve what is transacting at the national level, or want to cease support of a national entity, the oft-used threat of "withholding Cooperative Program funds" is raised. For years, conservative state leaders used this action with the SBC prior to the 1979 Conservative Resurgence. Today, the shoe is on the other foot, as some leaders of more moderate state conventions, such as the massive Baptist General Convention of Texas, chart their own destiny and do not grant undesignated offerings to the SBC.

These tensions and challenges remain today. Some state conventions have increased their giving percentages but others have decreased. Staff reductions make up for some lost monies, but the Cooperative Program is also reduced. Some Southern Baptists give to specific causes rather than the Cooperative Program. Moreover, methodological changes in the convention have produced tensional challenges. The preferences include individual versus corporate, society versus corporate, contemporary versus traditional, and young versus old.[15]

The future strategy for the Cooperative Program (as well as other agencies) is reflected in a process called Great Commission Advance. The strategy includes renewed emphases on prayer, vision, responsibility, positioning, partnerships, customization, and stewardship.[16]

North American Mission Board

The North American Mission Board (NAMB) experienced leadership angst in the early twenty-first century. After Larry Lewis retired, Robert Reccord succeeded him as the next president. He served from 1997 to 2006. Reccord, a former megachurch pastor who was used to free rein as an administrator, found it difficult to live under a more restrained structure. After a trustee investigation produced a scathing report of numerous examples of poor management, Reccord resigned as president in April 2006.[17] Geoff Hammond was unanimously selected as the next president. Yet Hammond also produced anguish among NAMB trustees after only a short period. Issues of autocratic leadership style and low staff morale led to his early departure. He served from 2007 to 2009.[18]

Kevin Ezell began his tenure as president in 2010. Thus, in only thirteen years NAMB was led by four different presidents. Ezell immediately embarked on an ambitious partnership with state conventions and local associations to see every SBC church planting other churches. This evangelical initiative is called God's Plan for Sharing (GPS). Other twenty-first-century emphases for NAMB include Send Network, a church planting ministry. Through Send Network, NAMB provides assessment, training, coaching, and church planter care support for Southern Baptist church planting missionaries. NAMB also helps equip churches for church planting and helps them discover and develop potential church planters in their congregation. Send Relief is NAMB's compassion ministry. Through Send Relief, NAMB helps pastors and churches become involved locally and nationally with compassion ministry. NAMB's focus in this area includes poverty, refugees and internationals, foster care and adoption, human trafficking and disaster response. Nevertheless, after ten years of leadership, Ezell has received increasing criticism. NAMB personnel, funding processes, and relationships have weakened considerably for at least six state conventions, particularly after NAMB announced the termination of cooperative agreements.[19]

By 2019, the number of NAMB missionaries stood at 5,200.[20] Almost $45 million was projected for home mission work. Furthermore, the annual Annie Armstrong Missions Offering provides a considerable amount of funds for the work. In 2019, the goal for this special offering was set at $70 million.[21] Ezell cites two priorities as NAMB faces the future. First, it is imperative that in the coming decades "champion pastors" are used to train other pastors and churches to be involved with missions. Second, NAMB must lead the way in planting churches where the people are. For example, over 80 percent of North America's population lives in larger urban areas.[22]

International Mission Board

The interest of international missions in the hearts and pocketbooks of Southern Baptists cannot be underestimated. Half of all

Cooperative Program money is channeled to the International Mission Board (IMB). Add to that the Lottie Moon Christmas Offering whose 2020 goal was $155 million, and the total money targeted for missions each year is an incredible 60 percent of all money coming to the SBC. The SBC maintains far and away the most extensive Protestant international mission work in the world.

After the retirement of Keith Parks, Jerry Rankin served seventeen years as president of the IMB (1993–2010). In 1993, nearly 4,000 missionaries helped start more than 2,000 churches in 142 countries. By 2010, more than 5,500 missionaries helped plant nearly 27,000 churches and engage 101 new people groups.[23] The largest controversy during Rankin's term was the requirement for all missionaries to sign the Baptist Faith and Message 2000. Several missionaries were convinced that this made the confession into a creed. It led to the eventual dismissal or resignation of 120 missionaries in the early 2000s.[24]

The next two presidents who followed Rankin served short tenures. Tom Elliff was selected to replace Rankin, but resigned after serving only three years (2011–2014). David Platt became the next president but lasted only from 2014 to 2018. Platt led the IMB through a significant time of transition due to budget constraints. By 2015, a $21 million budget deficit had to be addressed. Platt led the organization through numerous cutbacks which included more than 1,100 missionaries and staff who took early retirement or were laid off. Platt also made other changes to the qualifications for those who can serve as missionaries. One change was lifting the ban on speaking in tongues. Platt's platform focused on four foundational principles—exalting Christ (through accomplishing the Great Commission), mobilizing Christians (to see the doors God opens to missions), serving the church (through making disciples and multiplying churches), and playing our part (the obligation and ambition to preach the gospel where Christ is not known).[25] One of Platt's last decisions in office was to initiate sexual abuse investigations.[26]

Missionaries are now called "Church Planters." They form the core of missionary presence around the world. They are field-based and fully-funded by the IMB. The "Journeyman Program" is an IMB-funded program for recent college graduates between the ages of twenty-one and thirty. Journeymen serve in church planting roles on an IMB missionary team for two to three years. "Support roles" are field-based professional roles that support the administration, operations, communications, and technology needs of IMB personnel around the world.

Professionals, students, and retirees are targeted for IMB work. These three groups can reach people and places that traditional missionaries cannot.[27]

Paul Chitwood was tabbed as the thirteenth IMB president in 2018. Thus, similar to NAMB, the IMB shuffled four presidents in less than ten years, although with minimal conflict. As a first order of business, Chitwood promised to implement any sexual abuse recommendations. The number of missionaries at the conclusion of 2020 stood at 3,558.[28]

LifeWay Christian Resources

By convention action the Baptist Sunday School Board became LifeWay Christian Resources of the Southern Baptist Convention, or LifeWay. Jimmy Draper retired in 2006. Thom Rainer, the dean of the Billy Graham School of Evangelism at Southern Seminary, succeeded Draper. He would serve in the role of LifeWay president from 2006 to 2019.

LifeWay juggles several ministries under its banner. Discipleship Training began as the Baptist Young People's Union in the 1890s for youth on Sunday evenings. The movement changed its name successively to Baptist Training Union in 1934 to include all ages, then to Church Training, and then to Discipleship Training. For all of the incredible growth witnessed in Sunday School, Discipleship Training has gone the other way. Many Southern Baptist churches (as well as most denominations) are impoverished in training disciples beyond Sunday morning. Consequently, many Southern Baptists are increasingly ignorant of the Southern Baptist heritage and doctrines.[29]

Another area of emphasis is Vacation Bible School. VBS influence increased after World War I. By the 1960s, most Southern Baptist churches had VBS. This enterprise also declined in the twenty-first century. Nevertheless, VBS retains a significant impact for Southern Baptists. Recent data reveals VBS was used in more than 25,000 Southern Baptist churches and reached more than 2.5 million people. VBS connects kids and parents to the church, serves as a venue to hear God's vocational call to ministry, and remains an effective evangelism strategy.[30]

Music is another ministry highlighted by LifeWay. Most hymnals produced by Southern Baptists prior to 1900 were compiled by local pastors. Then hymnals for all Southern Baptists began being published, including the *Baptist Hymn and Praise Book* (1904), *Broadman Hymnal* (1940), and the *Baptist Hymnal* (1956), which was revised in 1975, 1991, and 2008.[31] The latest revisions reflect local church desires for more praise songs and other contemporary worship songs. The *Baptist Hymnal* may be revised again someday, but more Southern Baptist churches utilize video technology.[32]

LifeWay, however, is centered around its ministry as a publishing house. The ministries above are underscored by the literature produced for them. Broadman Press was created in the 1920s. This action led to the development of Baptist bookstores. Broadman Press changed its name in 1994 to Broadman & Holman, and in 2006 to B & H Publishing.

Today, LifeWay offers Bible Studies for all age groups. Three Bible study approaches are available in CSB, NIV, KJV, or ESV. They may even be tailored around weekly sermons. The three are Explore the Bible (book-by-book Bible study), Bible Studies for Life (tackling real life issues), and The Gospel Project (chronological, Christ-centered Bible study).[33] In 1999, LifeWay announced the publication of the *Holman Christian Standard Bible* New Testament. The full Bible was completed in 2004, and revised in 2009. The HCSB was produced in part to offset costs for utilizing the *New International Version* in its literature. Yet its development was hastened because of NIV's revision in 2011 that included gender accurate language. The HCSB was thoroughly revised in 2017, and changed its name to the *Christian Standard Bible*.[34]

Although LifeWay sells products created by non–Southern Baptists, they must be from a decidedly conservative perspective that does not disagree with the 2000 Baptist Faith and Message. For example, in 2016, LifeWay pulled all books authored by Jen Hatmaker after she endorsed same-sex marriage.[35]

LifeWay's denominational impact may have lessened in recent years, but its influence continues into the twenty-first century. Several points may be made. First, LifeWay continues to provide religious education for laypeople within Southern Baptist (and other) churches, both in America and abroad. Second, the impact on missions and evangelism is evident. Their published literature used in Sunday Schools stressed missions and a conversion experience. Third, LifeWay has had a financial impact since Sunday School continues to be a conduit through which offerings are given. Fourth, LifeWay brings some unity amid diversity to Southern Baptist churches since most churches used

LifeWay literature. Fifth, the way a Southern Baptist church physically looks is influenced by LifeWay. Southern Baptist churches include "educational space" at nearly a two-one ratio to its worship space. Thus, LifeWay has even affected architecture. Sixth, LifeWay has influenced church staffing. Their literature includes such things as developing plural ministry positions in the churches. The staff position of minister of education or minister of discipleship maturity or minister of music or minister of worship all derive largely from the original need of Sunday School literature.[36]

Ranier, a prolific author, resigned in 2019 to pursue other ministry.[37] Ben Mandrell began his service as the new president of LifeWay in 2019. He immediately inherited tougher economic realities. Almost 4,000 employees worked for LifeWay in 170 stores. However, in 2019, after five years and $50 million loss of revenues, LifeWay closed all its brick and mortar stores. It now emphasizes online sales (see lifeway.com).

GuideStone Financial Resources

The Annuity Board changed its name to GuideStone Financial Resources in 2004. O.S. Hawkins has led the board since 1997. A significant decision was made to expand its scope of ministry to include evangelical churches and ministry organizations outside of the Southern Baptist Convention. This change enabled the board to welcome younger-aged participants into the program. The action leveraged its actuarial tables and lower health coverage liability against the aging Southern Baptist baby boomer pastors. In turn, this skyrocketed a record amount of assets. Total assets reported in 2020 was $14.9 billion. GuideStone's impact into the twenty-first century has been enormous. Years ago, Leon McBeth mentioned three benefits which have all increased in recent years: (1) a financial safety net for pastors and family; (2) its programs have caused ministers to ponder the monetary side of ministry; and (3) its unifying influence on Southern Baptists.[38] Hawkins retired in 2021 and was replaced by Hance Dilbeck.

Ethics and Religious Liberty Commission

The Christian Life Commission was changed to the Ethics and Religious Liberty Commission (ERLC) in 1997. This agency dramatically reflects the public shift from moderate to conservative policies. The name change paved the way for the agency to take a more active role in matters of religious liberty. Once the SBC dropped the Baptist Joint Committee on Public Affairs, they changed their name to the Baptist Joint Committee for Religious Liberty.[39]

ERLC's Richard Land kept Southern Baptists focused on conservative politics and policies through the first decade of the twenty-first century.[40] But Land never strayed too far from personal controversy during his tenure. Finally, a stormy 2012 saw Land accused of both racial insensitivity and plagiarism. He soon announced his retirement.[41]

Russell Moore took over the ERLC in 2013, and immediately began stamping his own brand upon it. He is a staunch conservative, but used more winsome rhetoric. Under his leadership, the SBC has embraced a broader public agenda and perhaps a little less partisan. Nevertheless, ERLC represents the political voice of the SBC and Republican causes are front and center. Yet Moore opposed Donald Trump's presidential run, opting to support other Republicans. Trump's victory prompted some leaders in the SBC to demand Moore's removal. More conservative-oriented Southern Baptists did not approve of Moore's approach because it sometimes sounded conciliatory to liberal causes. Yet other Southern Baptists, particularly younger ones, appreciated Moore. In 2021, however, Moore resigned.[42]

Woman's Missionary Union

The only commission to survive was the retooled ERLC. Another entity that was not outwardly affected was the WMU. Wanda Lee served as president of Georgia WMU from 1993 to 1996. She served as national president from 1996 to 2000. Lee was elected executive director of national WMU in 2000. She is the only woman in the history of WMU to hold these positions.[43] Sandra Wisdom-Martin has served as the executive director since 2016.[44] She brought twenty-five years of experience in state WMU and church and community ministry. The WMU maintains their mission emphasis with twelve magazines and numerous conferences, among other things. Their willingness to remain open to moderate Southern Baptist churches and entities and to other Baptist denominations for the sake of missions has produced friction with SBC in the recent past.

Southern Baptist Seminaries

The remainder of this chapter focuses on the six seminaries which were only briefly mentioned until now. Their stories will be summarized from their inauguration to 2021. The widespread suspicion cast upon the seminaries was the source of much of the conservative movement's power. Yet widespread suspicion of higher education has always been part and parcel for many Baptists. Southern Baptists remained ambivalent toward higher education throughout much of the nineteenth century. Oliver Hart and Richard Furman helped assuage fears in the eighteenth century. After 1800, religious awakenings prompted Baptists to observe the value of educating themselves. It was the well-educated pastors who could define and defend the historic Baptist faith against Campbellism and Methodists on the frontier.

The college movement began when Hart and Furman supported the development of the Charleston Fund to help students with money and books. Books were given to Furman University and eventually to Southern Seminary. Luther Rice also persuaded the Triennial Convention to give to Columbian College. The religious awakenings that occurred from 1800 to 1850 encouraged the starting of more colleges despite a persistent anti-educational bias. Furman University was founded in Edgefield, South Carolina, in 1825. By 1845, Baylor University in Waco, Texas, became the sixth Baptist college. By the 1890s, there were almost thirty Baptist colleges. The religious departments of these colleges were the incubators for the development of seminaries.[45]

Southern Baptist Theological Seminary

Many Baptist leaders recognized a need for a separate theological institution. A group of likeminded people met for planning in Augusta, Georgia, in 1856. The eventual result was that in 1859, the theological department of Furman University moved to Greenville, South Carolina. Four professors—James P. Boyce, John Broadus, Basil Manly, and William Williams—along with twenty-six students opened the seminary. Boyce was elected chair of the faculty (the title of president came later). The professors all signed a statement called the Abstract of Principles. Although limited to professors from this one school, it nevertheless became the oldest confession or statement of faith among Southern Baptists.[46]

4. A Heritage of Change

The economic devastation of South Carolina during the Civil War, coupled with postwar depression, led to a relocation of the school to Louisville, Kentucky, in 1877. The seminary endured what was called the Toy Controversy. Crawford H. Toy joined the faculty in 1869 after a two-year sabbatical study in Germany. Toy adopted the theory of evolution and higher biblical critical assumptions and methods promoted in Europe. By the mid–1870s his views on inspiration became controversial enough that he was forced to resign in 1879.[47] Boyce served capably as president from 1859 until his death in December 1888.[48]

Original Southern Seminary faculty member John A. Broadus accepted the role of president upon the death of Boyce in December of 1888. He served from 1888 to 1895. Not much is reported on his presidency except that he maintained the seminary and kept it moving forward. His death paved the way for William H. Whitsitt's presidency.[49]

Whitsitt became Southern Seminary's third president, serving from 1895 to 1899. William Mueller related that "everything else considered, the achievements under W.H. Whitsitt's all too brief administration were quite remarkable."[50] The "everything else considered" refers to the Whitsitt Controversy that forced his resignation from the presidency. Whitsitt arrived at Southern Seminary in 1872 to teach church history. Along the way he uncovered the actual origins of Baptists. In 1896, soon after he became president, Whitsitt published (anonymously at first) several articles in *Johnson's Universal Cyclopedia*. These articles ran counter to the thinking of a majority of Southern Baptists on the topic of Baptist beginnings. The Landmark view of historic succession of Baptist churches all the way back to Jesus, John the Baptist, and the Jordan River was the prevalent interpretation. Whitsitt claimed that baptism by immersion can be traced back only to 1641, and Baptists themselves can be traced back only to the early 1600s. The subsequent uproar forced Whitsitt to resign from the presidency and seminary in 1899. Whitsitt was questioned on his character, judgment, and fitness for office. His arrogance toward others and disdain for Landmarkism did not aid his situation. The controversy was nurtured by B.H. Carroll, whose grief over Whitsitt's views eventually prompted him to form another seminary in Fort Worth, Texas—Southwestern Baptist Theological Seminary.[51]

The result of these two early controversies at Southern Seminary hardened the suspicions of many Southern Baptists toward seminary education, the extent of the relationship between seminaries and the convention, and especially raised suspicions toward how much academic freedom professors had within the confessional commitments. These issues can be seen throughout this entire section on the seminaries.

Southern Seminary entered the twentieth century still reeling from the Whitsitt affair. E.Y. Mullins, however, proved to be a capable president. He served from 1899 to 1928. The school experienced unprecedented expansion during his tenure. He was also an influential theologian and denominational leader. Out of his classroom experiences a pivotal textbook, *The Christian Religion in Its Doctrinal Expression*, was published in 1917. Eventually, nine other books came forth, most notably among them, *The Axioms of Religion*. Mullins became one of the most influential Baptists of the twentieth century. His influence extended to all spheres of Southern Baptist life. From 1921 to 1924 Mullins served as the president of the Southern Baptist Convention. Mullins helped to develop the consensus doctrinal statement called the Baptist Faith and Message, adopted in 1925. Mullins's legacy, however, has produced two interpretations. For moderate Southern Baptists, Mullins attempted to balance theologically the extremes between fundamentalism and liberalism. For conservative Southern Baptists, especially the Calvinist-minded, Mullins bowed his knee more toward liberalism and Arminianism, and his heritage should not be as greatly honored today.[52]

Old Testament professor John R. Sampey was chosen as the next president. His service extended from 1929 to 1942. Sampey served during the challenging era of economic downturn in America and burgeoning world war. Thus, his tenure centered around finances. Sampey's hard work reduced the seminary's debt by $800,000. Gregory Wills states, however, that it was during this time that progressive theology infiltrated the seminary. Yet Sampey himself opted for the term "progressive conservatism." Wills also catalogs internal controversies during Sampey's term of office. Sampey retired near the age of eighty years.[53]

Ellis A. Fuller, an influential pastor from Atlanta, became the next president (1942–1950). He was decidedly more conservative, and elected for this reason. Wills writes, "Fuller faced enormous challenges. The most urgent demand was to expand the school's faculty and physical plant to meet the demands of an exploding student population. Fuller was an energetic and visionary leader, an irrepressible soul. He seemed precisely the right man for job."[54] Fuller led the seminary to develop degree programs to answer the need for both music and religious education leaders. Student body and budget doubled during this time. Fuller's term, however, was hampered by lack of faculty trust. He was concerned with the progressive theology of some of the faculty. But faculty members expected more faculty governance. Fuller, on the other hand, appealed more to his authoritative role as president. He died suddenly of a heart attack in 1950.[55]

Duke McCall served the longest of any seminary president, from 1951 to 1982. His longevity is impressive considering that much of the time it included discontent between faculty and administration. Like Fuller before him, McCall attempted to tighten the reins of more progressive-thinking faculty. Several rebelled, citing the normal governing independence from administration that included prerogatives of enlisting their own faculty appointments. The internal controversy exploded in 1958. It was called the Lexington Road Massacre because thirteen professors were fired. One was later reinstated. Other professors resigned, and some ended up at other Southern Baptist seminaries. McCall weathered the storm and achieved more administrative power. Yet toward the conclusion of his presidency, McCall received poor marks from Conservative Resurgence leaders. They accused him of maintaining the status quo (i.e., liberalism) at Southern Seminary.[56]

Roy L. Honeycutt seemed like a good fit to follow McCall. He was dean of the school of theology and provost before accepting the role as Southern Seminary's eighth president. He served from 1982 to 1993. But he faced immediate pressure. In 1982, professor Dale Moody's systematic theology opus, *The Word of Truth*, was published. It articulated a lack of confidence in the security of the believer. This was interpreted as too General Baptist ("Arminian") for modern tastes. The book, along with Moody's discomfort with the Abstract of Principles (the article on perseverance of the saints), and a history of progressive thinking, led to his contract not being renewed.[57]

The Conservative Resurgence was well under way by this time. Year by year the seminary elected more conservative trustees. Honeycutt was hamstrung and could not implement any lasting objectives. Moreover, Honeycutt's 1984 sermon "To Your Tents O Israel!" laid the gauntlet down and signaled that he would not bow quietly to conservatives taking over the seminary. In effect, he was calling the conservative takeover a holy war. Thus, Honeycutt became a target, along with several faculty members, particularly Glenn Hinson, Molly Marshall, Paul Simmons, and Ken Chafin. The Glorieta Statement of 1986 was accepted but to the conservatives' point of view, any concessions that Honeycutt and Southern Seminary faculty made were dishonest. Honeycutt attempted to appease Conservative Resurgence leaders with new conservative faculty appointments but he proved to be too slow in doing this. His decade-long battle as president ended with his retirement, made effective July 31, 1993.[58]

Trustees elected thirty-three-year-old R. Albert Mohler, Jr., in 1993 as Southern Seminary's ninth president. He was the editor of the Georgia Baptist Convention's state newspaper, and fully committed to the Conservative Resurgence. He hit the ground running, and implemented an abrupt conservative makeover of the institution. Mohler immediately enforced a strict adherence of the Abstract of Principles as he believed it was originally intended by Boyce back in 1856. In addition to the Abstract, correct stances on issues such as homosexuality, abortion, women's ordination, and the exclusivity of the gospel as the means of salvation were areas which Mohler listed as nonnegotiable. Citing the Abstract, he forced the resignation of Molly Marshall. Next, Diana Garland, head of the Carver School of Social Work, was targeted. She was fired and the Carver School was eliminated, eventually moving to Campbellsville University. Student enrollment plunged by half and Southern Seminary was placed on probation by accrediting agencies. By 1995, ten more faculty sought early retirement packages, and another ten retired early a few years later. Under Mohler's leadership almost 100 percent of faculty turned over within the first half-dozen years. The Lexington Road Massacre, Part 2, was a drawn-out affair.

Mohler reshaped Southern Seminary into a brand-new school. Faculty replacements included the best appointments among conservative evangelicals, committed to conservative theology. A new journal was launched titled *Southern Baptist Journal of Theology*. The Billy Graham School of Evangelism, Missions, and Church Growth was established. Enrollment had peaked in 1985 with 2,335 and then began to decline. It dropped sharply in Mohler's first years and 1998 saw 1,350 students enrolled. But enrollment eventually rebounded, and increased dramatically, hitting over 5,000 by 2017. Mohler himself has become a major spokesman for Southern Baptists on convention stances. He has spoken, written, and blogged on numerous issues.

Southern Seminary is often coined as the convention's flagship seminary due to its size, age, and academic credentials. Since Mohler, a Reformed Baptist, has been president, a noticeable shift toward more Reformed theology is observable in its graduates. Mohler's presidency will certainly become the longest of any other seminary president. His hostile entrance into leadership made everyone take notice. His longevity in leadership set the mold for the direction of many Southern Baptists for generations to come.[59]

Southwestern Baptist Theological Seminary

The motives for establishing a second Southern Baptist seminary included the spiritual needs of the west (west of the east coast anyway), the long distance from Louisville's seminary, and particularly the lingering displeasure with the Whitsitt Controversy. Texas pastor B.H. Carroll was dissatisfied with Whitsitt's influence over Southern Baptists. Carroll himself was moderate Calvinist with postmillennial sympathies, but he was also Landmarkist.[60] He founded Southwestern Seminary out of Baylor University's department of theology in Waco, Texas, in 1908. The school moved to Fort Worth in 1910, along with seven faculty and 126 students. Carroll's intellect and personality were great, and he greatly influenced Texas Baptists. He died in 1914.[61]

L. R. Scarborough was an evangelist, denominational statesman, and voluminous author.[62] His service as Southwestern Seminary's second president extended from 1914 to 1942. In addition to being president, he retained his "Chair of Fire" in the evangelism department. The departments of religious education and music were established soon after his tenure began. He proved to be a popular and influential figure in the Southern Baptist Convention. His terms as president of the Baptist General Convention of Texas and the Southern Baptist Convention underscore his influence. The most serious threat was the constant attacks by fundamentalist J. Frank Norris. Some historians point to the snub of Norris at not being considered a candidate as Carroll's successor to the presidency in 1914 as the underlying cause for his abuse. Whatever the reason, Norris made it part of his ongoing ministry to undermine and destroy Southwestern Seminary.[63] Scarborough effectively led the seminary through tough times.[64]

Scarborough was succeeded by Texas pastor E.D. Head. He served as president from 1942 to 1953. Coming out on the other side of the

Great Depression and World War II, Head led the seminary into prosperous times. Lingering debt was eliminated, and buildings and programs were built. Enrollment rose from 734 to 2,160, and the faculty grew from twenty-three to forty-two full-time members. Poor health resulted in his early retirement.[65]

Denominational leader J. Howard Williams became the fourth president of Southwestern Seminary. His service was brief, and he died after five years (1953–1958). Nevertheless, enrollment numbers dramatically increased during this time. Williams made thirty-seven additions to the teaching staff, and he set into motion plans for updated facilities, technologies, and library resources. Robert Baker's history of the school titled the chapter on Williams as "Five Golden Years."[66]

Pastor and denominational leader Robert Naylor succeeded Williams. Naylor's twenty-year tenure (1958–1978) produced unprecedented growth. Enrollment numbers swelled to an all-time high, making Southwestern Seminary the largest seminary in the world at that time. To accommodate this growth, Naylor expanded campus facilities and launched new structures as well. Faculty additions doubled during his service to the school. The Elliott and *Broadman Bible Commentary* controversies occurred during Naylor's term in office, and the inklings of a Conservative Resurgence surfaced toward the end. Naylor stressed to critics that the Baptist Faith and Message (1963) adequately reflected Southwestern's position.[67]

Russell H. Dilday served as president from 1978 until 1994. Financial successes, growth in enrollment, and new buildings and renovation characterized his presidency.[68] Nevertheless, the Conservative Resurgence changed everything. Dilday kept track of the Controversy and spoke infrequently about it. But in 1984, he preached a sermon titled "On Higher Ground" at the Southern Baptist Convention meeting in New Orleans. Dilday's message placed him squarely in the crosshairs of conservatives bent on reshaping the convention. Once conservative trustees were elected it was only a matter of time before a showdown between them and the president took place. Dilday promised to tone down his political activity. It was not enough, however, to salvage his job. The trustees fired Dilday in March 1994. His doctrine was sound and he was given a recent satisfactory job assessment. Yet Dilday was fired for being too sympathetic to moderate Southern Baptists and blocking conservative reforms at Southwestern. Paul Pressler asserted that firing Dilday was necessary. If he "had been allowed to remain, with the faculty retirements which would soon occur, he could appoint many to the faculty who were not sympathetic to the conservative theology."[69] Moderates, of course, were shocked. Grady Cothen explained that "the true nature and form of fundamentalism was starkly revealed and displayed in the Southwestern debacle."[70] Dilday's dismissal ignited a firestorm of protest from students, alumni, and donors and prompted a rebuke and two-year probation from accrediting agencies.[71]

Pastor and author Kenneth S. Hemphill became the seventh president. After the fallout with Dilday's termination, Hemphill regrouped and guided the seminary for nine years (1994–2003). The accrediting agencies restrictions were lifted, and enrollment rebounded. However, when the convention passed the Baptist Faith and Message 2000, around ten faculty members were forced to sign or resign.[72] Apparently, Hemphill himself resigned under pressure for supporting women in ministry. He hired Sheri Klouda as a Hebrew professor and supported the tenure of history professor, Karen Bullock. Conservative leadership looked down upon women teaching men.[73]

Paige Patterson served as the president of Criswell College in Dallas, Texas (1975–1992), and Southeastern Seminary (1992–2003) before arriving at Fort Worth to serve as Southwestern Seminary's eighth president. He served from 2003 to 2018. Patterson was the premier leader of the Conservative Resurgence. His conservativism and maverick leadership produced issues for the school, including an attempted lawsuit from one former female faculty member who was dismissed because she was a woman (Klouda).[74] Karen Bullock, along with Stephen Stookey, were both denied tenure, prompting their departures.[75] In 2014, Patterson was reprimanded for not following school bylaws in allowing a Muslim student into the doctoral program.[76] Finally, reports of his mishandling and dishonesty concerning a rape investigation during his previous tenure as president of Southeastern culminated in his immediate dismissal.[77]

Adam Greenway has served as president since 2019. Greenway took over Southwestern at a tumultuous time. The presidential turnover masked the underlying financial difficulties the seminary had experienced during the previous years. The music school was disbanded and five professors lost their jobs. Greenway arrived having served as evangelism professor and dean of the Billy Graham School of Missions, Evangelism, and Ministry at Southern Seminary. He promises a new day for Southwestern, and cites the school as a "big tent" seminary.[78]

New Orleans Baptist Theological Seminary

The Baptist Bible Institute was established in 1917 in New Orleans, Louisiana. It was the first theological institution to be created by the direct action of the Southern Baptist Convention. This was the fulfillment of a century-old dream to reach the city of New Orleans and to establish a missionary training school at the gateway to Latin America. Byron H. DeMent was unanimously elected as the first president. The school experienced a solid beginning under his leadership. He served from 1917 to 1928.[79]

DeMent stepped down yet retained his faculty status as New Testament professor. W.W. Hamilton became the next president, and his term spanned from 1928 to 1942. He steered the school during its struggle for survival during its financial crisis due in large part to the Great Depression. Hamilton resigned suddenly in 1942. This paved the way for twenty-nine-year-old Duke McCall to become president. McCall's service to the school was short (1943–1946), but he launched a significant financial campaign that renovated and expanded school properties. The school's name was officially changed to New Orleans Baptist Theological Seminary in 1946. McCall moved on to become the Executive Secretary-Treasurer of the SBC Executive Committee before landing as the president of Southern Seminary in 1951.[80]

The administration of Roland Q. Leavell came next. He served from 1946 to 1958. Under Leavell, the seminary relocated to its present site. He expanded and reorganized the school into three areas (theology, Christian education, and music). Leavell's tenure was an era of prosperity for the seminary. When Leavell retired, he gave way to H. Leo Eddleman, who served from 1959 to 1970. Eddleman's presidency was plagued by the national uncertainty of the 1960s. Eddleman was also very conservative, and disenfranchised alumni and faculty. In some ways, his experience offered a glimpse of the future Conservative Resurgence. Next, Grady C. Cothen left the presidency of Oklahoma Baptist University to serve as the seminary's sixth president. His tenure was short but he led the school in a massive curriculum revision study that abolished separate schools and formed five academic divisions. Cothen served New Orleans from 1970 to 1974 before moving on to become president of Southern Baptist Sunday School Board (1975–1984).[81]

Pastor Landrum P. Leavell, nephew of Roland, was selected as the next president. In his two-decade service (1975–1996), the seminary's enrollment more than quadrupled. Its endowment grew from $1.5 million to $23 million. Leavell rescued the school's undergraduate program from near collapse. In addition, his presidency established an extensive network of satellite centers across the Southeast where distant students can pursue seminary studies. Leavell arrived just as the Southern Baptist Convention was plunging into the Controversy. While other institutions were wracked by the uproar, Leavell managed to thread the seminary through the upheaval with relatively little turmoil, in large part because he himself was a theological conservative.[82] Nevertheless, Conservative Resurgence proponents complained of a few faculty members, particularly Fisher Humphreys's views on the atonement.[83]

Charles Kelley became the school's eighth president. His administration spanned 1996 to 2019. During his lengthy tenure, technology and distance learning were emphasized. The school endured the devastation brought by Hurricane Katrina in 2005. It caused $20 million damage to the seminary yet it was the only school in New Orleans that continued all its programs and all its classes that fall despite no access to the campus. Kelley completed a successful twenty-three years as president and thirty-five years as evangelism professor.[84]

Jamie Dew has served as New Orleans Seminary's president since 2019. Dew most recently served as vice president of undergraduate studies and distance learning at Southeastern Seminary. He closed his inaugural address with an exposition of the seminary's new mission statement: "New Orleans Baptist Theological Seminary and Leavell College prepare servants to walk with Christ, proclaim His truth, and fulfill His mission."[85]

Gateway Seminary

The vision of many faithful people for a seminary on the west coast eventually came to fruition in 1944. Pastor Isam B. Hodges founded Golden Gate Baptist Theological Seminary in a church in Oakland, California. Sixteen students enrolled. It almost folded after its first year, but enough money and students became available to proceed. Hodges reluctantly left after two years as the trustees pushed for a more experienced educator as president.[86]

The experienced educator was B.O. Herring, who served as the seminary's second president from 1946 to 1952. Herring moved the school to its first campus site in Berkeley. Enrollment jumped to 142 students within a few years, and the financial pressure lessened. The seminary was officially adopted by the Southern Baptist Convention meeting in Chicago in 1950. From its beginnings, Golden Gate Seminary stressed the blending of the academic with the practical nature of theological studies. However, Herring ultimately came into conflict with some faculty. Those teaching in the practical disciplines felt slighted by other faculty members. When Herring stepped in and asked one faculty member, F.M. Powell, to resign, the decision backfired. As a result, both Powell and Herring resigned.[87]

Harold K. Graves was selected to lead the seminary next. His twenty-five-year presidency (1952–1977) produced a lasting legacy. The campus moved from Berkeley to Strawberry Point in Mill Valley, eight miles north of the Golden Gate Bridge. After five years of construction, classes opened in 1959. Graves's stamp on Golden Gate was indelible. He oversaw the construction of new classroom buildings, office space, library, and student housing. Enrollment and finances grew steadily. Graves effectively navigated the racial and social changes that hit the west coast during the 1960s. Nevertheless, two faculty members left or were asked to leave in 1965 over their desires for a stronger seminary stance on racial equality and opposition to the Viet Nam war—LeRoy Moore and James McClendon. The first regional campus of Golden Gate was opened in Brea in 1973. More regional campuses followed.[88]

The presidencies of William Pinson, Jr. (1978–1983) and Franklin D. Pollard (1983–1986) were short, spanning less than ten years. Pinson inherited close to 500 students. The Pacific Northwest Campus (now in Vancouver, Washington) was added in 1980. The Doctor of Philosophy program opened in 1981. But Pinson left after five years to become the Executive Director of the Baptist General Convention of Texas. Pollard's presidency was likewise brief. The seminary was doing well and enrollment exceeded 800 in 1985.[89] The Conservative Resurgence, however, burst forth during their presidencies. It would not be a stretch to suggest their terms were shortened by their own desires to steer clear of controversy. Pollard resigned to reenter the pastorate. The presidency of Golden Gate Seminary was a prize that both moderates and conservatives coveted.

William O. Crews was selected as the seminary's next president, serving from 1986 to 2004. He was not a conservative activist but did receive the blessing of Conservative Resurgence leaders. Crews's administration was notable. Leroy Gainey became the second African

American to be trustee-elected faculty member in Southern Baptist life.[90] Multicultural ministry was emphasized and many future faculty appointments were non–Anglo. Crews accented the practical aspects of ministerial training. This lessened the academic rigor that many faculty members expected, and raised concerns. Crews's term also saw more extension campuses open in Phoenix, Arizona, and Denver, Colorado. All the extension campuses eventually became fully accredited regional campuses. The school purposefully distanced itself from the Controversy. However, academic dean Bob Cate was criticized by conservative leaders for a few publications. He left Golden Gate for Oklahoma State University in 1991. An internal controversy occurred in 1998 when Crews closed the music school. This led to the loss of three faculty members and distress among faculty and students. When Crews retired in 2004, he had left behind his own imprint for years to come.[91]

Jeff P. Iorg became the seventh president of the seminary in 2004. He is a pastor, denominational leader, and author who is committed to evangelism and cultural engagement. The qualities of leadership training stressed by Crews was complemented with Iorg's desire to raise academic standards that had slipped. The curriculum was revised to reflect this. The Doctor of Philosophy program, which closed in 1989, reopened in 2007. The Jonathan Edwards Center was opened in 2019. Iorg's lasting mark will certainly be his leadership in moving the campus. In 2016, Golden Gate Seminary moved over 400 miles south to Ontario, California. The move precipitated a name change—Gateway Seminary. The new facility came equipped with the cutting-edge technology for students to serve the next generation. Gateway Seminary continues to emphasize missions, Pacific Rim culture, ethnic diversity, church leadership, online delivery systems, and the development of regional campuses throughout the western United States.[92]

Southeastern Baptist Theological Seminary

Southeastern Seminary was authorized and adopted by the Southern Baptist Convention in 1951. It is located in Wake Forest, North Carolina. The motive for founding the school included the recognition of the loss that Southern Seminary's move to Louisville meant geographically for the Southeast. Classes began in the fall of 1951 with Sydnor L. Stealey as the first president. Eighty-five students were served by three faculty members. Stealey led the seminary its first dozen years

(1951–1963). When Wake Forrest University left its campus in 1956, Southeastern Seminary acquired it. Stealey's administration experienced a solid start to the school. By 1963, the school grew to 575 students and twenty-eight faculty.[93]

Olin T. Binkley served as the school's second president (1963–1974). He continued the renovation projects on the property initiated by Stealey. Four old buildings were removed and thirteen new ones were constructed. His term also added Master of Religious Education and Doctor of Ministry degrees. Binkley retired in good standing in 1974. Conservatives, however, considered Southeastern to be too progressive. This came to the forefront during the next president's administration.[94]

Randall Lolley served as Southeastern Seminary's third president from 1974 to 1988. Enrollment had reached 663 with twenty-four faculty members in 1974. The next decade continued to be prosperous for the school. Several renovation projects were started to meet the influx of ever-increasing enrollment. Seminary enrollment peaked in 1983 with almost 1,400 students and thirty-six faculty.[95] Southeastern Seminary, however, felt the brunt first and worst when the Conservative Resurgence began. The progressive-minded institution with their progressive-thinking faculty were an early target for conservative leaders. A Peace Committee subcommittee met at the school and heard concerns from conservative students. Some teachers were accused of universalism, belief in homosexuality, and profanity. Once the balance of trustees favored the conservatives, Lolley's days as president were numbered. In 1987, he chose to resign the following year rather than implement the trustee's conservative agenda. Four other administrators resigned as well.[96]

Lewis Drummond was selected as the next president. His service was short, lasting from 1988 to 1992, before he retired due to health reasons. His first appointment was Russ Bush as the new dean of faculty, despite the unanimous vote of opposition from the faculty. Internal conflict, therefore, continued until more conservative faculty were hired. Student enrollment declined by half, from about 1,400 to less than 800. Eighteen faculty and administrators resigned or retired early by the end of Drummond's time. The school was placed on academic probation by accrediting agencies.[97]

Paige Patterson was elected as Southeastern Seminary's fifth president. He served from 1992 until 2003, when he left to become Southwestern Seminary's president. With the Conservative Resurgence's architect in place as president, sweeping changes ensued at Southeastern. New curriculum, faculty, administrators, and vision produced a new day. Student enrollment increased. By 1997, they reached their highest numbers since 1983. The numbers would continue to climb. Patterson added the College at Southeastern in 1994 and the Doctor of Philosophy program in 1995. Faculty would eventually reach sixty in number. Upon his resignation, Patterson pointed to the unprecedented theological shift he helped to produce. "In all the history of Christianity, I know of no other case in which an institution that was formed originally as a liberal school ... returned to the faith of the fathers and became a conservative school."[98]

Daniel L. Akin became the new president and has served since 2004. Prior to his administration he served as a professor at Southeastern and Southern. Under Akin's realm, the last several years show consistent growth in enrollment up to more than 3,500 students. He added multiple endowed professorship chairs. Akin is known for his emphasis upon the Great Commission, and he writes and preaches regularly on international missions. He describes himself as a "four-point Calvinist."[99]

Midwestern Baptist Theological Seminary

Midwestern Seminary is located in Kansas City, Missouri. The seminary arose after Southern Baptists distanced themselves from another Kansas City seminary—Central Baptist Theological Seminary. The spark that lit the possibility of a competing Kansas City seminary occurred in 1950. The name change adopted by Northern Baptists to American Baptists, coupled with an invitation to unite together again under one banner was received poorly by Southern Baptists, who were doing just fine on their own. A few years later, the SBC was looking for a sixth seminary, and Kansas City won the geographical prize.[100]

Millard Berquist was elected as the first president in 1958. The first faculty members were drafted from Southern Seminary to form a core of professors. This caused angst among some Southern Baptists. One of those professors was Ralph Elliott. The Elliott Controversy erupted in 1961 over his book *The Message of Genesis*. It caused a storm among conservative Southern Baptists because the book accepted the historical-critical view of the Pentateuch that undercut views on Mosaic authorship and historical reliability of Genesis. Elliott was fired a year later not for the content of his book but for insubordination. The 1963 Baptist Faith and Message was a result of the controversy. Despite the furor, President Berquist was well-liked and enjoyed a fruitful term. He retired after fifteen years (1958–1972).[101]

Milton Ferguson was elected as the second president. He was formerly a professor at Southwestern Seminary, and served Midwestern from 1972 to 1995. Ferguson's accomplishments included renovation and expansion projects, a campus extension center, Doctor of Ministry program, and a new music program. The Conservative Resurgence prompted an earlier than expected retirement. Professors under fire from conservatives during this time included Temp Sparkman who was charged with universalism, which he denied. By 1991, Ferguson was faced with a majority of trustees elected by the Conservative Resurgence. They instituted rapid changes. Sparkman resigned soon afterward. Professor Wilburn Stancil became a new target, and he was denied tenure by the trustees. This prompted a visit from accrediting agencies who issued notations that included "inappropriate control over Administration and Faculty."[102] Stancil left the school the following year. With more professors seeking tenure soon (no doubt to face similar results), and coupled with the firing of fellow seminary president Russell Dilday at Southwestern, Ferguson chose to retire.[103]

Mark T. Coppenger was elected as Midwestern Seminary's third president in 1995. Under his leadership the Conservative Resurgence agenda was now in full swing. Coppenger became known for his outspoken stance against the ordination of women, his Calvinistic theology, and his commitment to the conservative program. Conservative faculty were hired and in due course enrollment blossomed from 500 to 700 students. By 1999, all the notations from accrediting agencies that surrounded the Stancil affair had been lifted. Nevertheless, after only five years (1995–1999), Coppenger was fired by the trustees for "expressions of anger" that have "irreparably damaged his ability to lead this seminary." His dismissal was effective immediately.[104]

After a short interim, R. Philip Roberts was selected to replace Coppenger, and he served from 2001 until 2012. In addition to renovating existing buildings, his term saw the acquisition of Charles Spurgeon's library from William Jewel College in 2006. Yet Roberts's eleven-year presidency proved to be troubling and trustees attempted three times to oust him. A forensic audit uncovered serious financial irregularities. "Trustee leaders said Roberts shuffled money between seminary accounts and misused designated funds in order to mislead trustees, auditors and SBC officials about the school's true financial status."[105] Roberts resigned before he was fired.[106]

Jason K. Allen was chosen as Midwestern Seminary's fifth president in 2013. He was a vice president at Southern Seminary before his selection. Allen has brought calm to a seminary that endured numerous controversies over its lifetime. His term has witnessed consistent growth. Allen also serves as associate professor for preaching and pastoral ministry, and he maintains writing and preaching ministries.

Conclusion

The Controversy and the subsequent "Covenant for a New Century" have dramatically reshaped the Southern Baptist Convention. This reshaping was not limited to retooling agencies and entities or dropping them altogether. The restructuring is evident in how Southern Baptists now think and believe. The final chapter will address the topic of theology.

Discussion Questions

1. The "Covenant for a New Century" restructured the Southern Baptist Convention beginning in 1995. What appear to the be the strengths of the restructuring? The weaknesses? Who or what agencies/entities came out winners? Who are the losers?
2. List some concrete ways that state conventions and associations can be organized for greater impact in the twenty-first century.
3. What are the strengths of the Cooperative Program? What are some weaknesses? List specific ways to inform your church about the Cooperative Program.
4. What are the challenges which the IMB and NAMB face in the twenty-first century? How can local Southern Baptist churches help (beyond the call for finances)?
5. The ERLC represents the SBC in the arena of ethics and religious liberty. What are the strengths of promoting partisan politics? What are the weaknesses?
6. Which SBC seminaries were hit the hardest by the Conservative

Resurgence? Which ones were impacted the least? List reasons why you think this happened.

7. List the controversies which each seminary experienced. Trace any common themes or characteristics. Do any of these themes or characteristics stand out?

8. Several seminary controversies revolved around the issue of the academic freedom to explore over against the boundaries of denominational theology. What are the strengths and weaknesses of this issue?

≋ 5 ≋

A Theological Heritage
A Confessional People

When Southern Baptists discuss issues of theology, the question raised most often is "What do Southern Baptists believe?" The concern may be about the Bible, God, the security of the believer, the church, religious liberty, or any one of numerous other topics. However, the question usually begins "What do Baptists believe about (fill in the blank)?"

We propose that this is not the place to begin. The starting point for a proper appreciation and understanding of Baptist theology ought to be "How do Baptists believe?" or "How do they arrive at theological or doctrinal statements?" Then, the place and the purpose of theological statements must be examined. Finally, the role of Baptist theology can be reviewed in the context of the previous issues.

This chapter begins with a definition of "theology" and related terms. A discussion of the sources for Christian theology will follow, which will include an examination of the correlation of the revelation of God and the faith experience, plus the role of the Scriptures and the church. The next section of the chapter will examine the role, the origin, and the development of confessions of faith among Baptists in England and America. Special attention will be given to the place of confessionalism among Southern Baptists. This will be followed by a discussion in terms of leadership models of the Southern Baptist denominational theologian.

The final section will examine Baptist beliefs categorized by the topics covered in the Baptist Faith and Message. Included will be a review of Baptist interpretations of each topic. Also, a historical review will be presented on those topics which have resulted in controversy among Baptists in general and Southern Baptists in particular.

Some Definitions

When discussing theological issues, several terms come to mind. "Theology" in a Christian context "is a discipline of study that seeks to understand the God revealed in the Bible and to provide a Christian understanding of that reality."[1] Theology is derived from two Greek words, *theos* (God) and *logos* (word). Although the term may be narrowly defined to describe our thoughts about God only, it has come to be used in relation to all serious religious thought. "Doctrine," which comes from the Latin *doctrina* (teaching), is used in reference to the theological teachings that are more or less accepted by a particular denomination or by the church as a whole. Subsequently, a person may speak of Baptist doctrine or Christian doctrine. A word not used often in Baptist circles is "dogma." It comes from a Greek verb that means "to seem" or "to seem good." The term refers to the basic truths of doctrine which are officially proclaimed and maintained by a church or denomination. Baptists often use the word in a negative sense when they speak of an authoritarian person as being "dogmatic." Of the three terms discussed here, theology and doctrine are less exact than dogma.[2]

Sources for Formulating Doctrinal Statements

The question of "How do Baptists arrive at theological or doctrinal beliefs?" is essential in understanding Baptist theology.[3] Five sources are essential in formulating theological statements: the revelation of God, the faith experience of the believer, the Scriptures, the church, and the culture.

The Revelation of God

Baptists believe and the Bible teaches that God reveals himself in nature and that humanity is able to comprehend this. More important for Baptists and other Christians than this general revelation is the special revelation of God. Baptists believe that God has chosen to make himself known through special revelation, especially in his redemptive work in the history of humanity. Of utmost significance is the fact that in such events, "God discloses Himself, not thoughts or facts about Himself."[4] The Bible teaches that God revealed himself to Abraham,

Isaac, Jacob, Moses, and the prophets. The ultimate revelation of God was in the person of Jesus Christ. In this instance, the revelation of God was not theological or philosophical principles or facts about himself or religious matters. It was the event in the history of humanity when the Word of God "became flesh and dwelt among us" (John 1:14; CSB). God made himself known to humanity in a very personal manner in the incarnation.

With this understanding of special revelation in mind, the Bible takes on a new meaning. It becomes the written testimony or the recorded witness of those inspired, ancient personalities to whom God had made himself known. Long ago, W.T. Conner, who taught theology at Southwestern Seminary, concluded that revelation preceded the writing of the Bible. He stated that as the biblical authors "lived their lives, wrestled with their problems, received in different ways thoughts of God, had experiences with God," then they produced a written record of those thoughts and experiences. In light of this, the Bible is first and foremost a product of revelation.[5] God revealed himself, and the inspired writers produced a written record of his revelation and the consequences or influences of the same.

The New Testament is an excellent example of this perspective. Jesus Christ appeared as the complete revelation of God. He came, lived, taught, died, and was raised from the dead. He left no written statements or teachings. Out of his life and ministry arose the movement of Christianity, which centered around and advanced through the ministry and witness of his disciples.

As problems or issues developed in the church, or when those eyewitnesses to God's revelation in Christ began to die or be killed, the practical needs arose to address the problems or to preserve the witness of those who had been with Jesus. Paul, to whom Christ revealed himself on the road to Damascus, wrote his letters to address the questions and respond to the problems and concerns in the churches. Soon after Paul's letters, the Gospels were composed. They provided a written record for those who did not have the privilege of hearing eyewitness accounts about Jesus and his ministry. The Gospels instruct readers regarding Christ's redemptive work. Out of these and other writings came the New Testament, an inspired, practical book whose validity rests upon the authority of God who had revealed himself, and its value to the church. Conner wrote, "The New Testament did not produce Christianity, but Christianity produced the New Testament," which "grew out of the fact that God had revealed Himself in Christ, a significant fact."[6]

The Experience of Faith

God's revelation of himself is the objective side of theology. There must be, however, a recipient of God's revelation. Hence, the subjective side of theology is the faith experience of the believer. The first and most important question that Baptists ask the individual is not "What do you believe?" It is "In Whom do you believe?" or "Do you know Jesus?" and "Have you had a faith experience with him?"[7]

Baptists have always insisted upon the necessity of personal faith, of a direct encounter or experience with the God who has made himself known. They have emphasized that each person is capable of receiving, comprehending, and responding to God's revelation of himself. They have taught that the indwelling Christ through the work of the Holy Spirit can direct each believer toward all spiritual understanding and truth. E.Y. Mullins borrowed Roger Williams's term "soul competency."[8] The implication of soul competency is that there is no authority, civil or ecclesiastical, magistrate or minister, law or creed, which can stand between the individual believer and God. The Lordship of Christ is the only absolute authority, not any institution, personality, or theological statement.

Soul competency is a doctrine specifically articulated in a Southern Baptist context, first by Mullins in *The Axioms of Religion* (1908). This view emphasizes that each person (soul) is individually and personally accountable to God and "competent" to relate to God without mediation through other humans or human institutions. It may be properly related to, but not the same as, the doctrine of the priesthood of all believers. One clue to the significance of *The Axioms of Religion* by Mullins is found in the subtitle: *A New Interpretation of the Baptist Faith*.

The effect of Mullins's emphasis on soul competency has been criticized by many contemporary Southern Baptists as planting the seeds of experientialism within the Southern Baptist Convention. Albert Mohler, for example, recognized soul competency as Mullins's enduring legacy, yet related "soul competency also serves as an acid dissolving religious authority, congregationalism, confessionalism, and mutual theological accountability."[9]

Nevertheless, theology cannot be imposed upon one by a creedal statement or an ecclesiastical authority, whether church or minister. Instead, theology is the result of the believer's attempt to communicate the faith experience through the medium of words. One definition of theology is "God-talk," the manner in which we speak about God and other related topics. This is implied in two often-used theological terms. The word "creed" is derived from the Latin term *credo*, which translates to "believe."[10] "Confession" is rooted in *confessio*, which translates "to acknowledge" or "to confess."[11]

Both of these terms, when used in their most constructive sense, imply that theological statements are positive expressions that communicate the believer's experience and the implications of that experience. Theology then is a result of one who can say, "On the basis of my faith experience with the living God whom I know primarily through the revelation in his Son as witnessed to in the Scriptures, this I believe...." Of utmost consequence is the recognition that in the heritage of Baptists, theology is the product of faith, not a test of faith. Faith comes first; then theology flows out of that faith experience.

The Scriptures

A third source as Baptists attempt to respond theologically through the faith experience to God's revelation is the Scriptures. They test their experience with the God of revelation by comparing it with the experiences of the authors of the Bible, which is understood as the supreme authority in matters of faith and practice. Because of this position, "soul competency" does not mean that one can believe anything and be a Christian or a Baptist. It does mean that every believer through the Lordship of Christ and the leadership of the Holy Spirit has the right and the responsibility to study and interpret the Scriptures. Through constant examination and prayer, Baptists trust God to bring them to a deeper, more complete understanding of his truth and their faith.

Baptists have confidence that God will direct them by his Spirit through the Scriptures more than they trust any theological statements of individuals or churches.[12] Confessional statements and continued dialogue with others on theological issues are important. But the starting point is the Bible and its unique nature. The Bible is the record and the witness of its many writers who provided a testimony of their life-changing experiences with the God who has revealed himself known to them. They received his revelation. They interpreted that revelation in light of the world in which they lived. And they preserved a record of that revelation for all who would read it. As believers study their testimony, God over and over again makes himself known to them. He reveals himself anew through the witness of the Scriptures to every generation.

The Church

Another source in efforts to "theologize" is the importance of the Christian community. Baptists must be cautious of the danger of an individualistic approach to theology. Certainly "soul competency" is characterized by an emphasis upon the individual's experience with God, but it also involves confirmation and direction by the community of believers, especially the local congregation.[13] The church is a participant in the convert's initial confession that Jesus is one's Lord and in the believer's symbolic confession of baptism. The congregation must also have a continuing, active role in the maturing process of the experience of the believer and in the formulation of the believer's theology. The same is true of the associations of Baptists, but the atmosphere is to be one of love, compassion, and understanding, not coercion or intimidation. In such a process, the believer and the community of believers can meaningfully and progressively dialogue and communicate to others the theological expression of their faith.

One final note is necessary concerning the experience of faith. True faith expresses itself in more ways than just theologically. It also expresses itself as the believer worships God, both corporately and individually. Mission and ministry are not only valid but essential demonstrations of one's faith. Individual and corporate ethics are also based upon the faith of the believer. The overemphasis or the neglect of any of these expressions of faith will result in a distorted and unbalanced image of faith. Thus, mature faith is concerned with how Baptists worship God, how and what they believe, how believers serve and minister, and how they live on a personal and social level.

Culture

For theology to be relevant a consideration of changing culture, knowledge, and history is essential. The faith and its theological expression have been shaped by the advancement of the church from its

Jewish heritage into a universal world affected by Greek thought and culture in a Roman society. Throughout the history of Christianity as the movement spread geographically and confronted numerous cultures, Christian thought has been influenced by the society of humanity often reshaped by war, political disputes, and scientific advancements in numerous fields such as biology, archaeology, geology, physics, and chemistry. Moreover, developments of new machines, new technologies and new advancements in medicine, communications, and even the advent of space travel account for some of the dramatic cultural changes. Christians find themselves constantly having to revisit their understanding of God, faith, the church, and the mission of proclaiming the Good News in light of the consistency of change. Paul's teaching in Galatians 5:1 that "it is for freedom that Christ has set us free" reflects the challenge of understanding and communication of the faith in a rapidly changing world. For Christianity to be relevant it must adapt, restate to a contemporary world, and follow the command of Jesus to go to the "ends of the earth" with its message.

Baptist Confessions of Faith

Baptists throughout their history have avoided the adoption of authoritative and binding theological statements, which are often called creeds.[14] A creed is defined as "a confession of faith for public use, or a form of words setting forth with authority certain articles of belief which are regarded by the framers as necessary for salvation, or at least for the well-being of the Christian Church."[15] In a strict sense, creeds are considered to be theological statements that are binding upon all believers of all ages and therefore unchangeable and uncompromisable.

The reluctance toward adopting confessions is due to a fear of charting a path toward creedalism, a primary issue for the creation of a people called Baptists. McBeth made several distinctions between confessions and creeds. Confessions designate what people do believe; they are voluntary, and serve to inform, educate, and inspire. They offer guidelines under the authority of Scripture. Creeds, on the other hand, designate what people must believe; they are required, and are used to discipline and exclude. Creeds become a binding authority that subtly displaces the Bible.[16] Timothy George reminds contemporary Baptists that venerable shapers of Baptist tradition used the word "creed" in a positive sense. Nevertheless, it is "true that Baptists have never advocated *creedalism*."[17]

Thus, Baptists have rejected the use of creeds and instead have taken a "confessional" approach. From their beginnings, they have responded in freedom to the necessity of producing doctrinal statements which they have labeled "confessions of faith." These confessions were written and distributed by individuals, single congregations, and associations of churches. Although many Baptist confessions of faith have been written, they traditionally have not been binding. William L. Lumpkin stated that Baptists have lacked an authority which could impose a confessional statement upon individuals, churches, or associational bodies. He concluded that even if such an authority did exist, the desire for doctrinal uniformity has never been strong enough to adopt authoritative creeds.[18]

Positively, Baptists have found value in the use of confessional statements. Confessions which appeared in the seventeenth century were used for apologetic or propaganda purposes. Usually these confessions were responses to criticism from the Church of England, other churches, Quakers, and occasionally other Baptist groups. These confessions were used by Baptists to distinguish themselves from others or to demonstrate kinship with other Baptists or Protestants. Confessions were also used as theological summaries for instructing members, as statements to refute heretical teachings, and for direction in the study of the Bible—but never as authoritative substitutes for the Bible.[19]

English and American Baptist Confessions of Faith

The first Baptist confessions of faith appeared among the English General Baptists in the early 1600s in Amsterdam, Holland. In 1609, John Smyth established the first General Baptist church. He became dissatisfied with his self-baptism and applied for admission to a group of Waterlander Mennonites. He apparently sent along a confession of faith composed of twenty articles which was anti–Calvinistic and anti-pedobaptist (against infant baptism). This theological statement was followed in 1610 by "A Short Confession of Faith" which was signed by Smyth and forty-one other members of his congregation.[20] Thomas Helwys, who assumed leadership of those General Baptists who chose not to follow Smyth, produced a confession of his church entitled "A Declaration of Faith of English People Remaining at Amsterdam in

Holland." This confession was composed of twenty-seven articles. Its purpose was to defend truth, to instruct members of the Helwys congregation, and to repudiate unjust charges.[21]

In 1644, the first Particular Baptist confession of faith known later as the First London Confession was adopted by seven churches in London. This document was published to reject charges that the Particular Baptists were Anabaptists and to distinguish the position of the seven churches from those of the Anabaptists and the General Baptists. Care was taken to point out that each of these churches was a distinct and independent congregation which had voluntarily chosen to subscribe to the statement. A total of fifteen representatives from these churches signed this Calvinistic confession which contained fifty-three articles.[22]

Other English Baptist confessions began to appear. They included the first General Baptist Confession of Faith (in terms of an association of churches) in 1651; the Somerset Confession in 1656 which was produced by sixteen Particular Baptist churches; the Standard Confession of General Baptists from 1660 (this was presented to King Charles II by representatives of twenty thousand Baptists who sought to convince the king that they were not anarchistic Anabaptists but rather law-abiding citizens); and the Orthodox Creed prepared by General Baptists in 1678 whose purpose was "to unite and confirm all true Protestants against the errors and heresies of Rome."[23]

The most influential Particular Baptist confession was the Second London Confession. Signed by representatives of 107 churches, it was published in 1677. A second edition appeared in 1688 and was approved in 1689 by the first English Particular Baptist General Assembly. It was based on the Presbyterians' Westminster Confession of Faith (1646), and its purpose was to show the agreement of the London Particular Baptists with Presbyterians and Congregationalists.[24]

Confessional statements by Baptists in America were produced primarily for instructional and propaganda purposes. Most appeared during times of crisis and controversy. American Baptists published, used, and discarded freely their confessions of faith, but in no instance has a confession "permanently bound individuals, churches, associations, conventions, or unions of Baptists."[25] The first formal adoption of a confessional statement was in 1742 by the Philadelphia Association. It published a new edition of the Second London Confession, along with the addition of two articles. One article described the singing of Psalms, hymns, and spiritual songs in terms of "divine institution." The other article determined that the laying of hands upon baptized believers was "an ordinance of Christ."[26]

The Philadelphia Confession eventually was adopted by many associations including the Ketockton Association of Virginia (1766), the Warren Association of Rhode Island (1767), the Charleston Association of South Carolina (1761), and some early associations in Kentucky and Tennessee. The Philadelphia Confession was significant not only because it was the first American confession, but because it highlighted a Calvinistic theological heritage.

In 1833, the Baptist Convention of New Hampshire adopted a new confession of faith in response to the rising influence of the Free Will Baptists. Like English General Baptists, Free Will Baptists stressed general atonement among other tenets. They attracted people who grew tired of the rigid Calvinism of some Baptists. The New Hampshire Confession contained a more moderate interpretation of Calvinism. This confession became well-known through its publication in 1853 in J. Newton Brown's *The Baptist Church Manual*. Brown revised it and added two additional articles to the original sixteen. The New Hampshire Confession became the most widely accepted theological statement of Baptists in America. It was accepted or adapted by several Baptist organizations in the twentieth century, including the General Association of Baptist Churches (a Landmarkist group which is now the American Baptist Association), the conservative General Association of Regular Baptist Churches, and the Southern Baptist Convention, which in 1925 revised and added to it in the first Baptist Faith and Message.[27]

Southern Baptist Confessions of Faith

Southern Baptists were cautious in adopting confessional statements. When the Southern Baptist Convention was established in 1845 in Augusta, Georgia, President William B. Johnson prepared a statement explaining the reasons for establishing a new convention. In stating that the new convention was continuing the traditions of the past, Johnson provided the theological perspective for Southern Baptists when he declared, "We have constructed for our basis no new creed; acting in this matter upon a Baptist aversion for all creeds but the Bible."[28] For many Baptist churches in the South, the Philadelphia Confession (1742) and New Hampshire Confession (1833) remained as unofficial guides.[29]

The first doctrinal statement by the convention was prepared in

1914, sixty-nine years later. Entitled "The Pronouncement of Christian Union and Denominational Efficiency," it was presented in the report of the Efficiency Committee. Its purpose was to oppose the union movement, which was similar to what is often called the ecumenical movement today. The "Pronouncement" included an incomplete theological statement, which was composed by Mullins, and which presented the Southern Baptist attitude toward the union movement.

The union movement remained an issue after World War I. In 1919, the "Fraternal Address of Southern Baptists" was prepared. Three members of the committee which had prepared the "Pronouncement," Mullins, J.B. Gambrell, and William Ellyson, were joined by L.R. Scarborough and Z.T. Cody. Together they comprised a committee tasked with preparing an address with two purposes. One was to open communications with Baptists and Baptist-like groups in Europe, which had come to the attention of Southern Baptists because of the war. The second purpose was to state again the opposition of Southern Baptists to the Christian union movement. The "Fraternal Address" was also an incomplete statement. It contained eight articles, and like the "Pronouncement," essentially reflected the theology of Mullins. It was never formally adopted by the convention and was widely ignored.[30]

1925 Baptist Faith and Message

The first complete confessional statement adopted by the Southern Baptist Convention occurred in 1925, eighty years after its origin.[31] The theory of evolution, especially as it was being taught in public schools, was the primary issue behind the adoption of this statement of faith. The most publicized example of the controversy was the Scopes trial. Tennessee passed a law in March 1925 making it illegal to teach biological evolution in the public schools. In a test case, John T. Scopes was tried and convicted for breaking the law, and was fined $100 in Dayton in the same year.[32]

Although concerns about doctrine on the minds of some, it was the evolution issue that was central to events that occurred at the 1924 Southern Baptist Convention meeting in Atlanta. R.K. Maiden, coeditor of *The Word and Way* (the Missouri Baptist state newspaper), and C.P. Stealey, editor of the *Baptist Messenger* (Oklahoma), presented to the convention separate theological statements for adoption. The Resolutions Committee did not recommend either statement, but after additional efforts by Stealey, recommended the appointment of a committee to prepare a doctrinal statement for consideration by the convention in 1925. The committee consisted of three presidents of educational institutions, three Baptist editors, and the editorial secretary of the Southern Baptist Convention. Mullins was appointed chairman of the committee, which included L.R. Scarborough, W.J. McGlothlin, Stealey, S.M. Brown, R.H. Pitt, and E.C. Dargan.

In 1925, Mullins presented the committee's report to the convention. It included an introductory statement prepared by the committee, a revised and enlarged version of the New Hampshire Declaration of Faith, and a statement written by Mullins on "Science and Religion" which had been adopted by the 1923 convention. The report was not signed by Pitt or Stealey. Furthermore, Stealey's minority report, which called for more explicit anti-evolutionary language, was not accepted. He also failed to amend the committee's report. The convention then adopted overwhelmingly its first Baptist Faith and Message.[33]

Southwestern Seminary adopted the confession. Its president, L.R. Scarborough, would require "the hearty endorsement of all of its teachers to its doctrinal content."[34] Nevertheless, although widely distributed, the confession was never used by state conventions prior to 1945 and was seldom used by associations or churches. W.W. Barnes, Southwestern Seminary church historian, wrote nine years after the adoption of the Baptist Faith and Message that it was "received by Southern Baptist churches generally with a tremendous outburst of silence."[35]

1963 BAPTIST FAITH AND MESSAGE

Controversy resulted from the publication in 1961 of Ralph Elliott's *Message of Genesis*. The book, published by the Sunday School Board, received strong criticism from many conservatives and led to demands for doctrinal integrity. Because of the uproar in 1962, the Executive Committee recommended the appointment of a committee to prepare a new confession of faith. Herschel Hobbs was appointed chairman of the twenty-four-member committee and proved to be one of its most influential members.[36] The revision of the Baptist Faith and Message was completed on March 1, 1963. The report of the committee was adopted without amendment at the 1963 convention in Kansas City, Missouri.[37]

Hobbs maintained that the committee spent more time on the "Preamble" than any one article. "Our concern was to protect the individual conscience and to guard against a creedal faith."[38] After 1963, Hobbs repeatedly reminded the convention in writing and from the convention platform that "if we disregard the 'Preamble' we do not need to get a creed; we already have one."[39] Conservatives, however, cited a "criterion loophole" in the 1963 confession. Moderates claimed that Jesus is the criterion by which to interpret the Bible, but "they ignore what Jesus actually says about the Bible."[40] Thus, when the Conservative Resurgence was accomplished, a more exacting interpretation of the Baptist Faith and Message arose.

Two publications from Broadman Press appeared in 1969 and contributed to the growing controversy over theology. W.A. Criswell's *Why I Preach That the Bible Is Literally True* brought criticism from the Association of Baptist Professors of Religion, an organization composed of Southern Baptist religion teachers who were from Baptist colleges, universities, and seminaries. As the Elliott Controversy had caused some Baptists to view the seminaries with suspicion, so too this controversy resulted in distrust by some Baptists of the colleges and universities.[41]

More furor was created by the publication of Volume 1 of the *Broadman Bible Commentary.* Immediate criticism came over the interpretations of G. Henton Davies, principal of Regent's Park College in Oxford, England, and author of the commentary on Genesis. Primary attention was given to Genesis 22:1–9, where Davies took the position that God did not command Abraham to sacrifice Isaac. At the 1970 annual meeting of the convention in Denver, the Sunday School Board was asked to withdraw Volume I and to have it "rewritten with due consideration to the conservative viewpoint." After Davies was asked to rewrite the Genesis commentary, the St. Louis convention of 1971 narrowly voted to ask that a new writer be selected. Clyde T. Francisco of Southern Seminary was chosen, and the revised edition was published in 1972.[42]

These controversies resulted in a more organized concern within the convention for theological orthodoxy. A group that took the name The Baptist Faith and Message Fellowship was organized in March 1973, in Atlanta, Georgia. The group insisted upon strict adherence to the 1963 confession and constantly opposed what it considered to be doctrinal deviations through publication of the non-convention independent newspaper entitled the *Southern Baptist Journal.*[43] Interestingly, convention moderates responded to these challenges by appealing to the preface of the 1963 Baptist Faith and Message. They interpreted the statement as a defense against encroaching creedalism.

1998 ARTICLE ON THE FAMILY

A preliminary step toward a more conservative interpretation of the Baptist Faith and Message occurred in 1998. SBC President Tom Elliff appointed a committee that would draft a statement on the role of women in light of the Conservative Resurgence. The members of the committee were Anthony Jordan, Damon Shook, Richard Land, Mary Mohler, Bill Elliff, John Sullivan, and Dorothy Patterson. The committee crafted a statement that accentuated male headship in the home. The phraseology includes "A wife must submit herself graciously to the servant leadership of her husband even as the church willingly submits to the headship of Christ." The statement was based on an analogy from Ephesians 5 where the husband heads the wife as Christ heads the church. The Article on the Family, an attachment to the BFM, was passed in 1998's convention in Salt Lake City, Utah. Again, from the perspective of conservatives this was a necessary action. For moderates, it encroached on personal freedom (see more discussion below).

2000 BAPTIST FAITH AND MESSAGE

Walter Shurden reported in 1979 that of the thirty-one (at the time) Southern Baptist state conventions, only seven had officially adopted the 1963 Baptist Faith and Message. None required its employees to sign the statement. The confession was used as "guidelines" by the Annuity Board. Candidates for service under the Foreign Mission Board were questioned about their familiarity with the statement and asked if they were in agreement with it. Some employees in key positions with the Sunday School Board were required to sign the confession. The six convention seminaries demonstrated a growing sensitivity to the statement and all except Southern had adopted it officially or in principle. At the same time, none of the six convention commissions had adopted the confession, nor were their employees required to subscribe to it.[44]

The reserved usage of confessional statements by Southern Baptist associations, agencies, and institutions is consistent with the historic Baptist tradition. All three Baptist Faith and Messages (1925, 1963, 2000) contain the following description which details the nature, function, and limitations of such statements:

1. That they constitute a consensus of opinion of some Baptist body, large or small, for the general instruction and guidance of our own people and others concerning those articles of the Christian faith

which are most surely held among us. They are not intended to add anything to the simple conditions of salvation revealed in the New Testament, viz., repentance towards God and faith in Jesus Christ as Savior and Lord.

2. That we do not regard them as complete statements of our faith, having any quality of finality or infallibility. As in the past so in the future Baptists should hold themselves free to revise their statements of faith as may seem to them wise and expedient at any time.
3. That any group of Baptists, large or small, have the inherent right to draw up for themselves and publish to the world a confession of their faith whenever they may think it advisable to do so.
4. That the sole authority for faith and practice among Baptists is the Scriptures of the Old and New Testaments. Confessions are only guides in interpretation, having no authority over the conscience.
5. That they are statements of religious convictions, drawn from the Scriptures, and are not to be used to hamper freedom of thought or investigation in other realms of life.[45]

The prefaces of the 1925 and 1963 confessions also state that "Baptists are a people who profess a living faith. This faith is rooted and grounded in Jesus Christ who is the 'same yesterday, today, and forever.' Therefore the sole authority for faith and practice among Baptists is Jesus Christ whose will is revealed in the Holy Scriptures."[46] When one examines the central teachings of Baptists and Southern Baptists, the Lordship of Christ is the theological foundation of each group. The authority of the living Lord supersedes all other authority.

Significantly, these principles are not included in the preface of the 2000 Baptist Faith and Message, and became an issue of concern for some Southern Baptists. The deletion of the position that the Lordship of Christ and his will as revealed in the Bible is the supreme authority for faith and practice among Baptists, and that confessions have "no authority over the conscience" appears to have been intentional. Members of the committee also added a sentence stating that "Baptist churches, associations and general bodies have adopted confessions of faith as a witness to the world accountability. We are not embarrassed to state before the world that these are doctrines that we hold precious and essential to the Baptist tradition of faith and practice." Critics of the 2000 BFM considered this more creedal than confessional. The change expressed their fears that the Scriptures would replace Christ as the ultimate authority for faith and practice for believers. As such, the understanding of Christ and his leadership in the lives of believers would be restricted to the Bible only, eliminating the leadership of his Spirit in dealing with contemporary issues not discussed in the Bible.

The prefaces of the 1925, 1963, and 2000 statements affirm that confessions have positive functions, not negative ones. Their role is to clarify the faith, illuminate the Bible, and encourage freedom in the development of theology. As such, they represent a continuance of traditional Baptist understanding and usage of confessions of faith.

The debate over the addition of Article XVIII on "The Family" in 1998 and the adoption of important revisions in 2000 to the Baptist Faith and Message reflected diversity on important theological issues and also questions related to the understanding of confessions of faith.

The Southern Baptist Denominational Theologian

The previous discussion raises an important question, "Who speaks theologically for Southern Baptists?" Shurden proposed that the role of the denominational theologian has undergone an evolution in the history of Southern Baptists.[47] He suggested that there have been three phases in this evolution.

The Farmer-Preacher and the Gentleman Preacher

Phase one covered the period from 1700 to 1859. The theologians of the denomination were the pastors. In the South they were the "ones interpreting the Christian faith to the denomination, defending the faith for the denomination, and arguing for the specific faith of the denomination."[48] Two types of pastors existed. The Baptist farmer-preacher model was represented by Shubal Stearns, Daniel Marshall, and Dan Taylor, who through their revivalistic preaching both individualized and emotionalized Southern Baptist theology. Shurden labels them as "the Baptist folk theologians of their time."[49]

The other pastoral model was "the gentleman preacher," who was described in E. Brooks Holifield's *The Gentlemen Theologians: American Theology in Southern Culture, 1795–1860*.[50] These preachers were educated, urbane, genteel, well-to-do, and completely professional. Familiar names include Richard Furman, R.B.C. Howell, and Basil Manly, Sr. They functioned, along with the Baptist farmer-preacher, as denominational theologians in several ways, including preaching, hymnody (especially hymnbooks), and apologetic writings. These Baptist pastors served as theologians of their respective church bodies.[51]

The Seminary Professor

Phase two, 1859–1960, saw the decline of the pastor and the rise of the seminary professor as the denominational theological spokesperson. The most significant theologian of this period, which began with the founding of Southern Seminary in 1859, was Mullins. Others included John A. Broadus, B.H. Carroll, L.R. Scarborough, and William O. Carver. Shurden proposed that the professors were among the most impressive Southern Baptist pulpiteers, which gave them credibility among Southern Baptists. They were denominational statesmen, saturating Southern Baptist life with their ideas, which became incorporated into denominational structures. The writings of these teachers were "more popular than scholarly, more denominationally directed than world-scholarship directed, and more homiletical and inspirational in tone than argumentative and rational."[52]

Mullins became the "theologian" of Southern Baptists through the publication of *The Axioms of Religion* (1908) and *Baptist Beliefs* (1912) and his leadership in the preparation of the 1925 Baptist Faith and Message. He was an outstanding preacher and denominational statesman. At the same time, it was his vocation as the president and professor of theology at Southern Seminary "which legitimized him as the denominational theologian."[53]

From 1872 to 1942, a seminary president or previously seminary-related teachers were chosen as president of the convention on twenty-four different occasions. However, no seminary or ex-seminary-related leader was elected president after 1942 until the 1998 election of Paige Patterson, president of Southeastern Seminary.

The Reemergence of the Pastor

Phase three, 1960–1980, was characterized by the reemergence of the pastor as the denominational theologian. Herschel H. Hobbs, pastor of First Baptist Church, Oklahoma City, Oklahoma, and for twenty years preacher of the *Baptist Hour Radio Program*, represented the change. Hobbs and Mullins had much in common. Hobbs was deeply influenced by Mullins's writings. Both were denominational statesmen who served as president of the convention. Both made a significant contribution to a major Southern Baptist confessional statement. Both were popular pulpiteers, and wrote for Baptist audiences.[54]

The trend toward the pastor as the major theological spokesperson cut across theological lines. Hobbs represented the middle-of-the-road Southern Baptists. To his left were pastors such as John Claypool and Carlyle Marney. W.A. Criswell, on the other hand, was the primary theological spokesman of more conservative Southern Baptists.[55] This trend has continued in the sense that convention presidents, beginning with Adrian Rogers in 1979 through the election of Patterson in 1998, were pastors who were nominated and elected on the basis of their theological positions.

Shurden suggested four reasons for the shift back from the seminarian to the pastor as the denominational theologian. First, theological controversies since the early 1960s raised suspicions about the seminaries. Second, pastors of large churches dominated Southern Baptist denominational life, especially through election as the president of the convention, while seminary personnel are not as denominationally visible as in the past. Third, the role of the media in Baptist life elevated the image of the pastor. Radio and television broadcasts increased the influence of some pastors of prominent churches over wide geographical areas, and Broadman Press has contracted pastors to publish theology from an inspirational and devotional perspective. Fourth, pastors popularized whereas seminary leaders specialized.[56]

The Denominational Politician-Theologian

A new phase in identifying the denominational theologian corresponded with the rise of the Controversy in 1979. The rise of the denominational politician-theologian was a major factor in the changes that swept across the Southern Baptist Convention during the last two decades of the twentieth century. Theological orthodoxy as determined by Southern Baptist Convention leadership became one of the most important issues in determining one's suitability for service and leadership in the denomination. Select pastors of leading churches, often of the megachurch model, educators, editors, and lay political activists assumed the political power in the denomination. This enabled them to evaluate the theological acceptability of persons nominated and elected not only as trustees of convention agencies and institutions but also as executive directors and high-level administrators of the same.

Agency personnel, professors and administrators at convention seminaries, and trustees on the boards of convention agencies and institutions who resisted changes taking place in the denomination were systematically replaced with persons supporting the Conservative Resurgence and accepting the theological tenets of the conservative leadership. Within the narrower theological parameters, there arose some disagreements. For example, some leaders wanted a return to the Reformed theology of John Calvin while others felt some inconsistency with this system and the denomination's evangelistic/missions heritage.

As the moderate movement arose in the convention, spokesmen also were shaped by political as well as theological issues. Former leaders of agencies and institutions, pastors, missionaries, educators, ministers, and laypersons defined Baptist beliefs and practices not only from a historical perspective but also in an initial attempt to regain leadership in the convention. When this proved unsuccessful, the moderates created new organizations characterized by commitments to theological, practical and organizational, and political causes. Whether intended or desired, both the conservatives and the moderates found themselves unavoidably influenced by the denominational politics of the last two decades of the twentieth century.

Conclusions on the Denominational Theologian

A recognition of the developmental stages of the denominational theologian should assist believers in understanding the contemporary theological scene in Baptist life. Furthermore, it should encourage pastors to recognize and appreciate the importance of the seminarians, whose contributions have been both essential and enormous to the expression of the faith in changing times. The seminarians and the professors of religion in Southern Baptist colleges, universities, and graduate and divinity schools must recognize the importance and influence of the pulpit and their need to be effective proclaimers and preachers. They must be aware of their responsibility to speak, write, and teach not only from a scholarly and academic perspective, but also in popular manner by which the average Southern Baptist can comprehend the issues of the day.[57]

Of profound significance is the need for a new emphasis on the responsibility of each Baptist to continually grow and mature in the faith and to express that pilgrimage theologically. There will always be theological spokespersons, but no Baptist should default on the freedom and responsibility to "confess" the faith by simply allowing others think and speak for him or her. Every Baptist should convey theologically the foundation and substance of a living, maturing faith.

The Baptist Faith and Message

This chapter's final section will discuss in a concise manner each of the topics included in the 1963 and 2000 editions of the Baptist Faith and Message. Controversial topics in Baptist life will be surveyed in light of historical developments. Neither the text nor the Scripture references on each topic are printed as published in the document. Readers should study both the text and suggested biblical passages in the Baptist Faith and Message. Readers are also reminded that use of this confession does not violate or replace the freedom and responsibility of every Baptist to communicate one's personal faith through the leadership of the Holy Spirit in the study of the Bible. Rather, it should assist in that process, as each Baptist attempts to say, "This I believe."[58]

The Scriptures

The Bible (from the Greek *biblos*) is composed of sixty-six books.[59] Thirty-nine of these comprise the Old Testament, which was written primarily in Hebrew, with some parts in Aramaic. The New Testament contains twenty-seven books, and was written in *Koine* (common) Greek. No original autographs exist. Hence, copies of available texts must be compared to determine the most suitable Hebrew and Greek texts of the Bible. These texts must be translated into the languages of contemporary readers.

Two significant changes appeared in the 2000 revision of the article on the Bible. First, the statement that the "Bible is the record of God's revelation of Himself to man" was removed and the phrase that the Bible "is God's revelation of Himself to man" replaced it. Second, the statement that "The criterion by which the Bible is to be interpreted is Jesus Christ" was changed to "All Scripture is a testimony to Christ, who is

Himself the focus of divine revelation." Critics complained that the Bible subtly was placed ahead of the authority of Christ.[60] The addition that "all Scripture is totally true and trustworthy" avoided arguments over the issues of inerrancy and infallibility.

Four Topics of Consideration

When discussing the Scriptures, four topics must be considered: revelation, illumination, inspiration, and interpretation. Revelation in respect to the Bible has been discussed thoroughly. In retrospect God revealed himself and his will to the biblical writers. Using their own language and with an awareness of their religious, political, social, and economic world, these inspired writers provided a written record of God's revelation. The Scriptures become a part of the revelatory process as God makes himself known anew through the Bible.

Illumination applies to both biblical writers and readers. One comprehends revealed truth as the Spirit enlightens one with spiritual understanding. Hence, the biblical writers recognized God's revelation and wrote a record of it. Readers are able through the working of the Spirit to grasp anew this revelation and apply it to their generation.

Baptists believe that the Bible was inspired (God-breathed), that through unique acts of the Holy Spirit the writers were given divine guidance to receive, interpret, and record God's revelation. The method of how God inspired the writing of the Bible has been greatly debated. Russell Dilday lists and defines eight different theories of inspiration.[61]

Most Southern Baptists hold to one of the following three views. First, verbal plenary inspiration states that God inspired the authors to use the exact words found in the Scriptures. This theory is applied to the Scriptures in the original languages and preserves the idea of an inerrant, infallible Bible. At the same time, it does not go as far as the dictation theory, which gives the authors a totally mechanical character with no personal involvement. This accent on verbal plenary inspiration can be traced to the first fifty years of Southern Baptist history. Early Southern Baptist theologians such as John L. Dagg, James P. Boyce, and B.H. Carroll were influenced by the then-popular Princeton Seminary position. The writings of Charles Hodge, A.A. Hodge, and B.B. Warfield included three elements: (1) all Scripture is inerrant; (2) this inerrancy applies to all matters in the text; and (3) inerrancy applies only to the autographs.[62] This view is followed by most Southern Baptists today. "Put simply, this means that the Bible's inspiration is *verbal*—extending to the very words themselves—and *plenary*, or full. Thus, we affirm that every word of the Bible is inspired and that every word is *fully* inspired."[63]

Second, plenary inspiration holds that the Bible is completely inspired. The writers utilized their background, experience, and knowledge, but were so controlled by the Holy Spirit that the Scriptures were produced without any errors. The inerrancy of the Bible is preserved, while the contributions of the writers are recognized.[64]

A third view held by many Southern Baptists has been called the dynamic theory of inspiration. This emphasizes that the work of the Holy Spirit in the writing of the Scriptures is found in the inspiration of the thought rather than the exact wording. The freedom, personality, language, style, and cultural environment of the authors are considered. The underlying message of the Scriptures is inspired, while the exact wording is dynamic. Thus, the message of the Scriptures more than the exactness of the words is emphasized.[65] One can see the beginnings of the dynamic understanding in the writings of E.Y. Mullins and W.T. Conner. Mullins felt that verbal inspiration reduced the human element in the process. "He explicitly rejected the notion that a single error in a scientific detail invalidated the authority of the Scripture."[66]

Since 1845, Southern Baptists have embraced one or more of these choices. Regardless of one's choice, Southern Baptists affirm that the writers of the Scriptures were inspired. A most important consideration is the purpose of inspiration. The inspiration of the Scriptures is practical and functional. According to Paul, "All Scripture is God-breathed and is useful for the teaching, rebuking, correcting and training in righteousness" for the purpose "that the servant of God may be thoroughly equipped for every good work" (2 Tim. 3:16–17 NIV). The emphasis is on the purpose, not the method, of inspiration. Baptists must not lose sight of this practical approach to the Bible amidst the polemic over procedure.

The question of interpretation requires that several issues be considered in attempting to understand and apply the biblical message to the contemporary situation. The purpose and intent of the author are important. To whom was he writing and why? What was the situation being addressed? What response was he seeking from his readers? The environment, the history, and the setting of a passage must be examined. How does this fit into the total biblical view? Interpretation requires knowledge of the biblical languages and the type of literature, such as law, history, wisdom, poetry, prophecy, gospel, epistle, or apocalypse is essential to proper interpretation.[67]

Finally, the Bible is primarily a religious book, not a book of science or history. Its reason for existing is religious. The person who seeks to interpret the Bible must be aware of these issues in order to understand and apply biblical teachings to the present generation.

CURRENT ISSUES

Southern Baptists engaged in a debate over the Bible beginning in earnest by the early 1960s.[68] The main issue was biblical inerrancy, which for many became a test of orthodoxy. The debate arose out of the Elliott and *Broadman Bible Commentary* controversies. The publication of *The Battle for the Bible* (1976) by Harold Lindsell, former editor of *Christianity Today*, provided support for those who maintained the inerrancy of the Bible in the original manuscripts.[69] In 1980, two professors at Southwestern Seminary, Russ Bush and Tom Nettles, published *Baptists and the Bible*, a lengthy historical interpretation on Baptists which supports biblical inerrancy.[70] In the late 1970s, political efforts appeared in an effort to elect a succession of Southern Baptist Convention presidents committed to the inerrancy of the Bible. The election of Adrian Rogers in 1979 initiated a pattern which resulted in the election of a series of presidents throughout the remainder of the twentieth century committed to this agenda. Since then, other studies have become available that attempt to delineate the Bible's authority and inerrancy.[71]

In evaluating the issue of the Bible in Southern Baptist life in recent years, several factors must be considered. First, the issue was not over acceptance or rejection of the Bible. The issue was over the Bible in the original manuscripts, not in what is now available. Second, most of the staunchest supporters of inerrancy recognized that there were some concerns with the available manuscripts. Hence, the issue over the Bible was concerned with the opinion that one had about the original manuscripts. Third, the original manuscripts are missing. Copies of any of the autographs are not available. All that are extant are copies of copies of manuscripts in the original languages.[72]

The relevant issue facing Southern Baptists is what should Baptists believe about what we have and what we do not have available. The ultimate concern is "Do Baptists accept the Bible as they have it now as authoritative; do they study it and seek to understand it; and do they attempt to live by its teachings, minister and serve in light of its instructions, and apply its message to the world in which we live?" The Bible, as now available, including its translation into different languages, has always been and always will be sufficient for faith and practice. Believers do not and probably never will have the original manuscripts. The Bible as now available, however, is sufficient, and that is the primary concern in relation to the Bible for Southern Baptists.

God

Baptists believe that there is one God (monotheism). He is personal, having such qualities of personality as love, self-awareness, intelligence, emotion, and moral judgment. Several names are used for God in the Bible. *Elohim* is a Hebrew word (*Theos* in the Greek New Testament) which translates God, and is a general term used not only by the Hebrews but in various derivations by neighboring peoples. *Adonai* (Hebrew) or *Kurios* (Greek) means Lord. *Yahweh* is the Hebrew term most frequently used for God. It distinguished the Hebrew's God from the gods of Israel's pagan neighbors.[73]

Mullins listed seven natural and four moral attributes of God. Among the natural attributes are self-existence, immutability, omnipresence, immensity, eternity, omniscience, and omnipotence. God's moral attributes include holiness, righteousness, truth, and love.[74] One attribute that was made stronger in the Baptist Faith and Message 2000 was omniscience. In response to "open theism" that has garnered interest among some evangelicals, the revision added the sentence, "God is all powerful and all knowing; and His perfect knowledge extends to all things past, present, and future, including the future decisions of His free creatures."[75]

Baptists maintain a monotheistic view of God but hold a "trinitarian" concept in which God reveals himself as Father, Son, and Holy Spirit.[76] The clearest concept of God as Father is revealed in the teachings of Jesus. He called God his Father and taught his disciples that God was their Father (John 20:17). The Lord's Prayer begins "Our Father who art in Heaven..." (Matt. 6:9). God through his creative activity and his attitude toward humanity is fatherly toward all, but his children know him through faith in his Son, Jesus Christ.

Baptists agree that Jesus of Nazareth was the Son of God. In Jesus, God became man (the incarnation). Baptist views are consistent with the decisions of the early church councils from Nicaea (AD

325) to Chalcedon (AD 451) which compositely taught that Jesus was fully divine, fully human, and one person with two natures (divine and human). Baptists believe that Jesus is co-eternal with the Father and was active in the creation of the universe; that he was born through the activity of the Spirit to the virgin Mary; that he was completely obedient to the will of the Father; and through his voluntary death he atoned for mankind's sin; that he was resurrected from the dead; that he now makes intercession for humanity; and that the present age will end with his return.

The Holy Spirit is the spiritual manifestation of God, and is referred to as the "Spirit of God" and the "Spirit of Christ." The Spirit is portrayed in the Bible as being active in creation, as the agent in the divine conception of Jesus in Mary, and as present at the baptism and temptation of Jesus. Traditionally, four specific works are attributed to the Spirit. The Spirit's activity is seen in revelation, inspiration, and illumination as they relate to the Scriptures. The Spirit also leads in administration. The Acts of the Apostles describes this work as convicting the lost of sin, righteousness, and judgment. The Holy Spirit empowers the sinner to turn in faith to Christ and to live the Christian life.

Southern Baptists in the 1960s and early 1970s experienced divisiveness in relation to the "charismatic movement." Disunity continued throughout the twentieth century. Issues related to the work of the Spirit included an emphasis by some on the baptism of the Spirit as a second blessing beyond conversion, speaking in tongues (*glossolalia*), healing, casting out demons, and prophecy. Many Southern Baptists considered such ideas as extremes in relation to the traditional Baptist understanding of the Spirit. Other Southern Baptists, however, accepted or at least tolerated a new emphasis on the person and work of the Holy Spirit.[77]

In conclusion, the word "Trinity" is not in the New Testament, but the concept is. Although the idea is difficult to comprehend through human rationality, Baptists who grow in their understanding of God as Father, Son, and Holy Spirit will surely mature in their understanding of the creative and redeeming God.[78]

Man

The creation of humanity was the climax of God's creative activity. Mankind was created in the "image" or likeness of God. Although the term is difficult to define, among the suggestions implied in the "image of God" are self-awareness, emotion, intelligence, moral awareness, self-determination, creativeness, and activity as a social being.

Concerning the nature of humanity, Baptists usually hold one of three major views. The first states that mankind is a "dichotomy" composed of a material body and an immortal soul. The second teaches that mankind is a "trichotomy," composed of a body, a soul, and a spirit. Both views reflect Greek concepts of the body, which is temporal, and the soul and spirit, which are immortal. A third view states that a person is a psychosomatic unity. Thus, mankind is a unity, a single-entity (body-soul) and is reflective of the Hebrew view of the nature of humanity.[79]

Mankind was created with dignity and value in a state of innocence, neither righteous nor sinful. In freedom humanity sinned and thus was separated from God. All of mankind has the same tendency to reject God's sovereign will. Although mankind has rejected God, God has not rejected mankind. Through the redemptive work of Jesus Christ, God's grace and love call all people back into fellowship with him.

Minimal changes were made between the 1963 and 2000 editions of the Baptist Faith and Message on the topic of humanity. A growing minority of Reformed Southern Baptists desired a stronger statement than mankind's inheritance of "a nature and an environment inclined toward sin." Their preference would include the idea of guilt prior to engagement in moral activities.[80] If Reformed Baptists continue to grow and influence the Southern Baptist Convention, then a future edition may alter this statement.

Salvation

Humanity was separated from God by sin, but God chose to offer salvation to all who come to him through faith in Jesus Christ. Modern theologians offer in-depth insights in understanding the breadth of salvation.[81] Long ago, W.T. Conner described salvation by three terms: regeneration, sanctification, and glorification.[82]

Regeneration describes a complete act or transaction. It is the event in which one is saved or born anew. Regeneration is the result of conviction and repentance of sin and acceptance of God's gift of salvation by faith in Jesus Christ. In regeneration the believer is declared righteous and justified before God. The one who has faith can state that he or she has been saved, fully and completely. The 2000 confession divided regeneration and justification, making a standalone paragraph for "justification."[83]

Salvation can also be described as a process called "sanctification." One who has been saved continues to be saved by the grace of God through faith in Jesus. God continues his redemptive activity as the believer grows in understanding and applying one's faith experience. The believer becomes "holy," which refers more to being set apart or dedicated to the service of God than to moral qualities. The Spirit empowers the Christian to develop and to be used by God. Many Southern Baptists in recent years have tended to overemphasize conversion and thus neglect the importance of sanctification as part of the salvation process.

Glorification describes the consummation of salvation. The believer who has been born again and is in the process of sanctification has the promise of glory and reward with God in heaven. God's redemptive work will be complete. Hence, the Christian can say concerning salvation, "I have been saved by the grace of God through faith in Christ; I continue to be saved in the same manner; and I shall be saved."

God's Purpose of Grace: Election

The Bible teaches that God, knowing that mankind would sin, purposed to show his grace and save humanity, even before creation. He took the initiative in predetermining a plan for redeeming humanity and in seeking out those separated from him. The concept of election describes God's activity in this regard.

Baptists and Southern Baptists have differed in their interpretations on the issue of election. Some have held to a rigid predestinarianism, maintaining that God predetermined before creation who would be saved and who would be lost. Others have stressed that God foreknew but did not predetermine the destiny of individuals. Some, using Ephesians 1, have emphasized the fact that in a general sense God had predetermined to save those who would be "in Christ," those who accepted his offer of salvation in Jesus. One becomes "in Christ" through personal faith. This position provides the most acceptable balance in terms of God's sovereignty and mankind's free will.[84]

Another factor related to election is the purpose of God. Time and again in the Old Testament and the New Testament, election is connected with service. God chose Israel to be a "kingdom of priests and a holy nation" (Exod. 19:6) or "a light to the nations" (Isa. 49:6). Jesus told his disciples that he had chosen them to "go and bear fruit" (John 15:16). Thus, Baptists must be cautious not to overemphasize salvation and neglect the concept of mission in the biblical view of election.

True believers will endure to the end. This is called perseverance. This does not mean that the believer will not sin, but that God will remain faithful to his commitment to save and keep those who are "in Christ." The believer's salvation (regeneration, sanctification, and glorification) depends upon God and not upon the individual.

The Church

The word "church" translates the Greek word *ekklesia.* In a secular sense, *ekklesia* described an assembly of citizens in a self-governing Greek city. It was used in the Septuagint, the Greek translation of the Old Testament, to translate the Hebrew term *qahal,* which described the assembly of Israel before God. In the New Testament, *ekklesia* was used primarily to describe a local congregation of Christians and less frequently to define the redeemed of all the ages.[85] The basis of Matthew 16:18, Baptists normally believe that it was the intention of Jesus to found his church.

Although Baptists recognize the general nature of the church in terms of the redeemed of all ages, they tend to place great emphasis on the local church. The local congregation is a complete and independent church. It knows no authority, ecclesiastical, civil or individual, save the Lordship of Jesus Christ. The local church operates as an institution through democratic procedures and is considered autonomous in nature in relation to other churches and organizations. Yet its spiritual ideal is to seek to worship, serve, minister, and function in light of the leadership of the living Lord. Local Baptist churches do cooperate with others in non-authoritative associations in order to fulfill the purpose and goals of the church which are demanded by the gospel.[86]

The mission of the church is to proclaim the gospel to the world. This task involves evangelism and missions. It also includes the teaching and nurturing of converts and the proclamation of ethical and social consequences of the gospel in relationship to contemporary society.

Southern Baptists hold that there are two officers in a New

Testament church: pastor and deacon. The office of pastor is equivalent to that of bishop or elder as found in the New Testament. Pastors are shepherds or overseers. Deacons are "servants," who assist the pastor and the church in material and spiritual matters.[87] Both offices are functional in nature rather than authoritative. The addition in 2000 of the statement that "the office of pastor is limited to men as qualified by Scripture" proved to be controversial.[88]

Baptism and the Lord's Supper

Southern Baptists believe that Jesus gave his church two ordinances: baptism and the Lord's Supper. These are not sacraments, which convey the grace of God to the participant and which must be administered by qualified persons. Ordinances are symbolic acts which portray the significance of Jesus' redemptive ministry, his continued activity in the life of believers, and the anticipation of his return.

"Baptism" is a transliteration of the Greek word *baptizo*, which means to immerse. John the Baptist baptized those who had repented from sins in anticipation of the coming kingdom of God. Jesus demonstrated approval of John's message and ministry by submitting to his baptism. Jesus did not baptize, but his disciples did. As the church launched forth at Pentecost on her worldwide mission, baptism was expected of the new converts to Christianity.

Southern Baptists teach and practice that New Testament baptism is for believers only. This excludes infant baptism. Positively, baptism symbolizes the salvation experience, but it is not a part of the regeneration process. It is a symbolic confession of faith and an act of covenantal obedience administered by the authority of the local church. It follows the conversion experience and the public confession of that faith experience. Symbolically, baptism testifies to Christ's redeeming work for and in the believer. Immersion is the New Testament mode of this ordinance. Although not essential to salvation, baptism is expected and necessary for fellowship in the local church.

The Landmark influence among Southern Baptists has caused many churches to reject "alien immersion." This refers to the immersion of believers by churches other than Southern Baptists, or more generally, churches of like faith and order. The emphasis is placed upon the proper administrator and proper authority of the church which is baptizing. However, the evaluation of valid New Testament baptism is left to the determination by each local church under the Lordship of Christ. As a result, the acceptance or rejection of baptism from another church is a policy established by each individual congregation.[89]

The Lord's Supper is the second ordinance held by Southern Baptists. It, too, is a symbolic and covenantal act whereby members of the church through partaking of the bread and the fruit of the vine memorialize the death of the Redeemer and anticipate his return. In order to avoid any sacramental implications, some Baptists speak of it as "just" a symbol. However, Jesus gave the command to his followers to practice this in order to remember clearly and powerfully his redemptive work and his voluntary sacrifice which was accomplished for them. Hence, the Lord's Supper is a beautiful and profound symbolic presentation of Jesus and is much more than "just" a symbol. The church which administers the Lord's Supper ought to practice it in obedience with dignity and respect as a profound and sensitive testimony to the grace of God, the ministry of Jesus, and the anticipation of his return.

Baptized believers participate in the Supper. Interpretation of this varies from church to church. Some Southern Baptists, through Landmark influence, hold to "close" (or "closed") communion, where only members of the particular, local congregation are allowed to partake. Others practice "closed intercommunion," allowing any member of any Southern Baptist church, or, in some instances any Baptist church, to participate in the ordinance. Still other Baptist churches with variations practice "open communion" and allow any Christian to participate who chooses to do so. Like the practice of baptism, each local congregation determines its own policy on the issue of the Lord's Supper.[90]

There was no change in wording between the 1963 and 2000 Baptist Faith and Message confessions on these two ordinances. Nevertheless, recent conservative interpreters prefer a stricter understanding. Thus, only those who follow immersion baptism should be considered for church membership and participate in the Lord's Supper. Moreover, according to the Baptist Faith and Message 2000, only closed communion is affirmed.[91]

Both ordinances, however, in their own manner symbolize the redemptive work of Christ and the unity of his followers. They should not be degraded by becoming sources of disunity between his believers who are called Baptists. Baptists should respect each other's position on the ordinances, individually and corporately, as they seek to determine Christ's will for their lives and for their churches.

5. A Theological Heritage

The Lord's Day

The Christians in the New Testament era were Jews and worshiped publicly on the Jewish Sabbath, which began at sundown on Friday and went to sundown on Saturday. Early on the church began to worship on Sunday as well (the first day of the week), the day in which the resurrection of Jesus occurred. Christians began to refer to this as the "Lord's Day," the day that they celebrated the event of the resurrection of Jesus and memorialized through worship not only the creative activity of God (as on the Sabbath) but also his redemptive work in Jesus.

As the church became predominately Gentile, Sunday became the accepted day of public worship. The day was to be a day of rest (a "sabbath"), but even more so it became a day to assemble, worship, and give witness to the risen Lord. Baptists, however, should not forget that every day is given by God. Thus, each day should be devoted to him. Interestingly, the 2000 BFM removed the statement that "Christians should refrain from worldly amusements" and revised it with "Activities on the Lord's Day should be commensurate with the Christian's conscience under the Lordship of Christ."[92]

The Kingdom

The kingdom of God refers to God's rule in the natural and spiritual universe, or his sovereignty. God claims sovereignty over his creation, and persons are given the opportunity to acknowledge his rule in their lives through faith in and obedience to Jesus Christ. In so doing, they enter the kingdom.

The kingdom is a spiritual kingdom, not an earthly one. Jesus refused to accept the temptation to receive earthly authority. He said that his kingdom "was not of this world" (John 18:36) and that "the kingdom of God is within you" (Luke 17:21 GNT). The New Testament presents the kingdom as coming in Jesus' time (Matt. 3:2), as present (Matt. 12:28), and as future (Matt. 25:31–34). Hence, the kingdom can be spoken of as coming in the appearance of Jesus, as present in the hearts of believers, and as consummated at the return of Christ.

The church is not to be equated with the kingdom of God, although Landmarkism sought to equate Baptist churches with the kingdom.[93]

The role of the citizen, according to the New Testament, is to proclaim the kingdom and to pray for its presence and God's will on earth as in heaven, but not to establish the kingdom. That work belongs to Christ through the Holy Spirit's activity.[94]

Last Things

Eschatology is the doctrine of last things. The New Testament speaks of the arrival and the presence of God's kingdom in Jesus, which C.H. Dodd described as "realized eschatology." Humanity can experience the power and rule of God as appropriated through the Lordship of Jesus Christ. At the same time, the Bible points to a consummation of God's working in humanity's history, when Christ will come in complete redemption for the saved and judgment for the unsaved. There are many passages in the New Testament which point to Christ's return, and many interpretations are related to these passages.[95]

Several theories are related to the concept of the millennium as found in Revelation 20:1–6.[96] Among Southern Baptists three basic interpretations have received the most support.[97] The first of these is premillennialism, which states that Christ will return to earth and then establish a rule of one thousand years. There are two types of premillennialism. "Historical" premillennialism holds that before the second coming of Christ a great apostasy will occur, accompanied by persecution of the church during a period of great tribulation. Christ will return and destroy the Antichrist, and the sheep and goat judgment (Matthew 25) will take place. The millennial kingdom will be established, Satan will be bound, and the unrighteous nations will be governed. Near the end of the millennium, Satan will again rise up and will suffer final defeat. Then the white throne judgment will occur (Rev. 20:7–15), followed by the establishment of the new heaven and the new earth and the eternal kingdom of God. "Dispensational" premillennialism reflects the teachings of J.N. Darby (1800–1882) and was popularized by C.I. Scofield (1843–1921). This viewpoint takes the symbols and images in Revelation as literally as possible. It teaches that the church will be raptured before the tribulation. God then works through converted Jews. After the tribulation, Christ will return with his church.[98] Dispensationalism divides the Bible into distinct periods and emphasizes the role of prophetic predictions that foretell the future of church history events.[99]

Amillennialism is the second view. It usually interprets Revelation in its historical context of the late first century. It affirms that the thousand years is not a future era of earthly history but a symbolic period when Satan will be prevented from deceiving the nations through emperor worship. The millennium therefore represents the time period between the first and second comings of Christ. Amillennialism holds to one general resurrection and one general judgment. Both are connected with Christ's second coming which brings to completion this world order and ushers in the eternal heavenly order.[100]

Third, postmillennialism reflects the optimistic period prior to World War I. Through Christian agencies, the gospel will be most effective in permeating the entire world, a condition that will continue for a thousand years. During this period, Jews will be converted. Then there will follow a brief apostasy and tribulation. Finally, Christ will return, the general resurrection and judgment will occur, the old world will be destroyed by fire, and the new heaven and the new earth will be revealed.

There are Southern Baptists who follow each one of these eschatological perspectives. Changes in the BFM that accent one view over another is unlikely. In general, Baptists anticipate the return of Christ, the resurrection of the dead, final judgment, and eternal life. The timing of these events is not known, but Christians are expected to be prepared for their arrival and active in proclaiming the gospel of Jesus Christ.

Evangelism and Missions

From the time of the Evangelical Awakening in England and the Great Awakening in the colonial period in the American colonies, Baptists have been characterized by evangelism. Since the beginning of the modem mission movement with William Carey, Ann and Adoniram Judson, and Luther Rice, Baptists consistently and organizationally have been committed to the cause of missions at home and abroad.

Every Christian is given the responsibility to be a witness for the faith. The witness proceeds individually, as a part of the local church, and as a part of the various associations of Southern Baptists (regional, state, and national). In fact, it is the commitment to fulfill the Great Commission (Matt. 28:18–20) which is the central factor that binds the approximately 14 million Southern Baptists together. This mission of taking the gospel to all the world is accomplished as Baptists serve, support, and cooperate to fulfill the teachings of Jesus.[101] Chapter 2 of this book discussed in detail the various expressions of this commitment. The 2000 BFM appended a specific preference in which the gospel witness is to be communicated. The addition of the phrase "by verbal witness undergirded by a Christian lifestyle" could be interpreted to minimize the concept of "lifestyle evangelism."[102]

Education

One mission of the local church and the Southern Baptist Convention is the education of its people. The Sunday School program, the Discipleship Training program, and teaching from the pulpit are among the many activities of the local church in assisting its people to comprehend the faith and its expressions of worship, theology, and ministry.

Southern Baptists have been most active in establishing colleges, universities, and other institutions of learning. The convention operates six seminaries, and the state conventions operate over fifty junior colleges, senior colleges, and universities, as well as several theological schools and academies.

In Christian education there should be a proper balance between academic freedom and academic responsibility. Freedom in any orderly relationship of human life is always limited and never absolute. The freedom of a Christian school, college, or seminary teacher is limited by the preeminence of Jesus Christ, by the authoritative nature of the Scriptures, and by the distinct purpose for which the school exists.

Southern Baptist educational institutions have felt the tensions of economic stress, the struggle for a balance between academic freedom and academic responsibility, and the continual need for a clear identity of purpose as denominational institutions. Even so, these institutions consistently educated lay and ministerial leaders of churches, agencies, and communities. Through the leadership of their graduates, the Southern Baptist Convention has responded to a changing world with a relevant message, the result of which has been the development of the leading denomination in the United States. If Southern Baptists are to remain strong, they must demonstrate constructive, not negative, criticism of these institutions, and must display trust and support through a loving and committed concern for their well-being.[103]

Stewardship

No revisions were made on this topic in the 2000 Baptist Faith and Message. Southern Baptists believe that God is the giver of life and all that is related to it. He is the provider and sustainer of humanity. The Scriptures teach that mankind is to be a steward of everything in life, one who is responsible for that which belongs to God. This includes material possessions, time, and talents.

Much debate has occurred over the issue of whether or not Jesus taught tithing in the Old Testament sense of one-tenth of one's increase. It is important to recognize that Jesus taught stewardship of God's gifts and that all things should be used to glorify God. His concern, as demonstrated in the story of the widow's mite, was not quantitative but qualitative. He measured the gift not in terms of amounts or percentages but in terms of the love and the sacrifice behind it.

Stewardship is also to be practiced corporately. The church is accountable to practice good stewardship in the administration of gifts received. Christians should give willingly, systematically, and liberally to advance the cause of Christ. Churches, associations, conventions, and institutions related to those churches must use these resources effectively and efficiently in the application and spread of the gospel.

Cooperation

Baptists historically have expressed an independent spirit. English Baptists practiced congregational polity and opposed ecclesiastical authority beyond the local church. Baptists began quite early in their history to work together freely and willingly, a development which was described in Chapters 1 and 2. Baptists in America organized for the first time on a national scale in 1814 when the Triennial Convention was established to respond to the foreign mission enterprise.

The Southern Baptist Convention was organized in 1845 in Augusta, Georgia. The primary purpose was cooperation of Baptists in the South for the cause of missions, both foreign and domestic. Today, approximately 14 million Southern Baptists cooperate at area, state, and national levels with the ultimate concern being a unified effort at fulfilling the demand to take the gospel into all the world.

In their diversity, Southern Baptists have found unity, which is not organic, but functional and spiritual. Associations do not exercise authority or control over their constituent churches or individuals. Rather, they implement the desire of Southern Baptists to pool their energies, resources, talents, and gifts in order to serve, minister, and do missions as efficiently and effectively as possible. While sharing a union of spirit with all Christians throughout the world, Southern Baptists have exercised a conservative caution against uniting in an organic sense in the various ecumenical movements that appeared in the twentieth century.[104]

The Christian and the Social Order

Because of an emphasis on the necessity of a personal conversion experience, Southern Baptists throughout their history have placed great emphasis upon the individual. At the same time Baptists have developed a rich historical heritage in relation to social concern and social justice. Charles H. Spurgeon, the great English Baptist minister of the nineteenth century, established orphanages. Several nineteenth-century Baptists were leaders in areas of social concern, such as Parliamentary reform, education, and liberty of conscience.[105]

Southern Baptists, beginning with recognition of the sinfulness of humanity and its consequences, have stressed the need of both individual regeneration and application of the gospel to social problems. Led by the Christian Life Commission (renamed the Ethics and Religious Liberty Commission in 1997), the denomination sought to educate its constituents on contemporary social issues and to propose courses for action on issues such as alcoholism, drugs, gambling, war, child abuse, business ethics, race relations, human rights, hunger, interpersonal relations between parents and children, and problems facing young people. The 2000 confession added statements opposing specific practices such as homosexuality, pornography, abortion, and euthanasia.[106]

Local churches and associations have also been active in responding to local or regional concerns. Most Southern Baptists are cautious about any attempts to establish the kingdom of God simply through social reform because of their recognition of human sinfulness. However, this has not and must not deter them from addressing and responding to social injustice and social problems.

Peace and War

Because of human sinfulness, nations of the world throughout history have been engaged in war with each other. Baptists have been patriotic citizens who have for the most part been loyal to their respective countries and served in their respective nations' armed forces in defense of what they have considered to be just causes. In fact, the credibility of Baptists was significantly enhanced by their contributions as soldiers in both the English Revolution in the seventeenth century and the American Revolution in the eighteenth century.

At the same time, Baptists recognize the secondary and temporal nature of governments and their wars. They are called to a higher eternal ideal of universal brotherhood and peace among humans and nations. The primary example of such an ideal is Jesus, the Prince of Peace, who called his followers to conquer by sacrifice. His kingdom is not temporal but spiritual and eternal. Paul (Romans 13) recognized the importance of the role of government in resisting the evil of the world and in maintaining peace and called us to "live peaceably with all" (Rom. 12:18). John in the Revelation warned us, "if anyone is to be slain with the sword, with the sword must he be slain" (Rev. 13:10 ESV).

As Christians, Baptists should seek to be persons of peace. They should proclaim the gospel in order that others might find peace with God and thus build a foundation to learn to live at peace with others. Christians should constantly promote peace among people and nations. No issue is more relevant to Christians than the potential danger of a nuclear, chemical, or biological holocaust. With the availability of nuclear weapons and other weapons of mass destruction which threaten humanity and the planet, the message of God's love in Christ and its consequent demand that we love one another takes on a new and profound seriousness for our generation. Baptists must study and proclaim the implications of the gospel as they relate to the need for love, peace, and sanity in the anxious generation in which we live.[107]

Religious Liberty

Historically, Baptists have held to and struggled for religious liberty for all people. Historical precedents are plentiful. At the beginning, Thomas Helwys published *A Short Declaration of the Mystery of Iniquity* in 1612. It is considered to be the first book in English to call for universal religious liberty and freedom of conscience. Names like Roger Williams, John Leland, and Isaac Backus represent Baptists in America who led the struggle for religious freedom in the American colonies and for guarantees of the same in the Constitution of the United States of America, and in the individual states.

Religious liberty is much more than toleration. It recognizes the right of every person to worship or not to worship God according to the dictates of one's conscience. It denies the right of any person, ecclesiastical authority, or civil authority to come between God and the individual. Such freedom has its theological roots in the proposition that God has created humanity free and responsible. The highest expression of responsible freedom comes to the individual who through faith acknowledges the Lordship of Jesus Christ. Furthermore, Baptists played an important role in preserving religious freedom in the civil realm, which is guaranteed in the First Amendment of the United States Constitution. The First Amendment, which guarantees freedom of speech, press, assembly, and petition, states that "Congress shall make no law respecting an establishment of religion, or prohibiting the free exercise thereof." This means that "church and state should be separate" (BFM), that government is not to become involved in establishing religion in any form, nor is it to prohibit the belief and practice of one's religious convictions.[108] Finally, Baptist emphases upon soul competency and the priesthood of believers are expressions of the belief that the individual ultimately must answer only to God, not to any human authority.

Throughout much of the twentieth century, Southern Baptists struggled to preserve religious liberty through the activities of the Baptist Joint Committee on Public Affairs. The Controversy and the restructuring of the convention, however, resulted in withdrawal of support from the BJCPA and the assignment of religious liberty responsibilities to the Ethics and Religious Liberty Commission. These changes reflected a growing diversity on the issue of separation of church and state. Today, some Baptists advocate a strict separation of church and state whereas others adopt an accommodationist position (see Chapter 3).[109]

The Family

In 1998, the Southern Baptist Convention approved a new BFM article entitled "The Family." Southern Baptists agreed upon the importance of the family in both biblical teachings and society. However, a major dispute arose over a statement based upon Ephesians 5:22–25, which called upon the wife "to submit herself graciously to the servant leadership of her husband even as the church willingly submits to the leadership of Christ. She being in the image of God as is her husband and thus equal to him, has the God-given responsibility to respect her husband and to serve as his helper in managing the household and nurturing the next generation."[110]

Many Southern Baptists approved of the statement.[111] Leo Garrett noted that articles on marriage and family life were included in some early Baptist confessions. But the 1998 Southern Baptist Convention amendment "was seemingly the first such in a major Anglo-American Baptist confession for three centuries."[112]

Others, however, voiced their opposition, pointing out that the previous verse 21 (the beginning of the Greek paragraph and where the verb is located) calls for mutual submission: "Submit yourselves to one another because of your reverence for Christ" (Eph. 5:21 GNT). Therefore, only one viewpoint on the role of women was being espoused. Those Southern Baptists who followed mutual submission or egalitarianism in their homelife saw their views diminished. Only the complementarian point of view became acceptable. Wifely submission became the Southern Baptist standard.[113] Adoption of the article resulted in the resignation or retirement of some professors at Southwestern Seminary, who refused to sign the revised Baptist Faith and Message.[114] A few years later, after the 2000 Baptist Faith and Message passed, several International Mission Board personnel were also fired.[115]

The 2000 document can be criticized for confusing confessionalism with creedalism. The preface included the statement that Baptists "have adopted confessions of faith as a witness to the world, and as instruments of doctrinal accountability." It added that Baptists "deny the right of any secular or religious authority to impose a confession of faith upon a church or body of churches." Despite the claim that such a confession could not be imposed, some Southern Baptists have used the 2000 revision to demand what they believe is "doctrinal accountability."

Conclusion

Southern Baptist theology in its highest ideal is positive. It remains in a state of maturation as Baptists from person to person and from generation to generation seek to communicate to others their faith experience in light of the revelation of God. At the center of their faith in God's nate revelation in Jesus Christ rests the Scriptures. By the Scriptures all believers can examine, evaluate, and express their experience in comparison with the witness of the writers of the Bible.

Because of the personal nature of the faith experience, Baptists theologically are a diverse people. At the same time, Baptists are able to reach a general consensus on theological issues while allowing for diversity. Their theological unity rests not on doctrinal statements as tests of orthodoxy. It rests upon a commitment of faith in the living God, an acceptance of the Scriptures as an inspired testimony to God's revelation of himself, especially in Jesus Christ, and a belief that through the study of the Bible under the leadership of the Holy Spirit Christians will be drawn closer together in their theological beliefs.

Theology is an important and legitimate concern for every Southern Baptist. Baptist confessionalism is a positive and powerful approach to theology. It is an expression of faith, not a test of faith. Confessional theology is so important that Baptists should not entrust their beliefs to any person or organization but only to the test of the Scriptures in the context of the community of faith under the Lordship of Christ. Through confessionalism, Southern Baptists can continue with a maturing, vibrant theology and focus on their ultimate concern of obedience to the biblical command to take the gospel to the whole world.

Discussion Questions

1. The term "confession" is important in Baptist life. For example, a person confesses faith in Jesus as Lord. What do you think of the idea that theologically Baptists "confess" their faith rather than adhere to a set of theological beliefs?
2. Do you see the interrelatedness of the five "Sources for Formulating Doctrinal Statements?" If any of these are neglected does this have an effect on one's overall expressions of faith?
3. Why do Baptists refer to their theological statements as "confessions?" What are the implications to the individual believer, the church, and cooperative organization through a confessional rather than a creedal approach?
4. List several differences between a confession and a creed.
5. How are confessions of faith influenced by circumstances that arise during the discussion of and adoption of confessional statements? Provide a specific example.

6. Why do you think it took eighty years before Southern Baptists adopted the first Baptist Faith and Message in 1925? Consider William B. Johnson's statement during the founding of the SBC in 1845. Are there other reasons you can think of?

7. What were the reasons behind the adoption of the three major confessions of faith called the Baptist Faith and Message in 1925, 1963, and 2000? Why do you think that questions over the interpretation of Genesis played such a significant role in 1925 and 1963?

8. Reread carefully the preface to the 1925 and 1963 BFM confessions. What does the preface mean to you and your church? Do the changes to the Introduction of the 2000 BFM affect the way that confessional statements are seen in the SBC?

9. After reading the section describing the individual articles of the BFM, do you think it would be good to have your church develop its own confessional statement? Are the articles all needed by your church? Should new ones be added? If you wrote you own church confession, how would you deal with issues on which members disagreed—such as interpretations of last things, salvation in terms of election or free will, or religious liberty and separation of church and state? Should the majority rule or should language be compromised to attempt to include all or most of the views of the people while respecting the individual interpretation?

10. Do the people in your church really care about theological debate? Do you think that they would like the confessional approach rather than the creedal approach?

Conclusion

A Growing Heritage:
Southern Baptists and the Future

The idea of a growing heritage for Southern Baptists appears apt since we are always in flux. With forty years of a new Southern Baptist Convention now past, what will the next generation be like? What will their leaders do? What will they emphasize? What will they create and develop? This conclusion relates recent updates, reflections, and future challenges for twenty-first-century Southern Baptists to consider and discuss.

Moderate Organizations

Moderate Southern Baptists who left the convention found identity with new organizations. In 1987, the Southern Baptist Alliance was organized. Stan Hastey was elected to lead the organization and a small number of moderates identified with it. The Alliance expanded its outreach to other Baptist groups and eventually changed its name to the Alliance of Baptists in 1993.[1]

The Cooperative Baptist Fellowship (CBF) was formed in 1991.[2] It arose out of dissatisfaction following the defeat of Dan Vestal by Morris Chapman for president of the convention in New Orleans in 1990. The CBF elected Cecil Sherman as its first coordinator. Upon retirement he was succeeded by Vestal, then Suzii Paynter, and in 2019 by Paul Baxley. The CBF is the most successful of the moderate organizations that were connected to Southern Baptists. It serves, as Fletcher states, like an umbrella for other initiatives, such as the Alliance, Women in Ministry, and the publication *Nurturing Faith Journal* (formerly *Baptists Today;*

SBC Today).[3] Other moderate entities that were birthed out of the Controversy include the Baptist Theological Seminary at Richmond, Baptists Committed, Smyth and Helwys Publishing, and *Associated Baptist Press* (now *Baptist News Global*).[4] These entities are possible links for the larger group of Southern Baptists to engage, debate, and coexist. Nevertheless, after forty years since the Controversy began, few if any efforts to coalesce—by either moderates or conservatives—have taken place.[5]

Other Developments

Restructuring did not end with the "Covenant for a New Century." State conventions, associations, and local churches reexamined and redefined relationships with all Baptist organizations, including the Southern Baptist Convention. New conservative state conventions appeared, such as those in Virginia and Texas.[6] The rise of new divinity and theological schools was one result of Controversy. Colleges, universities, and societies established stronger or new relationships with state conventions and churches, in particular. Independent, voluntary societies took on new life and responsibilities. Again, all of these are potential avenues for a larger contingent of Southern Baptists—moderate and conservative—to participate.

Overtures for a reunion between moderate and conservative Southern Baptists appears hopeless at the present time. Perhaps a new generation of Southern Baptists will soften some hardened stances of early conservatives. Similarly, perhaps moderate Southern Baptists who left the convention can set aside raw feelings for the opportunity to dialogue again. Nathan Finn posits three priorities for post–Conservative Resurgence Southern Baptists.[7] One priority is what Finn tabs "Graciously Confessional Cooperation." He takes note that there are numerous groups of people that make up the SBC—fundamentalists, revivalists, traditionalists, orthodox evangelicals, Calvinists, contemporary church practitioners, culture warriors, Landmarkers, Cooperative Program apologists, and miraculous gifts advocates. The tensions among these groups are obvious. The SBC needs to embrace a confessional basis for cooperation with its churches, one that perhaps does not make adherence to the restrictions to the Baptist Faith and Message as the final say.[8] Will a new generation allow more progressive-minded churches to join these numerous groups?

Conclusion

Final Reflections and Future Challenges

The battles that surrounded the Controversy are over. A generation has come and gone. Nevertheless, several issues that sparked or perpetuated the Controversy were never fully resolved. Southern Baptists are debating and should continue to debate debatable topics.

The Status of Women in Southern Baptist Life

The ever-changing roles for women are evident throughout Baptist history. Women have served as deaconesses, eldresses, preachers, and even lead pastors of individual churches. Their service increased and decreased throughout the four centuries of Baptist life.[9] Each Baptist denominational expression has developed a pattern for placement of women in church and service. The role of women formed a major issue for the Controversy, and was discussed in Chapter 3. Yet roles for women cannot be forever decidedly fixed with a majority vote from a small percentage of Baptists who decide to attend an annual convention in June. Like the Baptist Faith and Message itself, women in ministry remains a fluid topic of discussion. Whether they are complementarian or egalitarian, Southern Baptists in the twenty-first century must continue to engage one another on the status, roles, and ministries of women.[10]

Southern Baptists and the Gifts of the Holy Spirit

Another issue for Southern Baptists to continue to discuss is the gifts of the Spirit. Charismatic Baptists are not as prominent as they were during the charismatic renewal of the 1960s and 1970s. Before and since that time Southern Baptists have generally followed a cessationist approach to speaking in tongues and miraculous healing.[11] This cessationist method led to a rejection of the phenomena. Associations in Texas, California, Ohio, Louisiana, and Oklahoma disfellowshipped churches. A spate of books was published in the 1970s, some affirming but most condemning the charismatic practices.[12] Yet disapproval moved to ambivalence and has now turned more toward acceptance in the past decade. A LifeWay study reported that half of SBC pastors believe that God gives some Christians a private prayer language. Yet the other half (41 percent) of SBC pastors think that the gift of tongues passed away with the death of the apostles.[13]

174

Conclusion

In 2006, the IMB passed standards for missionaries which would disqualify those who engaged in speaking in tongues or had a "private prayer language."[14] Yet in 2015, less than a decade later, the IMB reversed these standards and began admitting missionary candidates who spoke in tongues.[15] In response, NAMB has stated it now take no position on this question.[16] Dwight McKissic's sermon provides another example. This Southern Baptist pastor preached in chapel at Southwestern Seminary in 2006 on the baptism and filling of the Holy Spirit. President Paige Patterson called the message "harmful to the churches" and removed the recording from the seminary archives. In 2018, however, Southwestern Seminary restored the recording to its archives.[17] Southern Baptists are experiencing a healthy balance of both cessationists and non-cessationists within their ranks. Therefore, this issue should continue to be a subject of lively debate.[18]

Southern Baptists and Calvinism

A major looming doctrinal issue is what will the official SBC stance become in regard to the growing numbers of Reformed Baptists within their ranks? For the past forty years, the resurgence of Calvinism has accompanied the resurgence of conservatives. A new generation of Reformed Baptists has graduated from a few SBC seminaries that accentuate Reformed positions. Yet for every Southern Baptist who enthusiastically welcomes the growing presence and popularity of this viewpoint, there is another Southern Baptist who is theologically troubled by it. Several books and white papers have been published, and conferences and debates have taken place.[19]

Calvinistic Baptists continue to spread their influence. In 2006, LifeWay research stated that 10 percent of SBC pastors consider themselves five-point Calvinists.[20] By 2013, LifeWay research stated about 30 percent of SBC pastors consider their churches Calvinist, but a much larger number—60 percent—are concerned "about the impact of Calvinism in our convention."[21] In response, a growing number of "Traditional" Southern Baptists have arisen. In 2017, these traditional Southern Baptists urged "loyal opposition" to Calvinism's encroachment on the denomination.[22]

The wisest course of action for Southern Baptists would be to continue to debate and interact or else risk splitting the convention again. If the convention can coexist over differences on the very nature of God's sovereignty and matters related to the doctrine of salvation, then perhaps other less significant issues of disagreement are worth ongoing collegial discussion.

The Decline in Membership and Baptisms

The Southern Baptist Convention faces a serious challenge in the twenty-first century. Heartier evangelism, the assumed consequence of the Conservative Resurgence, did not materialize. Southern Baptists currently face some sobering statistics (as do most mainline denominations). The number of churches cooperating with the SBC has grown year after year, but membership continues to decline. Since 2006, the SBC has lost 1.5 million members. Baptisms also declined, up to almost 30 percent fewer than in 2007.[23] Albert Mohler wrote that the decline of baptismal numbers is "both remarkable and lamentable."[24] This is a challenge that has demanded the attention of SBC leadership.[25] Evangelism is a core issue that all Baptists can center upon. Instead of separating over areas in which we disagree, perhaps all Southern Baptists can cooperate and renew afresh around the call for an unhindered gospel message.

The Challenge of Multiculturalism

This section relates two multicultural challenges. The first is the SBC's approach to race relations. The convention has made tremendous strides since its shameful slavery origins in 1845. In 1954, the SBC affirmed the Supreme Court's school desegregation ruling in Brown v. Board of Education. In 1968, messengers denounced racism following the assassination of Martin Luther King, Jr., and the subsequent riots it produced. Nevertheless, the convention missed an opportunity when it defeated a motion to affirm the Civil Rights Act of 1964. Then the convention's 150th anniversary triggered a 1995 resolution on racial reconciliation. Messengers lamented and repudiated historic acts of racism, and apologized "to all African-Americans for condoning and/or perpetuating individual and systemic racism in our lifetime."[26]

In 2012, Fred Luter became the SBC's first African American president. Current SBC President J.D. Greear made 48 percent of his committee appointments people of color. Yet work remains if the SBC is to live up to its 1995 resolution. Convention entities still seek to increase the number of non–Anglos on their ministry staffs. The International Mission Board set a goal of 75 African American missionaries by 2025. At the end of last year, the number stood at thirteen out of 3,600 career missionaries.[27]

In 2019, the SBC passed a resolution that the convention could use aspects of Critical Race Theory (CRT is a set of ideas about systemic racism; it understands society and its laws as inherently racist). Southern Baptists could utilize CRT as long as it was subordinated to Scripture.[28] Not all Southern Baptists agreed with the resolution. Then the six seminary presidents declared that CRT was incompatible with the Baptist Faith and Message.[29] In response, some African American pastors and their churches left the SBC.[30] Fred Luter observed that "some recent events have left many brothers and sisters of color feeling betrayed and wondering if the SBC is committed to racial reconciliation."[31] Fortunately, the blowback led to convention officials admitting it would have been better to include African Americans in the decision process. A subsequent meeting helped to moderate feelings.

Most Southern Baptists would agree that there is still a long road to travel on race relations. Racism is spiking in America.[32] For the SBC to take the lead in this area, then more widely held meetings, more concentrated effort, and more grassroots work must be done. Racial reconciliation remains a present challenge.[33]

There is a second challenge to multiculturalism for Southern Baptists. The center of Christian demographics has shifted to believers living below the equator. These indigenous believers are discovering their theological voices.[34] Southern Baptists must define themselves not solely with faithfulness to their heritage and Scripture. Baptists need to accept themselves as Baptists amid a world of diversity, constant change, and criticism. Baptists will benefit as they understand their calling in God's timing to be a missional movement of the Spirit to obey Christ as revealed in Scripture in a covenant community no matter the cost.

There is a growing shift in ethnic and global Baptist leadership. Non-Anglo Baptists are by far the fastest growing segment of Baptist life. In fact, 2017 statistics reveal that fully 20 percent of SBC churches are non–Anglo and 50 percent of church plants are non–Anglo.[35] Such statistics should energize twenty-first-century Southern Baptists to understand more clearly who they are (becoming) and where they should be going. These emerging Baptists will need to be assimilated into denominational leadership at the associational, state, and national levels in all expressions of Baptist life. The SBC has an opportunity to coordinate across its agencies worldwide to provide curriculum and training in languages. The agencies must find new levels of networking and sharing resources to enable all Baptists to have materials in their own language and culture.

Defining "Southern Baptist" for a New Century

Therefore, competing Baptist identities continue into the twenty-first century. Moderate Southern Baptists were alarmed at what they perceived the Conservative Resurgence was taking away. Among the lost distinctives were soul competency, strict separation of church and state, respect for non-conformity, local autonomy, cooperative spirit, diversity, freedom of academic inquiry, women's status, and freedom of the press.[36] By contrast, conservative Southern Baptists passionately defended their rescue of originally lost Baptist ideals, called for necessitating and maintaining high biblical and confessional beliefs, and charted pathways for the future challenges that Southern Baptists now faced.[37] The broad identity outlined in the introduction of this study is one that all Southern Baptists of every stripe can agree upon. We are a people of faith, a free people, a servant people, a diverse people, a confessional people, and a people of conflict and controversy.

The Controversy and the restructuring of the Southern Baptist Convention resulted in anxiety and confusion over the term "Southern Baptist." For those supportive of the leadership in the convention starting in the 1980s, being Southern Baptist meant close identification and agreement with the national organization. Southern Baptist Convention leadership defined what it meant to be a Southern Baptist in a narrower theological and ethical sense. The expectation was that state conventions, associations, and churches would duplicate what was accomplished at the national level.

Some Southern Baptists who opposed the new directions simply walked away from the convention. Many participated in new enterprises or joined other denominations with whom they found agreement. Others felt an anxious tension. They did not approve or support all that was happening in the Southern Baptist Convention. Yet, they felt a kinship with those Southern Baptists who had come before them. They seized upon traditional Southern Baptist ideals and doctrines, such as the priesthood of believers, religious liberty and separation of chu... and state, cooperative evangelism and missions, an open educational approach over an indoctrination approach to higher education, congregational polity but associational cooperation, and an atmosphere of liberty and accepted diversity.

These Baptists began to focus more upon their respective state conventions or the ministry and programs of their local churches. They interpreted "Southern Baptist" to mean something different and much more than that advocated by a few convention leaders. "Southern Baptist" defined the best of a rich heritage of beliefs and practices that was rooted in the history of the English and American Baptist movements in general and the rise of Southern Baptists in particular.

A problem with these diverse definitions is the confusion it caused not only for those within the tradition but those observing the people called Southern Baptists. Are Southern Baptists people who fight among themselves with a winner-take-all approach, or are they a group of people who find unity in diversity? Do they determine theology by vote of the majority, or draw from their historical confessional statements and recognize the responsibility of confessing in a relevant manner their Christ-centered and biblically-based convictions in a rapidly changing world? Are they a people who find unity in doctrinal and ethical conformity or in a commitment to minister, evangelize, educate, and serve, or in a balance between both?

The Controversy and the restructuring of the Southern Baptist Convention resulted in the participants involved in the struggles asking "Who are Southern Baptists?" The question continues to be most relevant in a new century and for the next generation.

Discussion Questions

1. After forty years of disagreement and distance, are there now available avenues for moderate and conservative Southern Baptists to engage one another? List possible ways at the local church level, associational level, state convention level, and denominational level.
2. What are the strengths for having both complementarians and egalitarians in the SBC? What are the weaknesses? What are some ways in which these two groups can coexist and grow together?

Conclusion

3. What are the strengths for having both cessationists and non-cessationists in the SBC? What are the weaknesses? What are some ways in which these two groups can coexist and grow together?
4. What are the strengths for having both Reformed and Arminian Baptists in the SBC? What are the weaknesses? What are some ways in which these two groups can coexist and grow together?
5. Brainstorm and list some concrete ways in which the SBC can grow in membership, vitality, and discipleship in the twenty-first century.
6. List specific ways in which the SBC can grow in multicultural contexts and in global contexts. What are specific things that you can do to bridge multicultural gaps?

Chapter Notes

Introduction

1. Several recent contributions have appeared that describe and define Southern Baptists. H. Leon McBeth's extensive *The Baptist Heritage: Four Centuries of Baptist Witness* (Nashville: Broadman Press, 1987), although dated, nevertheless contains a wealth of material on Baptists and Southern Baptists. More recent contributions include Bill J. Leonard, *Baptist Ways: A History* (Valley Forge: Judson, 2003); Anthony L. Chute, Nathan A. Finn, and Michael A. G. Haykin, *The Baptist Story: From English Sect to Global Movement* (Nashville: B & H, 2015); and David W. Bebbington, *Baptists through the Centuries: A History of a Global People*, 2nd ed. (Waco, TX: Baylor University Press, 2018). Studies centered more on Baptists in America include William H. Brackney, *Baptists in North America: An Historical Perspective* (Malden, MA: Blackwell, 2006), and Thomas S. Kidd and Barry Hankins, *Baptists in America: A History* (New York: Oxford University Press, 2015). Smaller and more popular works of value include Pamela R. Durso and Keith E. Durso, *The Story of Baptists in the United States* (Brentwood, TN: Baptist History and Heritage Society, 2006); Bruce T. Gourley, *A Capsule History of Baptists* (Atlanta: Baptist History and Heritage, 2010); and C. Douglas Weaver, *In Search of the New Testament Church: The Baptist Story* (Macon, GA: Mercer University Press, 2008). Moreover, The Baptist History and Heritage Society (baptisthistory.org) has published several pamphlet and video series. Studies emphasizing Southern Baptists include C. Brownlow Hastings, *Introducing Southern Baptists* (New York: Paulist Press, 1981); Albert McClellan, *Meet Southern Baptists* (Nashville: Broadman Press, 1978); Robert A. Baker, *The Southern Baptist Convention and Its People, 1607–1972* (Nashville: Broadman Press, 1974); Jesse C. Fletcher, *The Southern Baptist Convention: A Sesquicentennial History* (Nashville: Broadman & Holman, 1994); and Roger C. Richards, *History of Southern Baptists*, rev. ed. (Nashville: CrossBooks Publishing, 2015).

2. "Preamble and Constitution of the Southern Baptist Convention," in *Annual of the Southern Baptist Convention, 1845*, 3–5, taken from http://media2.sbhla.org.s3.amazonaws.com/annuals/SBC_Annual_1845.pdf.

3. See Keith Hinson, "Southern Baptists: Calvinism Resurging among SBC's Young Elites," *Christianity Today*, 6 October 1997.

4. Walter B. Shurden, *Not a Silent People: Controversies that Have Shaped Southern Baptists*, rev. ed. (Macon, GA: Smyth & Helwys, 1994).

5. The phrase comes from the first sentences of the preamble and constitution of the Southern Baptist Convention of 1845: "We the delegates from Missionary Societies, Churches, and other religious bodies of the Baptist Denomination, in various parts of the United States, met in Convention, in the city of Augusta, Georgia, for the purpose of carrying into effect the benevolent intentions of our constituents, by organizing a plan

for eliciting, combining and directing the energies of the whole denomination in one sacred effort, for the propagation of the Gospel...." See http://media2.sbhla. org.s3.amazonaws.com/annuals/SBC_ Annual_1845.pdf.

Chapter 1

1. McBeth, *Baptist Heritage*, 49–63.
2. Robert G. Torbet (*A History of the Baptists*, 3rd ed. [Valley Forge: Judson Press, 1973,] 20–21) appealed to a "spiritual kinship theory" which is similar to this viewpoint.
3. Shurden, *Not a Silent People*, 9–17.
4. W. Morgan Patterson, *Baptist Successionism: A Critical View* (Valley Forge: Judson Press, 1969). This book is an excellent, constructive examination of the history, methodology, and evaluation of the theory of Baptist successionism. See also James E. McGoldrick, *Baptist Successionism: A Crucial Question in Baptist History* (Metuchen, NJ: Scarecrow Press, 1994); and James E. Tull, *High-Church Baptists in the South: The Origin, Nature, and Influence of Landmarkism*, rev. ed. (Macon, GA: Mercer University Press, 2000.)
5. Shurden, *Not a Silent People*, 12–17.
6. Glen Harold Stassen, "Opening Menno Simons's Foundation-Book and Finding the Father of Baptist Origins alongside the Mother-Calvinist Congregationalism," *Baptist History and Heritage* 33:2 (1998): 34–44; and "Revisioning Baptist Identity by Naming Our Origin and Character Rightly," *Baptist History and Heritage* 33:2 (1998): 45–54. Other scholars who show an affinity toward Anabaptist influence include A. C. Underwood, *A History of English Baptists* (London: Kingsgate Press, 1947); Ernest Payne, *Thomas Helwys and the First Baptist Church in England* (London: Baptist Union, 1961); W. R. Estep, *The Anabaptist Story: An Introduction to Sixteenth-Century Anabaptism*, 3rd ed. (Grand Rapids: Eerdmans, 1995); and Malcolm B. Yarnell III, ed., *The*

Anabaptists and Contemporary Baptists (Nashville: B & H, 2013).
7. Torbet (*History of the Baptists*, 33–40) provides an adequate treatment of the rise of the General Baptists. Henry C. Vedder (*A Short History of the Baptists* [Valley Forge: Judson Press, 1907]) is an older but helpful treatment of Baptist history. A recent entry and update is found in William Brackney, *The Early English General Baptists and Their Theological Formation* (London: Regent's Park College, 2017).
8. Leonard, *Baptist Ways*, 25.
9. For an overview on Helwys, see John Inscore Essick, "Thomas Helwys," in *Witnesses to the Baptist Heritage*, ed. Michael E. Williams Sr. (Macon, GA: Mercer University Press, 2015), 1–7. For a full biography of Helwys, see Joe Early, Jr., *The Life and Writings of Thomas Helwys* (Macon, GA: Mercer University Press, 2009).
10. For an overview on Particular Baptist origins, see Chute, Finn, and Haykin (*Baptist Story*, 20–27); McBeth (*Baptist Heritage*, 39–44); and Torbet (*History of Baptists*, 40–43).
11. Information on Blunt's activities comes from the "Kiffen Manuscript." See Chute, Finn, and Haykin (*Baptist Story*, 23) for a transcript of the manuscript.
12. Early, *Life and Writings of Thomas Helwys*, 209.
13. Leonard (*Baptist Ways*, 14–15) effectively notes the evolving history that coalesced into the Baptist church.
14. McBeth (*Baptist Heritage*, 99–122) interrelates religious and political history for this period.
15. Besides Torbet and Vedder, there are three books by English Baptist historians which are helpful to the student of English Baptist history: Underwood, *History of the English Baptists*; W. T. Whitley, *A History of English Baptists* (London: Charles Griffin, 1923); and Roger Hayden, *English Baptist History and Heritage*, 2nd ed. (Didcot, Oxfordshire: Baptist Union of Great Britain, 2005). Most of the material in this section is drawn from these writings.
16. Torbet, *History of Baptists*, 44.
17. B. R. White, "The English

Particular Baptists and the Great Rebellion, 1640–1660," *Baptist History and Heritage* 9:1 (1974): 20–24. See Leonard, *Baptist Ways*, 52–53.

18. Slayden A. Yarbrough, "The Origin of Baptist Associations Among the English Particular Baptists," *Baptist History and Heritage* 23:2 (1988): 14–24.

19. See McBeth, *Baptist Heritage*, 291–307.

20. See Torbet, *History of Baptists*, 45–46.

21. See McBeth (*Baptist Heritage*, 113–22) and Torbet (*History of Baptists*, 46–57) for a discussion of this period.

22. See Torbet (*History of Baptists*, 61–83, 111–34) for detailed information about these four developments.

23. See Michael Dain, "Dan Taylor," in Williams, *Witnesses to the Baptist Heritage*, 44–49; Frank W. Rinaldi, *The Tribe of Dan: The New Connexion of General Baptists, 1770–1891: A Study in the Transition from Revival Movement to Established Denomination* (Milton Keynes, UK: Paternoster, 2008).

24. Historians have traced similar tendencies to Anglican Tobias Crisp and Presbyterian Joseph Hussey. Both McBeth (*Baptist Heritage*, 173–74) and James Leo Garrett, Jr. (*Baptist Theology: A Four-Century Study* [Macon, GA: Mercer University Press, 2009], 89–90) conclude that hyper–Calvinism invaded Particular Baptists from these outside sources.

25. There are several excellent studies on Fuller's life and theology, including Sheila Klopfer, "Andrew Fuller," in Williams, *Witnesses to the Baptist Heritage*, 50–57; Paul Brewster, *Andrew Fuller: Model Pastor and Theologian* (Nashville: B & H, 2010); and Peter J. Morden, *Offering Christ to the World: Andrew Fuller (1754–1815) and the Revival of Eighteenth-Century Particular Baptist Life* (Waynesboro, GA: Paternoster, 2003).

26. See Terry Carter, "William Carey," in Williams, *Witnesses to the Baptist Heritage*, 66–72; Timothy George, *Faithful Witness: The Life and Mission of William Carey* (Birmingham, AL: New Hope, 1991).

27. See McBeth, *Baptist Heritage*, 300–302.

28. Garrett, *Baptist Theology*, 264–78; McBeth, *Baptist Heritage*, 302–7.

29. There are numerous biographies on Spurgeon. Two recent entries may be mentioned. First, Spurgeon's career through the lens of his spirituality is developed in Peter J. Morden, *Communion with Christ and His People: The Spirituality of C. H. Spurgeon* (Oxford: Regent's Park, 2010). Second, Tom J. Nettles published *Living by Revealed Truth: The Life and Pastoral Theology of Charles Haddon Spurgeon* (Fearn, Scotland: Mentor, 2013). It is a massive interpretive biography that accents Spurgeon's Particular Baptist-Calvinist-Reformed theology.

30. Much of the material in this section is summarized from McBeth (*Baptist Heritage*, 123–50, 200–287); Torbet (*History of Baptists*, 201–53, 266–97); and Vedder (*Short History of Baptists*, 287–334).

31. A capable biography of Williams is found in Edwin S. Gaustad, *Liberty of Conscience: Roger Williams in America* (Grand Rapids: Eerdmans, 1991).

32. See Bruce Gourley, "John Clarke," in Williams, *Witnesses to the Baptist Heritage*, 8–15; Louis Franklin Asher, *John Clarke* (Pittsburgh, PA: Dorrance, 1997).

33. See Elliott Smith, *The Advance of Baptist Associations Across America* (Nashville: Broadman Press, 1979), 21–42.

34. Nevertheless, Edwards was excommunicated for a period of time due to "Immoral Conduct, and Disorderly Walk," a charge that referred to intoxication and intemperate language. See Leonard, *Baptist Ways*, 116. A small group of German Baptists called the Dunkers or Dunkards also settled in Pennsylvania. They called themselves the Brethren. They practiced triune immersion (dipping three times in the name of the three persons of the Trinity) and laid the candidate face down in the water. See Donald F. Durnbaugh, *Fruit of the Vine: History of the Brethren*, 2nd ed. (Elgin, IL: Brethren Press, 1996).

35. See Kidd and Hankins, *Baptists in America*, 19–38.

36. See Scott Bryant, "Shubal Stearns," in Williams, *Witnesses to the Baptist*

Heritage, 31–37. An excellent discussion of the Sandy Creek tradition is William L. Lumpkin, *Baptist Foundations in the South* (Nashville: Broadman Press, 1961).

37. See Brad Creed, "John Leland," in Williams, *Witnesses to the Baptist Heritage*, 58–65; John A. Ragosta, *Wellspring of Liberty: How Virginia's Religious Dissenters Helped Win the American Revolution and Secured Liberty* (New York: Oxford University Press, 2010).

38. See David Holcomb, "Isaac Backus," in Williams, *Witnesses to the Baptist Heritage*, 38–43; Stanley Grenz, *Isaac Backus, Puritan and Baptist: His Place in History, His Thought, and Their Implications for Modern Baptist Theology* (Macon, GA: Mercer University Press, 1983).

39. Kidd and Hankins, *Baptists in America*, 77.

40. On the Judsons, see Delane Tew, "Adoniram Judson," in Williams, *Witnesses to the Baptist Heritage*, 79–86; Phyllis Rodgerson Pleasants, "Beyond Translation: The Work of the Judsons in Burma," *Baptist History and Heritage* 42:2 (2007): 19–35; Jason G. Duesing, ed., *Adoniram Judson: A Bicentennial Appreciation of the Pioneer American Missionary* (Nashville: B & H, 2012); and Rosalie Hall Hunt, *Bless God and Take Courage: The Judson History and Legacy* (Valley Forge, PA: Judson Press, 2005). On Rice, see Evelyn Wingo Thompson, *Luther Rice: Believer in Tomorrow* (Nashville: Broadman Press, 1967); and John Mark Terry, "Luther Rice: Dreamer and Doer," *Southern Baptist Journal of Theology* 6:4 (2002): 40–57.

41. For discussion on the anti-missions controversy, see Garrett, *Baptist Theology*, 249–57; Kidd and Hankins, *Baptists in America*, 110–16; Shurden, *Not a Silent People*, 19–28; and Michael E. Williams, Sr., "Baptist 'Anti' Movements and the Turn toward Progressivism: 1820/1832/1845," in *Turning Points in Baptist History: A Festschrift in Honor of Harry Leon McBeth*, ed. Michael E. Williams, Sr., and Walter B. Shurden (Macon, GA: Mercer University Press, 2008), 141–52.

42. For discussion on slavery and its contribution to the creation of the Southern Baptist Convention, see Baker (*Southern Baptist Convention*, 153–72); Chute, Finn, and Haykin (*Baptist Story*, 152–61); McBeth (*Baptist Heritage*, 381–91); and Shurden (*Not a Silent People*, 29–38). Bebbington (*Baptists Through the Centuries*, 139–56) devotes a full chapter to the gospel and race among Baptists. See also Terry Carter, "Baptists and Racism and the Turn Toward Segregation: 1845," and Sandy Dwayne Martin, "Baptists and Race and the Turn from Slavery to Greater Institutionalization among African-American Baptists, 1850–1880," in Williams and Shurden, *Turning Points*, 167–77, 194–203.

43. The meeting occurred at the First Baptist Church of Augusta. See Bruce T. Gourley, *A Journey of Faith and Community: The Story of the First Baptist Church of Augusta, Georgia* (Macon, GA: Mercer University Press, 2017).

44. The information that follows summarizes Walter B. Shurden, "The Southern Baptist Synthesis: Is It Cracking?" *Baptist History and Heritage* 16:2 (1981): 2–11. This is an excellent article in terms of an overview of Southern Baptist sources and developments.

45. See Michael E. Williams, Sr., *Isaac Taylor Tichenor: The Creation of the Baptist New South* (Tuscaloosa, AL: University of Alabama Press, 2005).

46. McBeth, *Baptist Heritage*, 461.

47. See James A. Patterson, *James Robinson Graves: Staking the Boundaries of Baptist Identity* (Nashville: B & H, 2012). Patterson provides background study that attempts to understand Graves's contemporary issues; issues that provoked him toward Landmarkism.

48. H. Leon McBeth, "The Texas Tradition: A Study in Baptist Regionalism, Parts I and II," *Baptist History and Heritage* 26:1 (1991): 37–57. This is developed more fully in McBeth, *Texas Baptists: A Sesquicentennial History* (Dallas, TX: Baptistway Press, 1998).

49. Shurden, "Southern Baptist Synthesis," 8–9.

50. A thorough overview of the Civil War and the Reconstruction period in relation to Southern Baptists is found in

Baker, *Southern Baptist Convention*, 226–55. Also valuable is Kidd and Hankins, *Baptists in America*, 117–39.

51. For discussions on Landmarkism, see Baker (*Southern Baptist Convention*, 208–19, 248–49, 277–84); McBeth (*Baptist Heritage*, 447–63); and Shurden (*Not a Silent People*, 39–51).

52. Shurden, "Southern Baptist Synthesis," 9; McBeth, *Baptist Heritage*, 432–40.

53. See Walter K. Knight, *Southern Baptists Nationwide* in *The Baptist Heritage Series* published by the Historical Commission of the Southern Baptist Convention; Shurden, "Southern Baptist Synthesis," 9–10; and Baker, *Southern Baptist Convention*, 342–89.

54. Baker, *Southern Baptist Convention*, 393–96.

55. Baker, *Southern Baptist Convention*, 397–400, 416–17; Chute, Finn, Haykin, *Baptist Story*, 282–91; Fletcher, *Southern Baptist Convention*, 259–305; and Leonard, *Baptist Ways*, 414–16.

56. Baker, *Southern Baptist Convention*, 414–23; Leonard, *Baptist Ways*, 416.

Chapter 2

1. An excellent treatment of this theme is James E. Carter, "Missions and Evangelism: The Strings That Tie Southern Baptists Together," *The Quarterly Review* 43:2 (1983): 68–74.

2. For a discussion on the priesthood of believers, see E. Y. Mullins, *The Axioms of Religion* (Philadelphia: Griffith and Rowland Press, 1908), 59–69; Herschel Hobbs and E. Y. Mullins, *The Axioms of Religion* (Nashville: Broadman Press, 1978), 75–90; and E. Glenn Hinson, *Soul Liberty* (Nashville: Convention Press, 1975). Mullins introduced the idea of "soul competency." What the priesthood of believers does for Christians, soul competency does for all people.

3. James Leo Garrett, Jr., "The Priesthood of All Believers," *The Baptist Standard* 76 (January 15, 1965). See Peter L. Tie, *Restore Unity, Recover Identity, and Refine Orthopraxy: The Believers' Priesthood in the Ecclesiology of James Leo Garrett, Jr.* (Eugene, OR: Wipf & Stock, 2012).

4. Timothy George, "The Priesthood of All Believers and the Quest for Theological Integrity," *Criswell Theological Review* 3 (1989): 283–94.

5. See Jerry Sutton (*Baptist Reformation: The Conservative Resurgence in the Southern Baptist Convention* [Nashville: Broadman & Holman, 2000], 425–38) for his take on the 1988 convention resolution on "priesthood of all believers."

6. Malcom B. Yarnell III, "Changing Baptist Concepts of Royal Priesthood: John Smyth and Edgar Young Mullins," in *The Rise of the Laity in Evangelical Protestantism*, ed. Deryck W. Lovegrove (New York: Routledge, 2002), 236–52. See also Malcolm B. Yarnell III, "The Priesthood of Believers: Rediscovering the Biblical Doctrine of Royal Priesthood," in *Restoring Integrity in Baptist Churches*, ed. Thomas White, Jason G. Duesing, and Malcolm B. Yarnell III (Grand Rapids: Kregel, 2007), 221–44; Chad Owen Brand and David E. Hankins, *One Sacred Effort: The Cooperative Program of Southern Baptists* (Nashville: B & H, 2005), 14–21; and Jonathan Leeman, "A Baptist View of the Royal Priesthood of All Believers," *Southern Baptist Journal of Theology* 23:1 (2019): 113–35.

7. Walter Shurden, *The Doctrine of the Priesthood of Believers* (Nashville: Convention Press, 1989). See also Reggie McNeal, "The Priesthood of All Believers," in *Has Our Theology Changed? Southern Baptist Thought Since 1845*, ed. Paul A. Basden (Nashville: Broadman & Holman, 1994), 204–29; and Fisher Humphreys, *The Way We Were: How Southern Baptist Theology Changed and What It Means to Us All*, rev. ed. (Macon, GA: Smyth & Helwys, 2002), 32–34.

8. For thorough treatments of Baptist polity, see W. W. Barnes, *The Southern Baptist Convention: A Study in the Development of Ecclesiology* (Fort Worth, TX: Seminary Hill Press, 1934); James L. Sullivan, *Baptist Polity as I See It*, rev. ed. (Nashville: Broadman & Holman, 1998); and Norman H. Maring, Winthrop S. Hudson, and David Gregg, *A Baptist*

Manual of Polity and Practice, 2nd rev. ed. (Valley Forge: Judson Press, 2012). A resource that stresses church discipline is Mark Dever, ed., *Polity: Biblical Arguments on How to Conduct Church Life* (Washington, D. C.: Center for Church Reform, 2001).

9. Franklin M. Segler, *A Theology of Church and Ministry* (Nashville: Broadman Press, 1960), 3–22.

10. See http://www.sbc.net/BecomingSouthernBaptist/pdf/FastFacts2019.pdf.

11. Helpful treatments on Baptist associationalism include F. Russell Bennett, Jr., *The Fellowship of Kindred Minds* (Atlanta: Home Mission Board of the Southern Baptist Convention, 1974); Elliott Smith, *The Advance of Baptist Associations across America* (Nashville: Broadman Press, 1979); and Paul Stripling, *Turning Points in the History of Baptist Associations in America* (Nashville: B & H, 2006). See also the brief offerings of Gregory Tomlin, "Baptist Associations to Celebrate 300th Anniversary," *Baptist Press*, 19 February 2007; and Walter B. Shurden, "Baptist Associations and the Turn Toward Denominational Cooperation: 1640s/1707," in Williams and Shurden, *Turning Points*, 63–73.

12. *1999 Book of Reports of the Southern Baptist Convention* (Nashville: Executive Committee, 1999), 7.

13. Lyle Garlow and Susan Ray, *Oklahoma Southern Baptists Working Together* (Oklahoma City: Arthur Davenport and Associates, 1980), 35–37.

14. See https://www.nwbaptist.org/regions/.

15. See http://www.sbc.net/BecomingSouthernBaptist/pdf/FastFacts2019.pdf.

16. Ed Stetzer, "The Future of the SBC–Local Associations," *Christianity Today*, 21 June 2016.

17. Josh Ellis, "Baptist Associations: The Next Era of Baptist Associations," *SBC Life*, 1 May 2013.

18. E. C. Routh, "Convention, The State Baptist," *Encyclopedia of Southern Baptists*, 1:313–14. This resource will use the abbreviation ESB hereafter.

19. See http://www.sbc.net/BecomingSouthernBaptist/pdf/FastFacts2019.pdf.

20. "Preamble and Constitution," 3–5.

21. "Preamble and Constitution," 117–18.

22. "Preamble and Constitution," 120.

23. McBeth, *Baptist Heritage*, 388–91. Chute, Finn, and Haykin (*Baptist Story*, 159) relate that the SBC received a jumpstart with 4,126 churches and 351,951 members.

24. Robert A. Baker, *A Baptist Source Book* (Nashville: Broadman Press, 1966), 117.

25. See Brand and Hankins, *One Sacred Effort*, 145–59.

26. Taken from https://www.bwanet.org. See Richard V. Pierard, ed., *Baptists Together in Christ 1905–2005: A Hundred-Year Anniversary of the Baptist World Alliance* (Falls Church, VA: Baptist World Alliance, 2005).

27. For a history of the Cooperative Program, see Cecil Ray and Susan Ray, *Cooperation: The Baptist Way to a Lost World* (Nashville: Stewardship Commission, 1985); and Brand and Hankins, *One Sacred Effort*.

28. See Brand and Hankins, *One Sacred Effort*, 93–99, 110–17; and Frank S. Page, "The Cooperative Program and the Future of Collaborative Ministry," in *The SBC and the 21st Century*, ed. Jason K. Allen (Nashville: B & H, 2016), 9–20.

29. Early treatments of the history of the Home Mission Board include J. B. Lawrence, *History of the Home Mission Board* (Nashville: Broadman Press, 1958) and Arthur B. Rutledge, *Mission to America*, rev. ed. (Nashville: Broadman Press, 1960). See also John Caylor, "Home Mission Board," *ESB*, 1:635–46; Hugo H. Culpepper, "Home Mission Board," *ESB*, 3:1759–62; and Walker L. Knight, "Home Mission Board," *ESB*, 4:2271–73. The material in this section is digested primarily from these sources.

30. See Williams, *Isaac Taylor Tichenor*, 97–128.

31. Fletcher, *Southern Baptist Convention*, 150.

32. Nevertheless, the HMB continued to struggle to delineate and maintain its mission. McBeth (*Baptist*

Heritage, 640) noted that as late as 1959, the SBC voted to allow the HMB "to continue to exist as a separate agency of the Convention."

33. Fletcher, *Southern Baptist Convention,* 213–14.

34. Fletcher, *Southern Baptist Convention,* 266.

35. Actually, three members of the original search committee (M. A. Winchester, Lula Walker, and Troy Morrison) refused to resign and were included in the new search committee.

36. See Sutton, *Baptist Reformation,* 258–68.

37. Fletcher, *Southern Baptist Convention,* 273–75.

38. *2000 Book of Reports of the Southern Baptist Convention* (Nashville: Executive Committee, 2000), 121.

39. Resources on the history of the Foreign Mission Board include Baker James Cauthen and Frank K. Means, *Advance to Bold Mission Thrust: A History of Southern Baptist Foreign Missions, 1845–1980* (Nashville: Broadman Press, 1981); and W. R. Estep, *Whole Gospel, Whole World: The Foreign Mission Board of the Southern Baptist Convention, 1845–1995* (Nashville: Broadman & Holman, 1995). See also E. C. Routh, "Foreign Mission Board," *ESB,* 1:457–74; Eugene L. Hill, "Foreign Mission Board," *ESB,* 3:1700–1702; and Thomas W. Hill, "Foreign Mission Board, SBC," *ESB,* 4:2205–11. The material in this section is compiled primarily from these sources.

40. Estep (*Whole World,* 83–111) sketches the progress amid challenges that Taylor's administration experienced.

41. When Tupper made his first annual report to the convention in 1872, he addressed for the first time to Southern Baptists the needed role of women in missions. See Cauthen and Means, *Advance,* 29–30; Estep, *Whole World,* 118–23.

42. Cauthen and Means, *Advance,* 33–37; Fletcher, *Southern Baptist Convention,* 148–49, 156.

43. Estep, *Whole World,* 221.

44. See Jesse C. Fletcher, *Baker James Cauthen: A Man for All Nations* (Nashville: Broadman Press, 1977).

45. On the Rüschlikon incident, see Estep, *Whole World,* 359–68; Sutton, *Baptist Reformation,* 274–85.

46. *1999 Book of Reports,* 65, 75.

47. Two treatments on the heritage of the Sunday School Board are Robert A. Baker, *The Story of the Sunday School Board* (Nashville: Convention Press, 1966); and Walter B. Shurden, *The Sunday School Board: Ninety Years of Service* (Nashville: Broadman Press, 1981). See also Clifton J. Allen, "Sunday School Board," *ESB,* 2:1317–39; Howard P. Colson. "Sunday School Board," *ESB,* 3:2000–2009; and Gomer R. Lesch, "Sunday School Board, SBC," *ESB,* 4:2498–2507. Material in this section is digested primarily from these sources, unless otherwise indicated.

48. Shurden, *Sunday School Board,* 11–19.

49. Frost provided the first history of the board: James M. Frost, *The Sunday School Board, Southern Baptist Convention: Its History and Work* (Nashville: Sunday School Board, 1914).

50. McBeth, *Baptist Heritage,* 644–46.

51. Baker, *Story of the Sunday School Board,* 124.

52. Shurden, *Sunday School Board,* 55–71.

53. Baker (*Story of Sunday School Board,* 200–202) provides a brief sketch of church music development.

54. Sutton, *Baptist Reformation,* 287.

55. Shurden (*Sunday School Board,* 8) offered broad strokes that characterized board leadership: Frost (Builder), Bell (Fighter), Van Ness (Educator), Holcomb (Pastor), Sullivan (Balancer), and Cothen (Bible Promotor).

56. Grady Cothen, *What Happened to the Southern Baptist Convention?* (Macon, GA: Smyth & Helwys, 1993), 319.

57. See Fletcher, *Southern Baptist Convention,* 296–97, 310–11; Cothen, *What Happened?* 318–33; James C. Hefley, *The Conservative Resurgence in the Southern Baptist Convention* (Garland, TX: Hannibal Books, 2005), 259–82; Sutton, *Baptist Reformation,* 287–308.

58. John Perry, *Walking God's Path: The Life and Ministry of Jimmy Draper*

(Nashville: Broadman & Holman, 2005), 210–24.

59. For a history of the Annuity Board see Robert A. Baker, *The Thirteenth Check* (Nashville: Broadman Press, 1968). See also Retta O'Bannon, "Relief and Annuity Board," *ESB*, 2:1140–45; John D. Bloskas, "Annuity Board," *ESB*, 3:1569–71; and John Bloskas and John Dudley, "Annuity Board, SBC," *ESB*, 4:2084–86. The material in this section is compiled primarily from these sources.

60. Fletcher, *Southern Baptist Convention*, 229.

61. Cothen, *What Happened?*, 358.

62. Fletcher, *Southern Baptist Convention*, 355.

63. McBeth, *Baptist Heritage*, 655.

64. The information on the Brotherhood Commission is compiled from McBeth, *Baptist Heritage*, 655–56; Archie E. Brown, "Brotherhood, Baptist," *ESB*, 1:196–99; Darrell C. Richardson, "Brotherhood, Baptist," *ESB*, 3:1621–24; and Roy Jennings, "Brotherhood Commission, SBC," *ESB*, 4:2131–33.

65. Fletcher, *Southern Baptist Convention*, 355.

66. Resources for this section include McBeth, *Baptist Heritage*, 656–58; Walter B. Shurden, "The Christian Life Commission: Evolved Conscience of the Southern Baptist Convention," *The Quarterly Review* 42 (1981): 63–75; A. C. Miller, "The Christian Life Commission," *ESB*, 1:260–61; Floyd A. Craig and Foy D. Valentine, "The Christian Life Commission," *ESB*, 3:1645–48; and Foy D. Valentine, "Christian Life Commission, SBC," *ESB*, 4:2154–56; Jerry Sutton, *A Matter of Conviction: A History of Southern Baptist Engagement with the Culture* (Nashville: B & H, 2008).

67. Quote from the *Annual, Southern Baptist Convention*, 1961, 60 as found in Shurden, "Christian Life Commission," 74.

68. Sutton (*Baptist Reformation*, 309–12) describes Valentine's pro-choice views on abortion.

69. Cothen, *What Happened?*, 349–50; Fletcher, *Southern Baptist Convention*, 286; Hefley, *Conservative Resurgence*, 55–56; David T. Morgan, *The New Crusades, The New Holy Land: Conflict in the Southern Baptist Convention, 1969–1991* (Tuscaloosa, AL: University of Alabama Press, 1996), 115–16; Sutton, *Baptist Reformation*, 312–14.

70. Fletcher, *Southern Baptist Convention*, 295; Hefley, *Conservative Resurgence*, 69–70; Morgan, *New Crusades*, 116; Sutton, *Baptist Reformation*, 315–19.

71. Fletcher, *Southern Baptist Convention*, 328–29.

72. Two excellent books on the Education Commission are H. I. Hester, *Southern Baptists in Christian Education* (Murfreesboro, NC: Chowan College School of Graphic Arts, 1968); and H. I. Hester, *Partners in Purpose and Progress* (Nashville: The Education Commission, 1977). See also R. Orin Cornett, "Education Commission of the Southern Baptist Convention," *ESB*, 1:392–94; Rabun L. Brantley, "Education Commission of the Southern Baptist Convention," *ESB*, 3:1685–86; and Arthur L. Walker Jr., "Education Commission, SBC," *ESB*, 4:2191–92. The material in this section is digested from these sources.

73. McBeth, *Baptist Heritage*, 653.

74. In 2006, the Association of Southern Baptist Colleges and Schools added "International" to the front of its name (see baptistschools.org).

75. Information on the American Baptist Seminary Commission is found in McBeth, *Baptist Heritage*, 654; L. S. Sedberry, "American Baptist Theological Seminary," *ESB*, 1:42–44; Herman F. Burns, "American Baptist Theological Seminary," *ESB*, 3:1568; and George C. Capps, "American Baptist Theological Seminary," *ESB*, 4:2081–82.

76. Information on the Historical Commission is digested from H. I. Hester, *Southern Baptists and Their History* (Nashville: Historical Commission, SBC, 1971); Judson Boyce Allen, "Historical Commission of the Southern Baptist Convention," *ESB*, 1:623–25; Lynn E. May Jr., "Historical Commission of the Southern Baptist Convention," *ESB*, 3:1756–57; A. Ronald Tonks, "Historical Commission, SBC," *ESB*, 4:2267–68; Fletcher, *Southern Baptist Convention*, 191–92; McBeth, *Baptist Heritage*, 658–59.

77. Tonks, "Historical Commission," 4:2268.

78. Material on the Radio and Television Commission is digested from Theodore Lott, "Radio and Television Commission," *ESB*, 2:1130–31; Clarence Duncan, "Radio and Television Commission," *ESB*, 3:1932–33; and Bonita Sparrow, "Radio and Television Commission, SBC," *ESB*, 4:2432–33.

79. Material on the Stewardship Commission is summarized from Merrill D. Moore, "Stewardship Commission of the Southern Baptist Convention," *ESB*, 3:1989–92; and A. R. Fagan, "Stewardship Commission, SBC," *ESB*, 4:2489.

80. Baker, *Southern Baptist Convention*, 438.

81. Baker, *Southern Baptist Convention*, 443; McBeth, *Baptist Heritage*, 661–62.

82. See Baker, *Southern Baptist Convention*, 444–45; McBeth, *Baptist Heritage*, 662–66; Bobbie Sorrill, *WMU—A Church Missions Organization* (Birmingham, AL: Woman's Missionary Union, 1981); Rosalie Hall Hunt, *We've a Story to Tell: 125 Years of WMU* (Birmingham, AL: Woman's Missionary Union, 2013); Juliette Mather, "Woman's Missionary Union," *ESB*, 2:1506–27; Betty Brown, "Woman's Missionary Union," *ESB*, 3:2054–56; and June Whitlow, "Woman's Missionary Union, Auxiliary to SBC," *ESB*, 4:2550–52.

83. *1999 Book of Reports*, 168.

84. *1999 Book of Reports*, 22.

85. That is, all agencies except the six seminaries. They will be discussed in Chapter 4.

Chapter 3

1. Mark Wingfield, "Houston Convention Forever Changed Baptist Life," *Baptist Standard*, 9 June 1999, 1.

2. For example, Walter B. Shurden, ed., *The Struggle for the Soul of the SBC: Moderate Responses to the Fundamentalist Movement* (Macon, GA: Mercer University Press, 1993); Walter B. Shurden and Randy Shepley, eds., *Going for the Jugular: A Documentary History of the*

SBC Holy War (Macon, GA: Mercer University Press, 1996); Bill J. Leonard, *God's Last and Only Hope: The Fragmentation of the Southern Baptist Convention* (Grand Rapids: Eerdmans, 1990); Cothen, *What Happened?*; Robison B. James, *The Takeover in the Southern Baptist Convention* (Decatur, GA: SBC Today, 1989); Barry Hankins, *Uneasy in Babylon: Southern Baptist Conservatives and American Culture* (Tuscaloosa, AL: University of Alabama Press, 2002); and Morgan, *New Crusades*.

3. For example, Sutton, *Baptist Reformation*; James C. Hefley, *The Truth in Crisis*, 5 vols. (Dallas: Criterion Publications; Hannibal, MO: Hannibal Books, 1986–1990); Hefley, *Conservative Resurgence*; Paige Patterson, *Anatomy of a Reformation: The Southern Baptist Convention 1978–2004* (Fort Worth, TX: Seminary Hill Press, 2004); Paul Pressler, *A Hill on Which to Die: One Southern Baptist's Journey* (Nashville: Broadman & Holman, 1999); Richards, *History of Southern Baptists*, 319–38; and Chute, Finn, and Haykin, *Baptist Story*, 275–91. More resources are found in the bibliography. The titles of the works in this note and the previous note underscore their perspectives. In addition, historian Gregory Wills is publishing a history of the SBC soon. His conservative credentials are on display in *Southern Baptist Seminary, 1859–2009* (New York: Oxford University Press, 2010). His forthcoming contribution will certainly be the most recent and detailed work on Southern Baptist history from a conservative perspective.

4. Fletcher, *Southern Baptist Convention*, 259–305; Garrett, *Baptist Theology*, 491–513.

5. Hefley, *Conservative Resurgence*, 29–35; Garrett, *Baptist Theology*, 457–73, 486–88.

6. Gregory A. Wills, "Progressive Theology and Southern Baptist Controversies of the 1950s and 1960s," *Southern Baptist Journal of Theology* 7:1 (2003): 12–31. Wills catalogs other controversies and faculty dismissals. For conservatives, then, the Elliott Controversy was only the tip of the iceberg of previous and ongoing

issues of progressive theology infiltrating the convention. See also Paige Patterson, "Theological Drift—World War II-1979," *Southwestern Journal of Theology* 54:2 (2012): 150–64; and Chute, Finn, and Haykin, *Baptist Story*, 278–79.

7. Fletcher (*Southern Baptist Convention*, 243–44) and Sutton (*Baptist Reformation*, 68–84) discuss the background of both Pressler and Patterson.

8. Sutton (*Baptist Reformation*, 18–30) and Wills ("Progressive Theology," 14–25) listed several examples of "continued theological drift."

9. Morgan, *New Crusades*, 191.

10. Toby Druin, "Patterson Group Seeks Long Range Control of SBC," *Baptist Press*, 21 April 1980, 1–5. Patterson (*Anatomy of a Reformation*, 3–5) recognized the necessity of utilizing the system. The key was to organize conservatives "in the methods to effect change and the necessity for doing so." He concluded "if you want to reform a church or association or convention to glorify God, you should work toward being known, getting organized, and knowing politics."

11. The roles of many of the players in the "Controversy" are described in the works by Fletcher (*Southern Baptist Convention*, 219–359) and Hefley (*Conservative Resurgence*, 25–91). Shurden and Shepley (*Going for the Jugular*) contains a treasure of primary source material from the participants in the "Controversy."

12. W. A. Criswell, *Why I Preach That the Bible Is Literally True* (Nashville: Broadman Press, 1969). Criswell mentions no names but the controversy over the *Broadman Bible Commentary* was the historical backdrop.

13. See W. A. Criswell, *Standing on the Promises: The Autobiography of W. A. Criswell* (Waco, TX: Word, 1990).

14. Actually, Pressler (*A Hill to Die*, 78–82) gives credit to Bill Powell (founder of the Baptist Faith and Fellowship) for helping him understand how the Southern Baptist system worked.

15. Sutton, *Baptist Reformation*, 78.

16. Tom Miller, "Committee Appointments the Key," *Religious Herald*, 18 September 1980, 8–10. See Shurden and Shepley, *Going for the Jugular*, 56.

17. Honeycutt's title for the 1984 sermon was "To Your Tents O Israel." See Shurden and Shepley, *Going for the Jugular*, 124–34.

18. "Hobbs Motion to Reaffirm the Baptist Faith and Message and Its Statement on the Bible," *SBC Annual 1981*, 35, 45.

19. "Motion to Establish SBC 'Peace Committee,'" *SBC Annual 1985*, 64–65.

20. "The Glorieta Statement," dated 22 October 1986, is found in Shurden and Shepley, *Going for the Jugular*, 195–96.

21. Dan Martin, "Sherman Resigns Peace Committee," *Baptist Press*, 24 October 1986, 5–6. See Shurden and Shepley, *Going for the Jugular*, 197–99.

22. Steve Maynard and Julia Duin, "SBC Fundamentalists Win Victory on Bible's Inerrancy," *Houston Chronicle*, 24 October 1986, in Fletcher, *Southern Baptist Convention*, 287.

23. Sutton (*Baptist Reformation*, 171–75) details reasons why conservatives backed away from the Glorieta Statement.

24. "The SBC Peace Committee Report," *SBC Annual 1987*, 232–42.

25. Sutton (*Baptist Reformation*, 152–79) details the ups and downs of the Peace Committee effort from the conservative viewpoint. Cothen (*What Happened?*, 207–26) does the same from the moderate perspective.

26. Herschel H. Hobbs, *My Faith and Message: An Autobiography* (Nashville: Broadman & Holman, 1993), 252.

27. Nancy Tatom Ammerman, *Baptist Battles: Social Change and Religious Conflict in the Southern Baptist Convention* (New Brunswick, NJ: Rutgers University Press, 1990), 78–80.

28. Wayne Grudem (*Systematic Theology: An Introduction to Biblical Doctrine* [Grand Rapids: Zondervan, 1994], 90) offers a succinct definition: "The inerrancy of Scripture means that Scripture in the original manuscripts does not affirm anything that is contrary to fact."

29. Ammerman, *Baptist Battles*, 80–84. See Hefley, *Truth in Crisis*, 3:35–54.

30. Ammerman, *Baptist Battles*, 84–87. See Cothen, *What Happened?*,

110–39; Hankins, *Uneasy in Babylon*, 4–6; Morgan, *New Crusades*, 43–45.

31. Druin, "Patterson Group Seeks Long Range Control," 5.

32. "Resolution No. 10—On Affirming Religious Liberty and Separation of Church and State," *SBC Annual 1981*, 56.

33. See Cothen, *What Happened?*, 153–55, 354–57; Sutton, *Baptist Reformation*, 124, 143–44, 311–12, 318–19.

34. Ammerman, *Baptist Battles*, 99–103.

35. Ammerman, *Baptist Battles*, 103–6. Cothen (*What Happened?*, 145–57) discusses abortion and prayer in public schools. Hankins (*Uneasy in Babylon*, 121–27; 140–49) describes the growing popularity of accommodationism and prayer in schools.

36. See Charles W. Deweese, *Women Deacons and Deaconesses: 400 Years of Baptist Service* (Macon, GA: Mercer University Press, 2005); and Curtis W. Freeman, ed., *A Company of Women Preachers: Baptist Prophetesses in Seventeenth-Century England* (Waco, TX: Baylor University Press, 2011).

37. Brad Creed, "Church Leaders," in Basden, *Has Our Theology Changed?*, 198–99.

38. Deweese (*Women Deacons*, 123–48) devotes a whole chapter to Southern Baptist churches who accepted women deacons and subsequent responses during the 1980s.

39. W. A. Criswell, *The Doctrine of the Church* (Nashville: Convention Press, 1980), 79.

40. Fletcher, *Southern Baptist Convention*, 225–26.

41. Ammerman, *Baptist Battles*, 89.

42. Hefley, *Conservative Resurgence*, 52.

43. Fletcher, *Southern Baptist Convention*, 272. See "SBC Resolution on Ordination and Role of Women," *SBC Annual* 1984, 65, in Shurden and Shepley, *Going for the Jugular*, 122–23.

44. Fletcher, *Southern Baptist Convention*, 292–93. See Cothen, *What Happened?*, 142–45. Leonard (*God's Last Hope*, 152) observed that "Few people apparently noticed that a similar

literalistic hermeneutic was operative in 1845 in the 'biblical' defense of human slavery."

45. Fletcher, *Southern Baptist Convention*, 271–72.

46. Jann Aldredge Clanton, "Why I Believe Southern Baptist Churches Should Ordain Women," *Baptist History and Heritage* 23:3 (1988): 50–55; Dorothy Kelley Patterson, "Why I Believe Southern Baptist Churches Should Not Ordain Women," *Baptist History and Heritage* 23:3 (1988): 56–62. These two articles are mentioned in Creed, "Church Leaders," 201. Deweese (*Women Deacons*, 25–32) includes them in a list of four point-counterpoint articles.

47. Ammerman, *Baptist Battles*, 96–97.

48. Ammerman, *Baptist Battles*, 97–98. See Susan M. Shaw, "Of Words and Women: Southern Baptist Publications and the Progress of Women in the 1970s," *Baptist History and Heritage* 42:2 (2007): 69–84; Joseph E. Early Jr., "The Role, Place, and Purpose of Southern Baptist Women, 1979–1987," *Baptist History and Heritage* 54:2 (2019): 8–21.

49. Ammerman, *Baptist Battles*, 100–102.

50. Hankins, *Uneasy in Babylon*, 192. See Morgan, *New Crusades*, 152–55; Sutton, *Baptist Reformation*, 309–23.

51. Hankins, *Uneasy in Babylon*, 192.

52. Ammerman, *Baptist Battles*, 108–9.

53. Ammerman, *Baptist Battles*, 108–10.

54. Fletcher, *Southern Baptist Convention*, 143.

55. Cothen, *What Happened?*, 157. A minority report attempted to add an article on the fall of man that included the statement "and not by evolution." See Fletcher, *Southern Baptist Convention*, 143.

56. Hefley, *Conservative Resurgence*, 30–31; Sutton, *Baptist Reformation*, 414–16.

57. Sutton, *Baptist Reformation*, 103–4.

58. Pressler, *A Hill to Die*, 105–8. See also Hefley, *The Truth in Crisis*, 1:69–71.

59. Sutton, *Baptist Reformation*, 114.

60. Leonard, *God's Last Hope*, 53. Leonard added that Marse Grant, editor of the *Biblical Recorder*, observed, "They're booing Herschel Hobbs. Am I at the Southern Baptist Convention? They're booing Herschel Hobbs. What is happening to us?"

61. Slayden Yarbrough, "Is Creedalism a Threat to Southern Baptists?" *Baptist History and Heritage* 18:2 (1983): 21–33.

62. "'Guidelines' of Belief Suggested by President," *Baptist Press*, 17 November 1983, 4.

63. Linda Lawson, "Issue among Baptist Polity, Cothen Warns," *Baptist Press*, 9 December 1983, 2. See Cothen, *What Happened?*, 157–63.

64. "Article XVIII: The Family," in The Baptist Faith and Message, Revised 1998 (Nashville: Lifeway Christian Resources, 1998), 21.

65. Toby Druin, "Southwestern Profs to Sign New Statement," *Baptist Standard*, 14 October 1998, 1. See Jeff B. Pool, *Against Returning to Egypt: Exposing and Resisting Credalism in the Southern Baptist Convention* (Macon, GA: Mercer University Press, 1998).

66. John Loudat, "Holiness Highlighted during New Mexico Convention," *Baptist Press*, 2 November 1999; Robert Dilday, "Va. Baptists Alter 169 Year Tie with University of Richmond," *Baptist Press*, 12 November 1999; and Art Toalston, "Texas Baptist Convention Counters SBC Stance on Marriage and Family," *Baptist Press*, 9 November 1999. These articles are available at Baptistpress.com

67. Mark Wingfield, "SBC to Review Faith and Message," *Baptist Standard*, 23 June 1999, 1.

68. "Adrian Rogers to Head Faith and Message Study Group," *Baptist Messenger*, 2 September 1999, 5.

69. For statistics see Ammerman, *Baptist Battles*, 110–12.

70. Dan Martin, "Doctrinal Unity, Program Unity Rise, Fall Together, Rogers, Says," *Baptist Press*, 14 May 1982, 6–7, in Shurden and Shepley, *Going for the Jugular*, 69.

71. See Brand and Hankins, *One Sacred Effort*, 164–65.

72. *Annual of the Southern Baptist Convention*, June 14–16, 1994 (Nashville: Executive Committee of the Southern Baptist Convention, 1994), 79, 103. See Brand and Hankins, *One Sacred Effort*, 166–69.

73. Marv Knox, "Southern Baptists of Texas Split from BGCT," *Baptist Standard*, 10 November 1998, 1; and "Conservatives Add 41 Churches to Virginia Convention," *Baptist Messenger*, 28 October 1999, 8.

74. Sutton, *Baptist Reformation*, 98. Sutton added that Robison was "perhaps the most caustic speaker during the Pastors' Conference" and "a man of deep passion." Robison declared concerning teachers who cast doubt on God's literal truth that "I would not tolerate a rattlesnake in my house.... And I would not tolerate a cancer in my body...."

75. Several professors are named in Leonard, *God's Last Hope*, 155–60; Sutton, *Baptist Reformation*, 6–30; Wills, "Progressive Theology," 12–31.

76. Fletcher, *Southern Baptist Convention*, 413–14.

77. See William H. Brackney (*A Genetic History of Baptist Thought* [Macon, GA: Mercer University Press, 2004], 385–429) for a brief history of Baptist schools.

78. Fletcher, *Southern Baptist Convention*, 309–10.

79. For the conservative understanding of *Baptist Press* reporting and the firings, see Pressler, *Hill to Die*, 207–24; Sutton, *Baptist Reformation*, 392–400. For the moderate take on these events, see Cothen, *What Happened?*, 232–45; Morgan, *New Crusades*, 157–61. In 2014, *Associated Baptist Press* merged with the *Religious Herald* to become *Baptist News Global*. See Baptistnews.com.

80. R. Albert Mohler, Jr., "A Conflict of Visions: The Theological Roots of the Southern Baptist Controversy," *Southern Baptist Journal of Theology* 7:1 (2003): 4–5.

81. See Ammerman, *Baptist Battles*, 112–17.

82. For example, Richard Land ("Pastoral Leadership: Authoritarian or Persuasive?" *Theological Educator* 37 [1988]:

75–82) understood the pejorative nature of the term "authoritarian" and thus opted for "authoritative." Contrastingly, Ralph H. Langley ("Pastoral Leadership: Authoritarian or Persuasive?" *Theological Educator* 37 [1988]: 83–92) defended the pastor-persuader model.

83. Leonard (*God's Last Hope*, 155) noted that some congregations accepted the authoritative model while other Baptists found it "incompatible with traditional Baptist congregationalism."

84. Jackson clashed with Paul Pressler over the conservative agenda. See Morgan, *New Crusades*, 92–112.

85. Conservatives purposed to address their understanding of the priesthood of believers at San Antonio in 1988. During the Pastors' Conference, W. A. Criswell proclaimed, "we have taken the doctrine of the priesthood of the believer and made it cover every damnable heresy you can imagine." See Morgan, *New Crusades*, 94.

86. "SBC Resolution on Priesthood of All Believers," *SBC Annual 1988*, 68–69.

87. Convention Bulletin, 15 June 1988, 5. Taken from Leonard, *God's Last Hope*, 155.

88. Fletcher, *Southern Baptist Convention*, 290–91. Pressler (*Hill to Die*, 141) recalled the action as "sophomoric, melodramatic gesture...." For him, freedom was not being extinguished since Baptists freely voted ten straight times to elect a conservative president.

89. Pressler (*Hill to Die*, 261–62) credited "two outstanding laymen—Judge Sam Currin of North Carolina and Congressman Albert Lee Smith of Alabama" for leading the drive to defund the BJCPA. See Cothen, *What Happened?*, 354–57; Morgan, *New Crusades*, 108–14; Sutton, *Matter of Conviction*, 291–311.

90. Fletcher, *Southern Baptist Convention*, 287–88.

91. Cothen, *What Happened?*, 339–42; Fletcher, *Southern Baptist Convention*, 314–16; Morgan, *New Crusades*, 180–82; Sutton, *Baptist Reformation*, 274–85.

92. Cothen, *What Happened?*, 329–31; Fletcher, *Southern Baptist Convention*, 310–11; Morgan, *New Crusades*, 117–21; Sutton, *Baptist Reformation*, 295–307.

93. Fletcher, *Southern Baptist Convention*, 295; Morgan, *New Crusades*, 115–16; Pressler, *Hill to Die*, 252–53; Sutton, *Baptist Reformation*, 312–19.

94. Fletcher, *Southern Baptist Convention*, 331–32; Sutton, *Baptist Reformation*, 216, 264.

95. Morgan, *New Crusades*, 68.

96. Tom R. Nettles, "Editorial: Understanding the Controversy," *Southern Baptist Journal of Theology* 7:1 (2003): 2–3. See also Mohler, "Conflict of Visions," 4–11; Russell D. Moore, "Resurgence vs. McWorld? American Culture and the Future of Baptist Conservatism," *Southern Baptist Journal of Theology* 7:1 (2003): 32–49.

97. Barry Hankins, "And the Answer Is, 'Yes!'" *Southern Baptist Journal of Theology* 7:1 (2003): 60.

Chapter 4

1. See Art Toalston, "SBC Executives Pose Questions Related to Proposed Changes," *Baptist Press*, 21 February 1995, 5–7. Larry Lewis, in particular, questioned strategic items. See Sutton, *Baptist Reformation*, 263–64, 475–78.

2. "Bylaws of the Southern Baptist Convention," *SBC Annual* 1995, 14. Specifically, Bylaw 20, section "I."

3. This comes from "Covenant for a New Century," in Program and Structure Study Committee Report to the Executive Committee of the Southern Baptist Convention, February 1995, under "Implementation." See "Transition Plan for Covenant for a New Century," *SBC Life*, 1 August 1996.

4. See Brand and Hankins, *One Sacred Effort*, 123–25.

5. See Kim Medley, "Historical Library and Archives to Continue Serving Baptists," *Baptist Press*, 4 February 1997.

6. See John S. Moore, "A 50th Anniversary History of the Southern Baptist Historical Society, 1938–1988," *Baptist History and Heritage* 23:2 (1988): 3–13; Carol Crawford Holcomb, "The History

of Southern Baptist History, 1938–1995," *Baptist History and Heritage* 34:3 (1999): 40–48; and http://www.baptisthistory.org/about/historyofbhhs.html

7. Tim Fields, "Report of the Annual Meeting of the Association of Southern Baptist Schools and Colleges, 9 June 1999," Waco, TX.

8. Ed Stetzer, "The Future of the SBC—State Conventions," *Christianity Today*, 22 May 2016. See also Paul Chitwood and John L. Yeats, "The Future of Baptist State Conventions," in Allen, *SBC in the 21st Century*, 51–65.

9. Michael Day, "The Future of State Conventions and Associations," in *Southern Baptist Identity: An Evangelical Denomination Faces the Future*, ed. David S. Dockery (Wheaton, IL: Crossway Books, 2009), 223–41.

10. Day, "Future of State Conventions," in Dockery, *Southern Baptist Identity*, 230–40.

11. Day, "Future of State Conventions," in Dockery, *Southern Baptist Identity*, 240.

12. Cooperative Program giving for any state convention back to 1925 is available at http://www.sbc.net/cp/.

13. McBeth, *Baptist Heritage*, 621–23.

14. Page, "Cooperative Program," in Allen, *SBC in 21st Century*, 12–13; McBeth, *Baptist Heritage*, 622.

15. Page, "Cooperative Program," in Allen, *SBC in 21st Century*, 16–18.

16. "Great Commission Advance," *SBC Life*, 1 September 2016. See Page, "Cooperative Program," in Allen, *SBC in 21st Century*, 19; Brand and Hankins, *One Sacred Effort*, 110–17.

17. "Bob Reccord Resigns as NAMB President," *Baptist Press*, 13 April 2006.

18. Mark Kelly, "NAMB President, 3 Associates, Resign," *Baptist Press*, 11 August 2009.

19. Scott Barkley, "6 State Conventions Speak Out on NAMB Cooperative Agreements," *The Christian Index*, 27 August 2020; Kevin Parker, "State Conventions Claim NAMB 'Abandons True Collaborative Partnership,'" *The Baptist New Mexican*, 22 October 2020.

20. https://www.namb.net/wp-content/uploads/2019/06/Ministry-Report-2019-FY17-FY18.pdf.

21. See https://www.anniearmstrong.com/faqs.

22. Kevin Ezell, "Every Church on a Mission: The North American Mission Board in the Twenty-First Century," in Allen, *SBC in the 21st Century*, 183–94.

23. Michael Logan, "IMB leader Jerry Rankin announces retirement," *Baptist Press*, 16 September 2009.

24. "Baptists Fire Missionaries: Thirteen Missionaries Fired and Twenty Resign over the Baptist Faith and Message," *Christianity Today*, 1 July 2003.

25. David Platt, "The Future of the IMB and Our Collaborative Great Commission Work," in Allen, *SBC in the 21st Century*, 169–81.

26. Art Toalston, "IMB's Platt Initiates Sexual Abuse Investigations," *Baptist Press*, 25 July 2018.

27. See https://www.imb.org/mission-opportunities/.

28. See IMB.org.

29. Andrea Higgins, "Urgency of Discipleship Underscored at Ridgecrest," *Baptist Press*, 7 August 2006.

30. Melita Thomas, "Vacation Bible School: What Stirs Churches to Do It?" *Baptist Press*, 7 June 2018.

31. See Harry Eskew, David W. Music, and Paul A. Richardson, *Singing Baptists: Studies in Baptist Hymnody in America* (Nashville: Church Street Press, 1994).

32. Aaron Wilson, "'Baptist Hymnal' Celebrates 10-Year Anniversary," *Baptist Press*, 7 August 2018.

33. See http://www.lifeway.com/n/-Bible-Study/Sunday-School-Groups.

34. E. Ray Clendenen and David K. Stabnow, *HCSB: Navigating the Horizons in Bible Translation* (Nashville: B & H, 2012), 83–95. See https://csbible.com/about-the-csb/history-of-the-csb/.

35. Kate Shellnut, "LifeWay Stops Selling Jen Hatmaker Books over LGBT Beliefs," *Christianity Today*, 27 October 2016.

36. See Brand and Hankins, *One Sacred Effort*, 133–35; McBeth, *Baptist Heritage*, 649–50; Shurden, *Sunday School Board*, 95–96.

37. LifeWay trustees filed a

lawsuit against Ranier who had signed a "non-compete" agreement. Ranier was publishing with Tyndale Press. The parties made a non-litigation settlement. See David Roach, "LifeWay, Ranier Settle Contract Dispute," *Baptist Press*, 6 October 2020.

38. McBeth, *Baptist Heritage*, 652. See Brand and Hankins, *One Sacred Effort*, 142–43; Roy Hayhurst, "Guide-Stone Financial Resources Serving Those Who Serve the Lord," *SBC Life*, 1 June 2011.

39. The BJC continues its mission without help from Southern Baptists. Executive director James Dunn retired in 1999. Brent Walker followed him (1999–2016). Amanda Tyler has served the position since 2017. See bjconline.org.

40. Sutton (*A Matter of Conviction*) documents a history of the CLC/ERLC from the conservative point of view.

41. David Gibson, "Richard Land, Controversial Southern Baptist leader, Gets a New Job," *Religious News Service* 12 April 2013.

42. Yonat Shimron and Bob Smietana, "Dispute over Russell Moore Spurs Pushback among Some Southern Baptists," *Religious News Service*, 20 February 2020.

43. Julie Walters, "WMU Exec. Director Wanda Lee Announces Retirement," *Baptist Press*, 13 January 2016.

44. Julie Walters, "National WMU Elects Sandra Wisdom-Martin," *Baptist Reflector*, 2 August 2016.

45. McBeth, *Baptist Heritage*, 666–68.

46. The inaugural address by James Boyce and the Abstract of Principles are found in H. Leon McBeth, *A Sourcebook for Baptist Heritage* (Nashville: Broadman Press, 1991), 305–15.

47. See Mikeal C. Parsons, *Crawford Howell Toy: The Man, the Scholar, the Teacher* (Macon, GA: Mercer University Press, 2019); Phyllis R. Tippit and W. H. Bellinger Jr., "Repeating History: The Story of C. H. Toy," *Baptist History and Heritage* 38:1 (2003): 19–35; William A. Mueller, *A History of Southern Baptist Theological Seminary, 1859–1959* (Nashville: Broadman Press, 1959), 135–42.

For harsher assessments of Toy see Gregory A. Wills, *Southern Baptist Theological Seminary, 1859–2009* (New York: Oxford University Press, 2009), 108–49; Paul R. House, "Crawford Howell Toy and the Weight of Hermeneutics," *Southern Baptist Journal of Theology* 3:1 (1999): 28–39; and L. Russ Bush and Tom J. Nettles, *Baptists and the Bible*, rev. ed. (Nashville: Broadman & Holman, 1999), 208–20.

48. Mueller (*A History of Southern Seminary*, 16–111) writes extensively of Southern's beginnings. See also Chute, Finn, and Haykin, *Baptist Story*, 180–84; Timothy George, "James Petigru Boyce," in *Theologians of the Baptist Tradition*, ed. Timothy George and David S. Dockery (Nashville: Broadman & Holman, 2001), 73–89; Tom J. Nettles, *James Petigru Boyce: A Southern Baptist Statesman* (Philipsburg, NJ: P & R, 2009).

49. Wills, *Southern Seminary*, 185–88; David S. Dockery, "The Broadus-Robertson Tradition," in George and Dockery, *Theologians of the Baptist Tradition*, 90–114. Dockery (96–97) suggests the added responsibility of the presidency coupled with his friend's death led to his own loss of buoyancy and health. See also David S. Dockery and Roger D. Duke, eds., *John A. Broadus: A Living Legacy* (Nashville: B & H, 2008).

50. Mueller, *A History of Southern Seminary*, 154.

51. Harsher evaluations of Whitsitt include Wills, *Southern Seminary*, 189–229; Joshua W. Powell, "'We Cannot Sit in Judgment': William Whitsitt and the Future of the Seminary," *Southern Baptist Journal of Theology* 13:1 (2009): 46–59. Moderate assessments on Whitsitt include Rosalie Beck, *The Whitsitt Controversy: A Denomination in Crisis* (Ann Arbor, MI: University Microfilms International, 1985); W. O. Carver, "William Heth Whitsitt: The Seminary's Martyr," *Review and Expositor* 51:4 (1954): 449–69; William E. Hull, "William Heth Whitsitt: Martyrdom of a Moderate," in *Distinctively Baptist: Essays on Baptist History: A Festschrift in Honor of Walter B. Shurden*, ed. Marc A. Jolley and John D. Pierce (Macon, GA: Mercer University Press, 2005), 237–78; James H. Slatton, *W.*

H. Whitsitt: The Man and the Controversy (Macon, GA: Mercer University Press, 2009); and Mueller, *A History of Southern Seminary*, 143–78.

52. For positive appraisals, see Russell Dilday, "Mullins the Theologian: Between the Extremes," *Review and Expositor* 96:1 (1997): 75–86; Fisher Humphreys, "Edgar Young Mullins," in George and Dockery, *Theologians of the Baptist Tradition*, 181–201; Mueller, *A History of Southern Seminary*, 179–210; William E. Ellis, *"A Man of Books and a Man of the People": E. Y. Mullins and the Crisis of Moderate Southern Baptist Leadership* (Macon, GA: Mercer University Press, 2003). For critical appraisals see R. Albert Mohler, Jr., "Introduction," in E. Y. Mullins, *The Axioms of Religion*, ed. Timothy George (Nashville: Broadman & Holman, 1997), 1–32; Russell D. Moore and Gregory A. Thornbury, "The Mystery of Mullins in Contemporary Southern Baptist Historiography," *Southern Baptist Journal of Theology* 3:4 (1999): 44–57; Tom J. Nettles, *By His Grace and Glory: A Historical, Theological, and Practical Study of the Doctrines in Baptist Life* (Grand Rapids: Baker, 1986), 244–64; Wills, *Southern Seminary*, 230–308.

53. Wills, *Southern Seminary*, 308–25; Mueller, *A History of Southern Seminary*, 211–16.

54. Wills, *Southern Seminary*, 327.

55. Wills, *Southern Seminary*, 325–50; Mueller, *A History of Southern Seminary*, 216–25.

56. Wills, *Southern Seminary*, 351–404, 423–36; Sutton, *Baptist Reformation*, 341–43. For McCall's personal insights into this controversy, see Duke McCall and A. Ronald Tonks, *Duke McCall: An Oral History* (Brentwood, TN: Baptist History and Heritage Society, 2001), 161–211.

57. See Timothy George, "Systematic Theology at Southern Seminary," *Review and Expositor* 82:1 (1985): 31–47; E. Glenn Hinson, "Dale Moody: Bible Teacher Extraordinaire," *Perspectives in Religious Studies* 14:4 (1987): 3–17; Wills, *Southern Seminary*, 410–13, 437–44; Slayden A. Yarbrough, "Academic

Freedom and Southern Baptist History," *Baptist History and Heritage* 39:1 (2004): 43–58.

58. Wills (*Southern Seminary*, 444–510) and Sutton (*Baptist Reformation*, 343–54) provide blow by blow accounts of Honeycutt's obscurantist presidency from the viewpoint of Conservative Resurgence leaders. Cothen (*What Happened?*, 295–306) relates the moderate perspective as trustees took control.

59. Wills, *Southern Seminary*, 511–47; Sutton, *Baptist Reformation*, 355–62; Fletcher, *Southern Baptist Convention*, 347–49; Hankins, *Uneasy in Babylon*, 25–29.

60. His younger brother, J. M. Carroll, published the oft-reprinted Landmark classic, *The Trail of Blood* (1931).

61. McBeth, *Baptist Heritage*, 669–70; Robert A. Baker, *Tell the Generations Following: A History of Southwestern Baptist Theological Seminary, 1908–1983* (Nashville: Broadman Press, 1983), 23–187. See Alan J. Lefever, *Fighting the Good Fight: The Life and Work of Benajah Harvey Carroll* (Austin, TX: Eakin Press, 1994); Glenn Jonas, "The Political Side of B. H. Carroll," *Baptist History and Heritage* 33:3 (1998): 49–56; Michael Crisp, "B. H. Carroll—Remembering His Life, Expanding His Legacy," *Southwestern Journal of Theology* 58:2 (2016): 159–81; James Spivey, "Benajah Harvey Carroll," in George and Dockery, *Theologians of the Baptist Tradition*, 163–80.

62. Scarborough published the first history of the seminary: L. R. Scarborough, *A Modern School of the Prophets: A History of the Southwestern Baptist Theological Seminary, a Product of Prayer and Faith, Its First Thirty Years, 1907–1937* (Nashville: Broadman Press, 1939).

63. Several biographies on Norris are available. The best among them are Barry Hankins, *God's Rascal: J. Frank Norris and the Beginnings of Southern Fundamentalism* (Louisville: University of Kentucky Press, 1996); Michael E. Schepis, *J. Frank Norris: The Fascinating, Controversial Life of a Forgotten Figure of the Twentieth Century* (Nashville: Westbow Press, 2012); and David R. Stokes, *The Shooting Salvationist: J. Frank Norris*

and the Murder Trial That Captivated
America (Hanover, NH: Steerforth Press,
2011).

64. Baker, *Tell the Generations*, 197–
280; Tom J. Nettles, "L. R. Scarborough:
Public Figure," *Southwestern Journal of
Theology* 25:2 (1983): 24–42; Glenn T.
Carson, *Calling Out the Called: The Life
and Work of Lee Rutland Scarborough*
(Austin, TX: Eakin Publications, 1996).

65. Baker, *Tell the Generations*, 285–
323; Alex Sibley, "SWBTS Legacy: E. D.
Head," Southwestern Seminary Legacy
Series; https://swbts.edu/news/releases/
swbts-legacy-ed-head/ 1 August 2019.

66. Baker, *Tell the Generations*, 329–
61; Katie Coleman, "SWBTS Legacy: J.
Howard Williams," Southwestern Seminary Legacy Series; https://swbts.edu/
news/releases/swbts-legacy-j-howard-
williams/ 8 August 2019.

67. Baker, *Tell the Generations*, 371–
436; Katie Coleman, "SWBTS Legacy:
Robert Naylor," Southwestern Seminary
Legacy Series; https://swbts.edu/news/
releases/swbts-legacy-robert-naylor/ 15
August 2019.

68. Baker, *Tell the Generations*,
445–80.

69. Pressler, *A Hill on Which to Die*,
145.

70. Grady Cothen, *The New SBC:
Fundamentalism's Impact on the South-
ern Baptist Convention* (Macon: Smyth &
Helwys, 1995), 119.

71. Bill J. Leonard, "Lone Star Baptists: Fallout at Southwestern Seminary,"
Christian Century 111:13, 20 April 1994,
404–6; Cothen, *The New SBC*, 101–20;
Sutton, *Baptist Reformation*, 363–80. Dilday's personal reflections can be found in
Russell H. Dilday, *Columns: Glimpses of
a Seminary under Assault* (Macon, GA:
Smyth & Helwys, 2004).

72. Brent Hoffman and Jim Jones,
"Seminary Professors Forced to Sign
Statement or Resign," *Daily Herald*, 4 May
2001, D2.

73. David Porter, "Hemphill Leaving
SWBTS to Lead SBC's 'Kingdom' Strat-
egy," *Baptist Press* 8 April 2003; "Paper's
Story on Hemphill Retirement Called
'Speculation,' 'Patently False,'" *Baptist
Press*, 24 April 2003; Dwight McKissic,

"The Case for Electing Beth Moore as
President of the Southern Baptist Convention," *Christianity Today*, 8 June 2018.

74. Hannah Elliott, "Dismissed Professor Files Lawsuit against Southwestern
Seminary," *Baptist Standard*, 30 March
2007.

75. Mark Wingfield, "Fate of South-
western Profs Unclear After Trustee
Meeting." *Associated Baptist Press*, 12
April 2003.

76. Kate Tracy, "Evangelical Seminary Explains Why It Enrolled First Muslim Student," *Christianity Today*, 20 May
2014.

77. Kate Shellnut, "Paige Patterson Fired by Southwestern, Stripped of
Retirement Benefits," *Christianity Today*,
30 May 2018; "SWBTS: Paige Patterson
Terminated 'Effective Immediately,'" *Baptist Press*, 30 May 2018.

78. James A. Smith, Sr., and Alex Sib-
ley, "Greenway Inaugurated as Ninth
Southwestern President," *Baptist Press*, 22
October 2019.

79. Claude L. Howe, Jr., "Providence
and Prayer for Seventy-Five Years: A Historical Overview," *Theological Educator*
47:1 (1993): 7–10.

80. Howe, "Providence and Prayer,"
10–17.

81. Howe, "Providence and Prayer,"
17–20; Cothen, *What Happened?*, 314.

82. Bruce Nolan, "Baptist Educator Landrum Leavell Dies," *The
Times-Picayune*, 27 September 2008.

83. Cothen, *What Happened?*, 314–
15; Sutton, *Baptist Reformation*, 382.

84. See https://www.drchuckkelley.
com/about.

85. Gary D. Myers and Marilyn
Stewart, "Dew Inaugurated as New Orle-
ans Seminary's Ninth President," *Baptist
Press* 31 January 2020.

86. Chris Chun and John Shouse,
Golden Gate to Gateway: A History
(Nashville: B & H, 2020), 12–20; Harold
K. Graves, *Into the Wind: Personal Reflec-
tion on the Early Years of Golden Gate
Baptist Theological Seminary* (Nashville:
Broadman Press, 1983), 30–67.

87. Chun and Shouse, *Golden Gate
to Gateway*, 20–28; Graves, *Into the Wind*,
68–122.

88. Chun and Shouse, *From Golden Gate to Gateway*, 32–64. The bulk of Graves's history (*Into the Wind*, 120–366) covers his own lengthy administration.

89. Chun and Shouse, *From Golden Gate to Gateway*, 65–88.

90. T. Vaughn Walker of Southern Seminary was the first, starting one year ahead of Gainey.

91. Chun and Shouse, *From Golden Gate to Gateway*, 89–134.

92. Chun and Shouse, *From Golden Gate to Gateway*, 40–41, 161–210.

93. L. Russ Bush, "Southeastern Baptist Theological Seminary," *American Baptist Quarterly* 18:2 (1999): 145–46.

94. Bush, "Southeastern Seminary," 146; Sutton, *Baptist Reformation*, 324.

95. Bush, "Southeastern Seminary," 146–47.

96. Sutton, *Baptist Reformation*, 324–29; Bush, "Southeastern Seminary," 146–48. Lolley and other administrators document their perception of events in W. Randall Lolley, Morris Ashcraft, Thomas Henry Graves, and Thomas A. Bland, *Servant Songs: Reflections on the History and Mission of Southeastern Baptist Theological Seminary, 1950–1988* (Macon, GA: Mercer University Press, 1994).

97. Bush, "Southeastern Seminary," 148–49; Cothen, *What Happened?*, 279–95; Sutton, *Baptist Reformation*, 329–34; Richards, *History of Southern Baptists*, 350–51.

98. Jason Hall, "Patterson Reflects on 11 Years of God's Grace at Southeastern," *Baptist Press*, 1 August 2003. See Sutton, *Baptist Reformation*, 334–39. Moderate Southern Baptists, of course would dispute Patterson's definitions of "liberal school," "faith of the fathers," and "conservative school." See Fletcher, *Southern Baptist Convention*, 362–64; Leonard, *God's Last Hope*, 157–60.

99. Jeff Robinson, "Akin Commends, Cautions Calvinist Advocates," *Baptist Press*, 9 July 2009.

100. Stephen R. Prescott, "Seminary Education in Kansas City: A Model of Diversity in Southern Baptist Life: Midwestern Baptist Theological Seminary," *Baptist History and Heritage* 34:3 (1999): 29–30.

101. See Jerry L. Faught II, "The Ralph Elliott Controversy: Competing Philosophies of Southern Baptist Seminary Education," *Baptist History and Heritage* 34:3 (1999): 7–20; Sutton, *Baptist Reformation*, 7–11. For Elliott's personal view see Ralph H. Elliott, "*The Genesis Controversy" and Continuity in Southern Baptist Chaos: A Eulogy for a Great Tradition* (Macon, GA.: Mercer University Press, 1992). The conservative appraisal of Elliott is found in Bush and Nettles, *Baptists and the Bible*, 333–37.

102. Sutton, *Baptist Reformation*, 389.

103. Cothen, *What Happened?*, 312–14; T. Patrick Hudson, "Former Midwestern President Milton Ferguson Dies at 89," *Baptist Press*, 21 December 2017; Prescott, "Seminary Education in Kansas City," 31–39; Sutton, *Baptist Reformation*, 383–90.

104. Herb Hollinger, "Midwestern Seminary Trustees Fire Mark T. Coppenger as President," *Baptist Press*, 15 September 1999.

105. Greg Warner, "Seminary President Resigns Ahead of Confrontation with Trustees," *Baptist Standard*, 10 February 2012. See Allen Palmeri, "Midwestern Seminary Pres. Phil Roberts Resigns," *Baptist Press*, 10 February 2012.

106. Richards, *History of Southern Baptists*, 355–57.

Chapter 5

1. Millard J. Erickson, *Christian Theology*, 3rd ed. (Grand Rapids: Baker, 2013), 3.

2. C. W. Christian, *Shaping Your Faith* (Waco, TX: Word Books, 1973), 28.

3. See Yarbrough, "Is Creedalism a Threat to Southern Baptists?," 25–28.

4. Dale Moody, *The Word of Truth* (Grand Rapids: Eerdmans, 1981), 38.

5. Walter Thomas Conner, *Revelation and God: An Introduction to Christian Doctrine* (Nashville: Broadman Press, 1936), 78.

6. Conner, *Revelation and God*, 79. For fuller discussion see Erickson, *Christian Theology*, 188–209. Conner is another Baptist scholar whose views

have been reassessed in light of the Controversy. Bush and Nettles (*Baptists and the Bible*, 286–91), for example, state that Conner's experiential focus on Scripture (from Mullins) led him to dismiss the concept of inerrancy.

7. See Grudem, *Systematic Theology*, 699–721.

8. Mullins, *Axioms of Religion*, 53–58: Hobbs and Mullins, *Axioms of Religion*, 48–50.

9. R. Albert Mohler, Jr., "Baptist Theology at the Crossroads: The Legacy of E. Y. Mullins," *Southern Baptist Journal of Theology* 3:4 (1999): 19. Two other articles in the same journal issue likewise disagree with Mullins's views on soul competency in favor of stricter authoritarian standards. See Tom J. Nettles, "E. Y. Mullins—Reluctant Evangelical," *Southern Baptist Journal of Theology* 3:4 (1999): 24–42; and Moore and Thornbury, "The Mystery of Mullins," 44–57.

10. "*Credo*," *Cassell's New Latin Dictionary*, ed. H. P. Simpson (New York: Funk and Wagnalls, 1960), 156.

11. "*Confessio*," *Cassell's New Latin Dictionary*, 131.

12. Wayne E. Ward, "No Creed? What Do Baptists Believe?" *The Quarterly Review* 37:2 (1977): 7.

13. Ward, "No Creed," 6. See Erickson, *Christian Theology*, 971–88; and Grudem, 853–72.

14. Excellent resources on this topic include William L. Lumpkin and Bill J. Leonard, eds., *Baptist Confessions of Faith*, 2nd rev. ed. (Valley Forge: Judson Press, 2011); Joseph Early, Jr., *Readings in Baptist History: Four Centuries of Selected Documents* (Nashville: B & H, 2008); and Timothy George and Denise George, eds., *Baptist Confessions, Covenants, and Catechisms* (Nashville: Broadman Press, 1996). An older but still valuable source is W. J. McGlothlin, *Baptist Confessions of Faith* (Philadelphia: American Baptist Publication Society, 1911).

15. Philip Schaff, *The Creeds of Christendom*, 3 vols. (New York: Harper & Brothers, 1877), 1:3–4.

16. McBeth, *Baptist Heritage*, 686–87.

17. George and George, *Baptist Confessions*, 2. See C. Douglas Weaver, "Baptists and Denominational Identity and the Turn toward Creedalism: 2000," in Williams and Shurden, *Turning Points*, 288–301.

18. Lumpkin and Leonard, *Baptist Confessions*, 16.

19. Lumpkin and Leonard, *Baptist Confessions*, 16–17.

20. Lumpkin and Leonard, *Baptist Confessions*, 95–105.

21. Lumpkin and Leonard, *Baptist Confessions*, 106–14.

22. Lumpkin and Leonard, *Baptist Confessions*, 131–60; George and George, *Baptist Confessions*, 8–9, 34–49.

23. Torbet, *History of the Baptists*, 45. See Lumpkin and Leonard, *Baptist Confessions*, 160–71, 184–98, 202–15, 298–348.

24. Lumpkin and Leonard, *Baptist Confessions*, 216–97.

25. Lumpkin, and Leonard, *Baptist Confessions*, 17.

26. Lumpkin and Leonard, *Baptist Confessions*, 363–69.

27. Lumpkin and Leonard, *Baptist Confessions*, 370–83; George and George, *Baptist Confessions*, 12–13, 131–35.

28. Baker, *Baptist Sourcebook*, 120. On the other hand, Tom J. Nettles ("How to Lose Your Way: A History Lesson in Confessions," in *Baptist Faith and Message 2000: Critical Issues in America's Largest Protestant Denomination*, ed. Douglas K. Blount and Joseph H. Woodell [New York: Rowman & Littlefield 2007], xxii) asserts that Johnson spoke for himself and not the other delegates at Augusta. Moreover, the adoption of the first Baptist Faith and Message (1925) was "bringing to fruition the confessional propensities of Southern Baptists, [and] established a sense of doctrinal responsibility that has generated substantial reform in times of doctrinal crisis."

29. George and George, *Baptist Confessions*, 11. The *Southwestern Journal of Theology* 51:2 (2009): 129–256 devoted the full issue to a commentary on the New Hampshire Confession of Faith by B. H. Carroll and Calvin Goodspeed.

30. See James E. Carter, "Southern Baptists' First Confession of Faith,"

Baptist History and Heritage 5:1 (1970): 24–28; James E. Carter, "A Review of Confessions of Faith Adopted by Major Baptist Bodies in the United States," *Baptist History and Heritage* 12:2 (1977): 75–91; James E. Carter, "The Fraternal Address of Southern Baptists," *Baptist History and Heritage* 12:4 (1977): 211–18; William L. Lumpkin, "The Bible in Early Baptist Confessions of Faith," *Baptist History and Heritage* 19:3 (1984): 33–41; Nettles, "A History Lesson in Confessions," in Blount and Wooddell, *BFM 2000*, xiii–xxv.

31. Early (*Readings in Baptist History*, 229–70) offers easy-to-compare columns of the 1925, 1963, and 2000 Baptist Faith and Messages.

32. See Mark A. Noll, "Scopes Trial," in *The Evangelical Dictionary of Theology*, 3rd ed., ed. Daniel J. Treier and Walter A. Elwell (Grand Rapids: Baker, 2017), 788–89.

33. Carter, "Review of Confessions," 84–85; Lumpkin and Leonard, *Baptist Confessions*, 407–8; Nettles, "A History Lesson in Confessions," in Blount and Wooddell, *BFM 2000*, xviii–xxi; and Shurden, *Not a Silent People*, 60–67.

34. Taken from Nettles, "A History Lesson in Confessions," in Blount and Wooddell, *BFM 2000*, xxi.

35. Walter B. Shurden, "Southern Baptist Responses to Their Confessional Statements," *Review and Expositor* 76:1 (1979): 69–85. The quote is from page 76.

36. Hobbs (*My Faith and Message*, 230–46) offers an insider's viewpoint on the background and effects of the 1963 Baptist Faith and Message. See Jerry Faught, "Herschel H. Hobbs," in Williams, *Witnesses to the Baptist Heritage*, 189–94.

37. Carter, "Review of Confessions," 85.

38. Hobbs, *My Faith and Message*, 241.

39. Hobbs, *My Faith and Message*, 241–42.

40. James T. Draper and Kenneth Keathley, *Biblical Authority: The Critical Issue for the Body of Christ*, rev. ed. (Nashville: Broadman & Holman, 2001), 67. Hefley (*Conservative Resurgence*, 30–31) stated the criterion is a "tip of the hat to neo-orthodoxy," and added that

conservatives did not realize how loosely some denominational employees took the phrase "truth, without any mixture of error." Another conservative critique of the preamble is found in Sutton (*Baptist Reformation*, 414–16).

41. Claude L. Howe, Jr., *Glimpses of Baptist Heritage* (Nashville: Broadman Press, 1981), 147.

42. Baker, *Southern Baptist Convention*, 416–17; Shurden, *Not a Silent People*, 75–79.

43. Howe, *Glimpses of Baptist Heritage*, 148; Walter B. Shurden, "The Problem of Authority in the Southern Baptist Convention," *Review and Expositor* 75:2 (1978): 225.

44. Shurden, "Southern Baptist Response," 80–81.

45. Lumpkin and Leonard, *Baptist Confessions*, 409–10.

46. Baptist Faith and Message, 1963, 5.

47. Walter B. Shurden, "The Pastor as Denominational Theologian in Southern Baptist History," *Baptist History and Heritage* 15:3 (1980): 15–22.

48. Shurden, "Pastor as Theologian," 16.

49. Shurden, "Pastor as Theologian," 16.

50. E. Brooks Holifield, *The Gentlemen Theologians: American Theology in Southern Culture, 1795–1860* (Durham, NC: Duke University Press, 1978).

51. Shurden, "Pastor as Theologian," 16–18.

52. Shurden, "Pastor as Theologian," 20.

53. Shurden, "Pastor as Theologian," 20.

54. Shurden, "Pastor as Theologian," 21.

55. Shurden, "Pastor as Theologian," 21.

56. Shurden, "Pastor as Theologian," 21–22.

57. For further study on individual denominational theologians, see Brackney, *Genetic History*, 488–526; Garrett, *Baptist Theology*, 515–47; and George and Dockery, *Theologians of the Baptist Tradition*, 163–360.

58. Resources for studying the

Baptist Faith and Message include Herschel H. Hobbs, *The Baptist Faith and Message*, rev. ed. (Nashville: Convention Press, 1996); George and George, *Baptist Confessions*; Blount and Wooddell, *BFM 2000*; and Charles S. Kelley Jr., Richard Land, and R. Albert Mohler, Jr., *The Baptist Faith and Message* (Nashville: Lifeway, 2007). Other helpful books include Walter Thomas Conner, *The Gospel of Redemption* (Nashville: Broadman Press, 1945); E. Y. Mullins, *The Christian Religion in Its Doctrinal Expression* (Valley Forge: Judson Press, 1917); Fisher Humphreys, *Thinking about God* (New Orleans: Insight Press, 1977). In addition, volume 4 of the *Encyclopedia of Southern Baptists* is very helpful on individual topics. The revised Baptist Faith and Message (2000) along with both the 1963 confession and the 1925 confession is available online at <http://www.sbc.net/2000_report.html>. The full report of the Baptist Faith and Message revision committee is included.

59. Resources on this topic include Russell H. Dilday Jr., *The Doctrine of Biblical Authority* (Nashville: Convention Press, 1982); Draper and Keathley, *Biblical Authority*; Bush and Nettles, *Baptists and the Bible*; Grudem, *Systematic Theology*, 47–137; and Dwight A. Moody, "The Bible," in Basden, *Has Our Theology Changed?*, 7–40.

60. Joseph D. Wooddell ("The Scriptures" in Blount and Wooddell, *BFM 2000*, 6–8) asserted that the "criterion" statement could be interpreted and applied in numerous ways. Thus, composers of the 2000 BFM narrowed the statement in order to eliminate this.

61. Dilday, *Biblical Authority*, 73–75. The eight theories presented by Dilday are the dictation theory; the natural theory; the general Christian inspiration theory; the theory of partial inspiration; the theory of levels of inspiration; the plenary theory; the verbal theory; and the dynamic theory.

62. See Moody, "The Bible," in Basden, *Has Our Theology Changed?*, 21–25; Bradley N. Seeman, "The 'Old Princetonians' on Biblical Authority," in *The Enduring Authority of the Christian Scriptures*, ed. D. A. Carson (Grand Rapids: Eerdmans, 2016), 195–237.

63. Kelley, Land, and Mohler, *Baptist Faith and Message*, 11.

64. Dilday, *Doctrine of Biblical Authority*, 75.

65. Dilday, *Doctrine of Biblical Authority*, 75.

66. Moody, "The Bible," in Basden, *Has Our Theology Changed?*, 26.

67. See Barry G. Webb, "Biblical Authority and Diverse Literary Genres," in Carson, *Enduring Authority of Christian Scriptures*, 577–614.

68. See Yarbrough, "Creedalism," 21–23 for a discussion of these developments.

69. Harold Lindsell, *The Battle for the Bible* (Grand Rapids: Zondervan, 1976).

70. L. Russ Bush and Tom J. Nettles, *Baptists and the Bible* (Chicago: Moody Press, 1980). This was revised and expanded in 1999 and published by Broadman & Holman, as previous footnotes mention. The authors highlight a multitude of famous Baptists and their views on the Bible, defending several and devaluing some.

71. See Norman L. Geisler, ed., *Inerrancy* (Grand Rapids: Zondervan, 1979); Duane A. Garrett and Richard R. Melick Jr., eds., *Authority and Interpretation: A Baptist Perspective* (Grand Rapids: Baker, 1987); Robison B. James, ed., *The Unfettered Word: Southern Baptists Confront the Authority-Inerrancy Question* (Waco, TX: Word Books, 1987); and the *Proceedings of the Conference on Biblical Inerrancy, 1987* (Nashville: Broadman Press, 1987).

72. Grudem (*Systematic Theology*, 96–97) cogently defends the need to appeal to the autographs. Over 99 percent of the modern text is accepted, but "it is extremely important to affirm the inerrancy of the original documents, for the subsequent copies were made by men with no claim or guarantee by God that these copies would be perfect."

73. Hobbs, *Baptist Faith and Message*, 32–39.

74. Hobbs, *Baptist Faith and Message*, 37–39.

75. See Douglas K. Blount, "God," in Blount and Wooddell, *BFM 2000*, 13–17.

76. The 2000 edition inserts the word "triune" between "eternal" and "God" in the first paragraph. Blount ("God" in Blount and Wooddell, *BFM 2000*, 13) relates that this makes "explicit the confession's commitment to orthodox Trinitarianism." According to Blount (17–18) the 1925 and 1963 editions failed to "affirm unequivocally the Baptist commitment to God's triunity."

77. See Howe, *Glimpses of Baptist Heritage*, 120–33; and Brand and Hankins, *One Sacred Effort*, 28–42.

78. See Erickson, *Christian Theology*, 291–313; 771–821; Grudem, *Systematic Theology*, 634–52.

79. See Erickson, *Christian Theology*, 423–37; Grudem, *Systematic Theology*, 472–86.

80. See Robert B. Stewart, "Man," in Blount and Wooddell, *BFM 2000*, 32–33.

81. For example, see Erickson, *Christian Theology*, 825–929.

82. See Conner, *Gospel of Redemption*, 139–43.

83. R. Albert Mohler, Jr. ("The Doctrine of Salvation," in Blount and Wooddell, *BFM 2000*, 42) reasoned that some evangelicals were confused concerning the doctrine of justification. Thus, this new edition "makes clear that sinners are justified by faith alone—on the basis of Christ's righteousness alone."

84. Daniel L. Akin ("God's Purpose of Grace," in Blount and Wooddell, *BFM 2000*, 45–53) approaches the topic from a Reformed Baptist perspective. The 2000 edition can resonate with most Reformed Baptists on four of the five points of Calvinism. The fifth point ("limited atonement") is better understood as "particular redemption," states Akin.

85. Hobbs (*My Baptist Faith and Message*, 244) asserted that the acceptance of the church "as the redeemed of all ages" meant that Landmarkists understood the necessity of what most Baptists believed.

86. See Bill J. Leonard, "The Church," in Basden, *Has Our Theology Changed?*, 159–79.

87. Hobbs, *Baptist Faith and Message*, 69–70.

88. For a defense of no women pastors or deaconesses, see Thomas White and Joy White, "The Offices and Women: Can Women Be Pastors? Or Deacons?" in *Upon This Rock: A Baptist Understanding of the Church*, ed. Jason G. Duesing, Thomas White, and Malcolm B. Yarnell III (Nashville: B & H, 2010), 33–55. For a history and defense in favor of Baptist women ministers, see Pamela R. Durso, "She-Preachers, Bossy Women, and Children of the Devil: Women Ministers in the Baptist Tradition, 1609–2012," *Review & Expositor* 110:1 (2013): 33–47.

89. See Hobbs, *Baptist Faith and Message*, 72–75. Several chapters in White, Duesing, and Yarnell, *Restoring Integrity*, address the ordinance of baptism, including Daniel L. Akin, "The Meaning of Baptism," 63–80; David Allen, "'Dipped for Dead': The Proper Mode of Baptism," 81–106; Thomas White, "What Makes Baptism Valid?," 107–18; and Jason K. Lee, "Baptism and Covenant," 119–36.

90. Hobbs, *Baptist Faith and Message*, 76–77.

91. For narrower interpretations of the Lord's Supper, see John S. Hammett, "Baptism and the Lord's Supper," in Blount and Wooddell, *BFM 2000*, 71–81; Thomas White, "A Baptist's Theology of the Lord's Supper," in White, Duesing, and Yarnell, *Restoring Integrity*, 137–61; and Emir F. Caner, "Fencing the Table: The Lord's Supper, Its Participants, and Its Relationship to Church Discipline," in White, Duesing, and Yarnell, *Restoring Integrity*, 163–78. For less strict views on the ordinances, see the articles in Walter B. Shurden, ed., *Proclaiming the Baptist Vision: Baptism and the Lord's Supper* (Macon, GA: Smyth & Helwys, 1999).

92. John S. Hammett ("The Lord's Day," in Blount and Wooddell, *BFM 2000*, 86) suggests that "Sabbath rest may be prudent or beneficial, but it is not commanded."

93. See McBeth, *Baptist Heritage*, 446–61.

94. There is no change in wording between the 1963 and 2000 editions. See Hobbs, *Baptist Faith and Message*, 84–86; Russell D. Moore, "The Kingdom," in Blount and Wooddell, *BFM 2000*, 89–97.

95. There is no change in wording between the 1925 and 2000 confessions. See Hobbs, *Baptist Faith and Message*, 87–92. In his discussion of this article, Paige Patterson ("Last Things," in Blount and Wooddell, *BFM 2000*, 99–109) stressed the eternal states of heaven and hell.

96. For a comparison of representative positions on this topic among Southern Baptists, see G. R. Beasley-Murray, Herschel H. Hobbs, and Ray Frank Robbins, *Revelation: Three Viewpoints* (Nashville: Broadman Press, 1976); and the articles in *SBC Life*, 1 June 2014: James W. Bryant, "Why I Am a Traditional Dispensational Premillennialist," Craig Blaising, "A View of Progressive Dispensationalism," Nathan A. Finn, "Why I Am a Historic Premillennialist," Thomas P. Johnston, "Why I Am a Mid-Trib Premillennialist," and Michael Kuykendall, "Why I Am an Amillennialist."

97. James Spivey ("The Millennium," in Basden, *Has Our Theology Changed?*, 230–62) traces the changing views among Southern Baptists on this subject. He notes postmillennial beginnings, an emerging premillennialism, followed by ascendant amillennialism, and a resurgence in premillennialism.

98. See Robert A. Baker, "Premillennial Baptist Groups," *ESB*, 2:1110–11; and Slayden Yarbrough, "Premillennialism among Baptist Groups," *ESB*, 4:2424.

99. An example of a commentary by a Southern Baptist who follows historic premillennialism is George R. Beasley-Murray, *The Book of Revelation*, New Century Bible Commentary (Greenwood, SC: Attic Press, 1974). An example from the dispensational viewpoint is Paige Patterson, *Revelation*, New American Commentary (Nashville: Broadman & Holman, 2012).

100. Two treatments of amillennialism by Southern Baptists are Ray Summers, *Worthy Is the Lamb* (Nashville: Broadman Press, 1951); and Edward A. McDowell, *The Meaning and Message of the Book of Revelation* (Nashville: Broadman Press, 1951).

101. See Hobbs, *Baptist Faith and Message*, 94–96.

102. See Keith E. Eitel, "Evangelism and Missions," in Blount and Wooddell, *BFM 2000*, 111–19.

103. The 2000 BFM added four sentences to its edition that praise the value of wisdom and knowledge.

104. The 2000 confession did not revise anything on the topic of cooperation from the 1963 confession. Chad Owen Brand, however, cautioned modern Southern Baptists that cooperation with other groups and even other Southern Baptists has its limits. See Brand and Hankins, *One Sacred Effort*, 53–77; Chad Owen Brand, "Cooperation," in Blount and Wooddell, *BFM 2000*, 143–49.

105. For a history of Southern Baptist engagement with the social order, see Timothy D. Gilbert, "Christian Ethics," in Basden, *Has Our Theology Changed?*, 284–305; and John Lee Eighmy, *Churches in Cultural Captivity: A History of the Social Attitudes of Southern Baptists* (Knoxville, TN: University of Tennessee Press, 1972).

106. C. Ben Mitchell ("The Christian and the Social Order," in Blount and Wooddell, *BFM 2000*, 151–62) discusses the necessity of adding these specific practices in the new edition.

107. A publication on this topic is *Baptist Peacemaker*, which is sponsored by the World Peacemaker Group at Deer Park Baptist Church of Louisville, Kentucky. See https://www.bpfna.org. The only revision in the 2000 confession is the addition of the phrase, "Christian people throughout the world should pray for the reign of the Prince of Peace."

108. Jerry A. Johnson ("Religious Liberty," in Blount and Wooddell, *BFM 2000*, 180) states "Religious liberty is thus good for the gospel, good for the church, good for the state, and good for the individual."

109. See *Baptist History and Heritage* 33:1 (1998): 4–96. The entire issue is on "The Changing State of Church and State." See also William M. Tillman Jr., "Religious Liberty," in Basden, *Has Our Theology Changed?*, 306–28.

110. See Dorothy Kelley Patterson, "The Family," in Blount and Wooddell, *BFM 2000*, 183–91.

111. See Sutton, *Baptist Reformation*, 233, 243, 246–47, 251, 255, 321.

112. Garrett, *Baptist Theology*, 506.

113. See Hankins, *Uneasy in Babylon*, 213–32; Sutton, *Baptist Reformation*, 243, 246.

114. Toby Druin, "Southwestern Profs to Sign New Statement," *Baptist Standard* 14 October 1998, 2.

115. "Baptists Fire Missionaries: Thirteen Missionaries Fired and Twenty Resign Over the Baptist Faith and Message," *Christianity Today*, 1 July 2003.

Conclusion

1. Fletcher, *Southern Baptist Convention*, 349; Morgan, *New Crusades*, 83–84. See Andrew Gardner, *Reimagining Zion: History of the Alliance of Baptists* (Macon, GA: Nurturing Faith, Inc., 2015).

2. Walter B. Shurden, "CBF's 'An Address to the Public," *The Baptist Identity*, 97–102, in Shurden and Shepley, *Going for the Jugular*, 266–70; Richards, *History of Southern Baptists*, 339–40.

3. Fletcher, Southern Baptist Convention, 312. See Terry Maples and Gene Wilder, *Reclaiming and Re-Forming Baptist Identity: Cooperative Baptist Fellowship* (Macon, GA: Nurturing Faith, Inc., 2017); Aaron D. Weaver, ed., *CBF at 25: Stories of the Cooperative Baptist Fellowship* (Macon, GA: Nurturing Faith Inc., 2016).

4. Editor Walter Shurden's book, *The Struggle for the Soul,* relates the origin of many of these new entities. Baptists Committed ceased operations in 2017, and the Baptist Theological Seminary at Richmond closed in 2019.

5. When moderates left the Southern Baptist Convention, the moderate voice went with them. The lack of a balancing voice resulted in the SBC becoming even more conservative than anticipated. Likewise, with no conservative voice to balance the CBF, that organization has opened itself up to more liberal stances.

6. Two state conventions were successful in resisting a conservative takeover—the Baptist General Convention of Virginia and the Baptist General Convention of Texas. In response, conservatives created alternative state conventions called Southern Baptist Conservatives of Virginia and Southern Baptists of Texas Convention. See Richards (*History of Southern Baptists*, 340–42) for battles in other state conventions.

7. Nathan Finn, "Priorities for a Post-Resurgence Convention," in Dockery, *Southern Baptist Identity*, 257–80.

8. Finn, "Priorities for a Post-Resurgence Convention," in Dockery, *Southern Baptist Identity*, 270–80.

9. See Charles Deweese and Pamela R. Durso, eds., *No Longer Ignored: A Collection of Articles on Baptist Women* (Atlanta: Baptist History and Heritage Society, 2007); David T. Morgan, *Southern Baptist Sisters: In Search of Status, 1845–2000* (Macon, GA: Mercer University Press, 2003).

10. There are numerous resources to continue the debate. Recent examples that maintain restrictions on women's roles include Dorothy K. Patterson, "The Role of Women as Missionaries," *Southwestern Journal of Theology* 57:1 (2014): 63–76; Jacob J. Prahlow, "Rules and Roles for Women: Vocation and Order in the Apostolic Fathers," *Southern Baptist Journal of Theology* 22:4 (2018): 77–100; White and White, "The Offices and Women: Can Women Be Pastors? Or Deacons?" in Deusing, White, and Yarnell, *Upon This Rock*, 33–55; and Andreas J. Köstenberger and Thomas R. Schreiner, *Women in the Church: An Interpretation and Application of 1 Timothy 2:9–15*, 3rd ed. (Wheaton, IL: Crossway, 2016). Resources that favor an openness toward Baptist women in ministry include Karen Bullock, "Baptists and the Turn toward Gender Inclusion," in Williams and Shurden, *Turning Points*, 204–221; and Pamela R. Durso, "Baptists and the Turn toward Baptist Women" in Williams and Shurden, *Turning Points*, 275–87. See also Baptist Women in Ministry at https://bwim.info/. One final resource to consider is James R. Beck, ed., *Two Views on Women in Ministry*, rev. ed. (Grand Rapids: Zondervan, 2005).

11. Cessationists believe that

spiritual gifts such as speaking in tongues and miraculous healing ceased operation in the apostolic age. Non-cessationists believe that these spiritual gifts continue into the present age.

12. For bibliography, see Howe, *Glimpses of Baptist History*, 120–33; and Garrett, *Baptist Theology*, 489–90.

13. Libby Lovelace, "LifeWay Releases Prayer Language Study," *Baptist Press*, 1 June 2007.

14. Will Hall, "Analysis: 2006 News in Review," *Baptist Press*, 4 January 2007.

15. Greg Horton, "Southern Baptists to Open their Ranks to Missionaries Who Speak in Tongues," *Religious News Service*, 14 May 2016.

16. "Baptists and Speaking in Tongues," 3 March 2016; https://www.namb.net/apologetics-blog/baptists-and-speaking-in-tongues/.

17. Rob Collingsworth, "McKissic Sermon Restored to SWBTS Website," *Southern Baptist Texan*, 26 October 2018.

18. For balanced treatments see Chad Owen Brand, ed., *Perspectives on Spirit Baptism: Five Views* (Nashville: B & H, 2004); Wayne Grudem, ed., *Are Miraculous Gifts for Today?* (Grand Rapids: Zondervan, 1996); and Craig S. Keener, *3 Crucial Questions about the Holy Spirit* (Grand Rapids: Baker, 1996). An historical resource is C. Douglas Weaver, *Baptists and the Holy Spirit: The Contested History with Holiness-Pentecostal-Charismatic Movements* (Waco, TX: Baylor University Press, 2019).

19. A few resources to start with, including pro and con views are John Revell, "Calvinism—Southern Baptist Perspectives," *SBC Life*, 1 October 2010; Fisher Humphreys, "Southern Baptists and Calvinism," *Theological Educator* 55:1 (1997): 11–26; E. Ray Clendenen and Brad J. Waggoner, eds., *Calvinism: A Southern Baptist Dialogue* (Nashville: B & H, 2008); Rodney S. Walls, *Calvinism and the Southern Baptist Convention: A Response to Non-Calvinist Objections* (Apollo, PN: Ichthus Publications, 2020); and David L. Allen and Steve W. Lemke, eds., *Whosoever Will: A Biblical-Theological Critique of Five-Point Calvinism* (Nashville: B & H, 2010).

20. Libby Lovelace, "10 percent of SBC pastors call themselves 5-point Calvinists," *Baptist Press*, 18 September 2006.

21. Greg Horton, "Are Southern Baptists Predestined to Fuss Over Calvinism?" *Baptist Standard*, 6 June 2013.

22. David Roach, "Connect316 Urges 'Loyal Opposition' to Calvinism," sbcannualmeeting.net, 22 June 2017.

23. Carol Pipes, "Giving Increases for SBC in 2018, Baptisms, Attendance Continue Decline, blog.lifeway.com 23 May 2019; Kate Shellnut, "Southern Baptists See Biggest Drop in 100 Years," *Christianity Today*, 4 June 2020.

24. See https://albertmohler.com/2019/05/31/the-future-of-the-southern-baptist-convention-the-numbers-dont-add-up.

25. See Thom S. Rainer, "A Resurgence Not Yet Realized: Evangelistic Effectiveness in the Southern Baptist Convention Since 1979," *Southern Baptist Journal of Theology* 9:1 (2005): 54–69; Thom S. Ranier, "Evangelism and Church Growth in the SBC," in Dockery, *Southern Baptist Identity*, 217–22; and Thom S. Ranier, "By the Numbers: What SBC Demographics Tell Us About Our Past, Present, and Future," in Allen, *SBC and 21st Century*, 21–32.

26. "Resolution on Racial Reconciliation on the 150th Anniversary of the Southern Baptist Convention," sbc.net., 1 June 1995.

27. David Roach, "Racial Reconciliation Not a 'Finished Project' 25 Years After Historic Resolution," *Baptist Press*, 19 June 2020.

28. "On Critical Race Theory and Intersectionality," sbc.net., 1 June 2019.

29. George Schroeder, "Seminary Presidents Reaffirm BFM, Declare CRT Incompatible," *Baptist Press*, 30 November 2020.

30. Mark Wingfield, "Houston Pastor Quits Southwestern and SBC Over Seminary Presidents' Statement on Race," *Baptist News Global*, 17 December 2020; Kate Shellnut, "Two Prominent Pastors Break with SBC After Critical Race Theory Statement," *Christianity Today*, 18 December 2020.

31. Adele Banks, "Southern Baptist

Leaders Meet After Critical Race Theory Statement Caused Controversy," *Religious News Service*, 9 January 2021.

32. Michael Balsamo, "Hate Crimes in U.S. Reach Highest Level in More than a Decade," *Associated Press*, 16 November 2020.

33. See Jarvis J. Williams and Kevin M. Jones, *Removing the Stain of Racism from the Southern Baptist Convention: Diverse African American and White Perspectives* (Nashville: B & H, 2017).

34. See Philip Jenkins, *The Next Christendom: The Coming of Global Christianity* (New York: Oxford University Press, 2002); Philip Jenkins, *The New Faces of Christianity: Believing the Bible in the Global South* (New York: Oxford University Press, 2006); Lamin Sanneh, ed., *The Changing Face of Christianity: Africa, the West, and the World* (New York: Oxford University Press, 2005).

35. http://www.sbc.net/ BecomingSouthernBaptist/pdf/ FastFacts2020.pdf

36. Examples include Walter B. Shurden, *Baptist Identity: Four Fragile Freedoms* (Macon, GA: Smyth & Helwys, 1993); Walter B. Shurden, "Baptists at the Twenty-First Century: Assessments and Challenges" in Williams and Shurden, *Turning Points*, 302–8; and Charles W. Deweese, *Defining Baptist Convictions: Guidelines for the Twenty-First Century* (Franklin, TN: Providence House Publishers, 1996).

37. Examples include R. Stanton Norman, *The Baptist Way: Distinctives of a Baptist Church* (Nashville: B & H, 2005); David Dockery, ed., *Southern Baptist Identity: An Evangelical Denomination Faces the Future* (Wheaton, IL: Crossway Books, 2009); and Jason K. Allen, ed., *The SBC and the 21st Century: Reflection, Renewal, and Recommitment*, rev. ed. (Nashville: B & H, 2019). Moreover, Brand and Hankins (*One Sacred Effort*, 178–204) list numerous future challenges. Tom J. Nettles (*The Baptists: Key People Involved in Forming a Baptist Identity*, 3 vols. [Fearn, Scotland: Mentor, 2005–2007]) covers Baptist convictions from British Baptists to American Baptists to modern Baptists with a definite accent toward Calvinist Baptists. Brian Talbot ("Can Baptists Be Identified in the Twenty-First Century?" *Baptist History and Heritage* 55:1 [2020]: 84–98) provides recent reflections with broader worldwide Baptist identity.

Bibliography

Books

Allen, Catherine B. *A Century to Celebrate.* Birmingham, AL: Woman's Missionary Union, 1987.

_____. *The New Lottie Moon Story.* 2nd ed. Birmingham, AL: Woman's Missionary Union, 1997.

Allen, David L., and Steve W. Lemke, eds. *Whosoever Will: A Biblical-Theological Critique of Five-Point Calvinism.* Nashville: B & H, 2010.

Allen, Jason K., ed. *The SBC and the 21st Century: Reflection, Renewal, and Recommitment.* Nashville: B & H, 2016.

_____. *The SBC and the 21st Century: Reflection, Renewal, and Recommitment.* Rev. ed. Nashville: B & H, 2019.

Ammerman, Nancy Tatom. *Baptist Battles: Social Change and Religious Conflict in the Southern Baptist Convention.* New Brunswick, NJ: Rutgers University Press, 1990.

Ammerman, Nancy Tatom, ed. *Southern Baptists Observed: Multiple Perspectives on a Changing Denomination.* Knoxville: University of Tennessee Press, 1993.

Asher, Louis Franklin. *John Clarke.* Pittsburgh: Dorrance, 1997.

Baker, Robert A. *The Southern Baptist Convention and Its People: 1607–1972.* Nashville: Broadman Press, 1974.

_____. *The Story of the Sunday School Board.* Nashville: Broadman Press, 1966.

_____. *Tell the Generations Following: A History of Southwestern Baptist Theological Seminary, 1908–1983.* Nashville: Broadman Press, 1983.

_____. *The Thirteenth Check: Jubilee History of the Annuity Board of the Southern Baptist Convention.* Nashville: Broadman Press, 1968.

Baker, Robert A., ed. *A Baptist Source Book.* Nashville: Broadman Press, 1966.

Barnes, W.W. *The Southern Baptist Convention: 1845–1953.* Nashville: Broadman Press, 1954.

_____. *The Southern Baptist Convention: A Study in the Development of Ecclesiology.* Fort Worth, TX: Seminary Hill Press, 1934.

Basden, Paul A., ed. *Has Our Theology Changed? Southern Baptist Thought Since 1845.* Nashville: Broadman & Holman, 1994.

Baugh, John G. *The Battle for Baptist Integrity.* Austin, TX: Battle for Baptist Integrity, 1995.

Beasley-Murray, George R. *The Book of Revelation.* New Century Bible Commentary. Greenwood, SC: Attic Press, 1974.

Beasley-Murray, George R., Herschel H. Hobbs, and Ray Frank Robbins. *Revelation: Three Viewpoints.* Nashville: Broadman Press, 1976.

Bebbington, David W. *Baptists Through the Centuries: A History of a Global People.* 2nd ed. Waco: Baylor University Press, 2018.

Bibliography

Beck, James R., ed. *Two Views on Women in Ministry*. Rev. ed. Grand Rapids: Zondervan, 2005.

Beck, Rosalie. *The Whitsitt Controversy: A Denomination in Crisis*. Ann Arbor, MI: University Microfilms International, 1985.

Bennett, F. Russell Jr. *The Fellowship of Kindred Minds*. Atlanta: Home Mission Board of the Southern Baptist Convention, 1974.

Birch, Ian. *To Follow the Lambe Wheresoever He Goeth: The Ecclesial Polity of the English Calvinistic Baptists 1640–1660*. Eugene, OR: Wipf & Stock, 2017.

Blount, Douglas, and Joseph Wooddell, eds. *Baptist Faith and Message 2000: Critical Issues in America's Largest Protestant Denomination*. New York: Rowman & Littlefield, 2007.

Brackney, William H. *Baptists in North America: An Historical Perspective*. Malden, MA: Blackwell, 2006.

_____. *A Capsule History of Baptist Principles*. Macon, GA: Mercer University Press, 2009.

_____. *The Early English General Baptists and Their Theological Formation*. London: Regent's Park College, 2017.

_____. *A Genetic History of Baptist Thought: With Special Reference to Baptists in Britain and North America*. Macon, GA: Mercer University Press, 2004.

_____. *Historical Dictionary of the Baptists*. 2nd ed. Metuchen, NJ: Scarecrow Press, 2009.

Brackney, William H., ed. *Baptist Life and Thought: A Source Book*. Rev. ed. Valley Forge, PA: Judson Press, 1998.

Brand, Chad Owen, ed. *Perspectives on Spirit Baptism: Five Views*. Nashville: B & H, 2004.

Brand, Chad Owen, and David E. Hankins. *One Sacred Effort: The Cooperative Program of Southern Baptists*. Nashville: B & H, 2005.

Brewster, Paul. *Andrew Fuller: Model Pastor and Theologian*. Nashville: B & H, 2010.

Bush, L. Russ, and Tom J. Nettles. *Baptists and the Bible*. Rev. ed. Nashville: Broadman & Holman, 1999.

Carson, D. A., ed. *The Enduring Authority of the Christian Scriptures*. Grand Rapids: Eerdmans, 2016.

Carson, Glenn T. *Calling Out the Called: The Life and Work of Lee Rutland Scarborough*. Austin, TX: Eakin Publications, 1996.

Cauthen, Baker James, and Frank K. Means. *Advance to Bold Mission Thrust: A History of Southern Baptist Foreign Missions, 1845–1980*. Nashville: Broadman Press, 1981.

Christian, C. W. *Shaping Your Faith*. Waco, TX: Word Books, 1973.

Chun, Chris, and John Shouse. *Golden Gate to Gateway: A History*. Nashville: B & H, 2020.

Chute, Anthony L. *Father Mercer: The Story of a Baptist Statesman*. Macon, GA: Mercer University Press, 2011.

Chute, Anthony L., Nathan A. Finn, and Michael A. G. Haykin. *The Baptist Story: From English Sect to Global Movement*. Nashville: B & H, 2015.

Clendenen, E. Ray, and Brad J. Waggoner. *Calvinism: A Southern Baptist Dialogue*. Nashville: B & H, 2008.

Clendenen, E. Ray, and David K. Stabnow. *HCSB: Navigating the Horizons in Bible Translation*. Nashville: B & H, 2012.

Conner, Walter Thomas. *The Gospel of Redemption*. Nashville: Broadman Press, 1945.

_____. *Revelation and God: An Introduction to Christian Doctrine*. Nashville: Broadman Press, 1936.

Copeland, E. Luther. *The Southern Baptist Convention and the Judgment of History: The Taint of an Original Sin*. Rev. ed. Lanham, MD: University Press of America, 2002.

Cothen, Grady. *The New SBC: Fundamentalism's Impact on the Southern Baptist Convention*. Macon, GA: Smyth & Helwys, 1995.

Bibliography

_____. *What Happened to the Southern Baptist Convention?* Macon, GA: Smyth & Helwys, 1993.

Cothen, Grady, and James M. Dunn. *Soul Freedom: Baptist Battle Cry.* Macon, GA: Smyth & Helwys, 2000.

Criswell, W A. *The Doctrine of the Church.* Nashville: Convention Press, 1980.

_____. *Standing on the Promises: The Autobiography of W. A. Criswell.* Waco, TX: Word, 1990.

_____. *Why I Preach That the Bible Is Literally True.* Nashville: Broadman Press, 1969.

Dallimore, Arnold. *Spurgeon: A New Biography.* Edinburgh: Banner of Truth, 1985.

Dever, Mark, ed. *Polity: Biblical Arguments on How to Conduct Church Life.* Washington, D.C.: Center for Church Reform, 2001.

Deweese, Charles W. *Baptist Church Covenants.* Nashville: Broadman Press, 1990.

_____. *Women Deacons and Deaconesses: 400 Years of Baptist Service.* Macon, GA: Mercer University Press, 2005.

Deweese, Charles W., ed. *Defining Baptist Convictions: Guidelines for the Twenty-First Century.* Franklin, TN: Providence House, 1996.

Deweese, Charles W., and Pamela R. Durso, eds. *No Longer Ignored: A Collection of Articles on Baptist Women.* Atlanta: Baptist History and Heritage Society, 2007.

Dilday, Russell H., Jr. *Columns: Glimpses of a Seminary Under Assault.* Macon, GA: Smyth & Helwys, 2004.

_____. *The Doctrine of Biblical Authority.* Nashville: Convention Press, 1982.

Dockery, David S., ed. *Southern Baptist Identity: An Evangelical Denomination Faces the Future.* Wheaton, IL: Crossway Books, 2009.

Dockery, David S., and Roger D. Duke, eds. *John A. Broadus: A Living Legacy.* Nashville: B & H, 2008.

Draper, James T., and Kenneth Keathley. *Biblical Authority: The Critical Issue for the Body of Christ.* Rev. ed. Nashville: Broadman & Holman, 2001.

Duesing, Jason G., ed. *Adoniram Judson: A Bicentennial Appreciation of the Pioneer American Missionary.* Nashville: B & H, 2012.

Duesing, Jason G., Thomas White, and Malcolm B. Yarnell III, eds. *Upon This Rock: A Baptist Understanding of the Church.* Nashville: B & H, 2010.

Durnbaugh, Donald F. *Fruit of the Vine: History of the Brethren.* 2nd ed. Elgin, IL: Brethren Press, 1996.

Durso, Keith E. *No Armor for the Back.* Macon, GA: Mercer University Press, 2007.

_____. *Thy Will Be Done: A Biography of George W. Truett.* Macon, GA: Mercer University Press, 2009.

Durso, Pamela R., and Keith E. Durso. *The Story of Baptists in the United States.* Brentwood, TN: Baptist History and Heritage Society, 2006.

Early, Joseph, Jr. *Readings in Baptist History: Four Centuries of Selected Documents.* Nashville: B & H, 2008.

Early, Joseph, Jr., ed. *The Life and Writings of Thomas Helwys.* Macon, GA: Mercer University Press, 2009.

Eighmy, John Lee. *Churches in Cultural Captivity: A History of the Social Attitudes of Southern Baptists.* Knoxville, TN: University of Tennessee Press, 1972.

Elliott, Ralph H. *"The Genesis Controversy" and Continuity in Southern Baptist Chaos: A Eulogy for a Great Tradition.* Macon, GA: Mercer University Press, 1992.

Ellis, William E. *"A Man of Books and a Man of the People": E. Y. Mullins and the Crisis of Moderate Southern Baptist Leadership.* Macon, GA: Mercer University Press, 2003.

Erickson, Millard J. *Christian Theology.* 3rd ed. Grand Rapids: Baker, 2013.

Eskew, Harry, David W. Music, and Paul A. Richardson. *Singing Baptists: Studies in Baptist Hymnody in America.* Nashville: Church Street Press, 1994.

Estep, William R. *The Anabaptist Story: An Introduction to Sixteenth-Century Anabaptism.* 3rd ed. Grand Rapids: Eerdmans, 1995.

209

Bibliography

_____. *Whole Gospel, Whole World: The Foreign Mission Board of the Southern Baptist Convention, 1845–1995*. Nashville: Broadman & Holman, 1995.

Farnsley, Arthur E. *Southern Baptist Politics: Authority and Power in the Restructuring of an American Denomination*. Harrisburg: Pennsylvania State University Press, 1994.

Ferguson, Robert U., Jr., ed. *Amidst Babel, Speak the Truth: Reflections on the Southern Baptist Convention Struggle*. Macon, GA: Smyth & Helwys, 1993.

Fisher, Linford D., J. Stanley Lemons, and Lucas Mason-Brown. *Decoding Roger Williams*. Waco, TX: Baylor University Press, 2014.

Fletcher, Jesse C. *Baker James Cauthen: A Man for All Nations*. Nashville: Broadman Press, 1977.

_____. *The Southern Baptist Convention: A Sesquicentennial History*. Nashville: Broadman & Holman, 1994.

Freeman, Curtis W., ed. *A Company of Women Preachers: Baptist Prophetesses in Seventeenth-Century England*. Waco, TX: Baylor University Press, 2011.

Gardner, Andrew. *Reimagining Zion: History of the Alliance of Baptists*. Macon, GA: Nurturing Faith, Inc., 2015.

Garlow, Lyle, and Susan Ray. *Oklahoma Southern Baptists Working Together*. Oklahoma City: Arthur Davenport and Associates, 1980.

Garrett, Duane A., and Richard R. Melick, Jr., eds. *Authority and Interpretation: A Baptist Perspective*. Grand Rapids: Baker, 1987.

Garrett, James Leo, Jr. *Baptist Theology: A Four Century Study*. Macon, GA: Mercer University Press, 2009.

Gaustad, Edwin S. *Liberty of Conscience: Roger Williams in America*. Grand Rapids: Eerdmans, 1991.

Geisler, Norman L., ed. *Inerrancy*. Grand Rapids: Zondervan, 1979.

George, Timothy. *Faithful Witness: The Life and Mission of William Carey*. Birmingham, AL: New Hope, 1991.

George, Timothy, and David S. Dockery, eds. *Baptist Theologians*. Nashville: Broadman Press, 1990.

_____, and _____. *Theologians of the Baptist Tradition*. Nashville: Broadman & Holman, 2001.

George, Timothy, and Denise George, eds. *Baptist Confessions, Covenants, and Catechisms*. Nashville: Broadman Press, 1996.

Gourley, Bruce T. *A Capsule History of Baptists*. Atlanta: Baptist History and Heritage, 2010.

_____. *The Godmakers: A Legacy of the Southern Baptist Convention?* Franklin, TN: Providence House, 1996.

_____. *A Journey of Faith and Community: The Story of the First Baptist Church of Augusta, Georgia*. Macon, GA: Mercer University Press, 2017.

Graves, Harold K. *Into the Wind: Personal Reflections on the Early Years of Golden Gate Baptist Theological Seminary*. Nashville: Broadman Press, 1983.

Grenz, Stanley. *Isaac Backus, Puritan and Baptist: His Place in History, His Thought, and Their Implications for Modern Baptist Theology*. Macon, GA: Mercer University Press, 1983.

Grudem, Wayne. *Systematic Theology: An Introduction to Biblical Doctrine*. Grand Rapids: Zondervan, 1994.

Grudem, Wayne, ed. *Are Miraculous Gifts for Today?* Grand Rapids: Zondervan, 1996.

Hammett, John S. *Biblical Foundations for Baptist Churches: A Contemporary Ecclesiology*. 2nd ed. Grand Rapids: Kregel, 2019.

Hankins, Barry. *God's Rascal: J. Frank Norris and the Beginnings of Southern Fundamentalism*. Louisville: University of Kentucky Press, 1996.

_____. *Uneasy in Babylon: Southern Baptist Conservatives and American Culture*. Tuscaloosa, AL: University of Alabama Press, 2002.

Hastings, C. Brownlow. *Introducing Southern Baptists*. New York: Paulist Press, 1981.

Bibliography

Hayden, Roger. *English Baptist History and Heritage.* 2nd ed. Didcot, Oxfordshire: Baptist Union of Great Britain, 2005.

Hefley, James C. *The Conservative Resurgence in the Southern Baptist Convention.* Hannibal, MO: Hannibal Books, 1991.

_____. *The Truth in Crisis.* 5 vols. Dallas: Criterion Publications; Hannibal, MO: Hannibal Books, 1986–1990.

Hester, H I. *Partners in Purpose and Progress.* Nashville: The Education Commission, 1977.

_____. *Southern Baptists and Their History.* Nashville: Historical Commission, SBC, 1971.

_____. *Southern Baptists in Christian Education.* Murfreesboro, NC: Chowan College School of Graphic Arts, 1968.

Hill, Samuel S. Jr. *Southern Churches in Crisis.* New York: Holt, Rinehart, and Winston, 1967.

Hinson, E. Glenn. *Soul Liberty.* Nashville: Convention Press, 1975.

Hobbs, Herschel, and E. Y. Mullins. *The Axioms of Religion.* Nashville: Broadman Press, 1978.

Hobbs, Herschel H. *The Baptist Faith and Message.* Rev. ed. Nashville: Convention Press, 1996.

_____. *My Faith and Message: An Autobiography.* Nashville: Broadman & Holman, 1993.

Howe, Claude L. Jr. *Glimpses of Baptist History.* Nashville: Broadman Press, 1981.

Humphreys, Fisher. *Thinking About God.* New Orleans: Insight Press, 1977.

_____. *The Way We Were: How Southern Baptist Theology Has Changed and What It Means to Us All.* Rev. ed. Macon, GA: Smyth & Helwys, 2002.

Hunt, Alma. *History of Woman's Missionary Union.* Nashville: Convention Press, 1964.

Hunt, Rosalie Hall. *Bless God and Take Courage: The Judson History and Legacy.* Valley Forge, PA: Judson Press, 2005.

_____. *We've a Story to Tell: 125 Years of WMU.* Birmingham, AL: Woman's Missionary Union, 2013.

James, Robison B. *The Takeover in the Southern Baptist Convention.* Decatur, GA: SBC Today, 1989.

James, Robison B., ed. *The Unfettered Word: Southern Baptists Confront the Authority-Inerrancy Question.* Waco, TX: Word Books, 1987.

James, Robison B., and David S. Dockery, eds. *Beyond the Impasse?* Nashville: Broadman Press, 1992.

Jenkins, Philip. *The New Faces of Christianity: Believing the Bible in the Global South.* New York: Oxford University Press, 2006.

_____. *The Next Christendom: The Coming of Global Christianity.* New York: Oxford University Press, 2002.

Johnson, Robert E. *A Global Introduction to Baptist Churches.* New York: Cambridge University Press, 2010.

Jolley, Marc A., and John D. Pierce, eds. *Distinctively Baptist: Essays on Baptist History: A Festschrift in Honor of Walter B. Shurden.* Macon, GA: Mercer University Press, 2005.

Jonas, W. Glenn Jr., ed. *The Baptist River: Essays on Many Tributaries of a Diverse Tradition.* Macon, GA: Mercer University Press, 2006.

Keener, Craig S. *3 Crucial Questions about the Holy Spirit.* Grand Rapids: Baker, 1996.

Kelley, Charles S., Jr., Richard Land, and R. Albert Mohler, Jr. *The Baptist Faith and Message.* Nashville: LifeWay, 2007.

Kidd, Thomas S., and Barry Hankins. *Baptists in America: A History.* New York: Oxford University Press, 2015.

Köstenberger, Andreas J., and Thomas R. Schreiner. *Women in the Church: An Interpretation and Application of 1 Timothy 2:9–15.* 3rd ed. Wheaton, IL: Crossway, 2016.

Lawless, Chuck, and Adam W. Greenway. *The Great Commission Resurgence: Fulfilling God's Mandate in Our Time.* Nashville: B & H, 2010.

Lawrence, J. B. *History of the Home Mission Board.* Nashville: Broadman Press, 1958.

Bibliography

Lee, Jason K. *The Theology of John Smyth: Puritan, Separatist, Baptist, Anabaptist.* Macon, GA: Mercer University Press, 2003.

Lefever, Alan J. *Fighting the Good Fight: The Life and Work of Benajah Harvey Carroll.* Austin, TX: Eakin Publications, 1994.

Leonard, Bill J. *Baptist Ways: A History.* Valley Forge, PA: Judson, 2003.

_____. *Baptists in America.* New York: Columbia University Press, 2005.

_____. *The Challenge of Being Baptist: Owning a Scandalous Past and an Uncertain Future.* Waco, TX: Baylor University Press, 2010.

_____ *God's Last and Only Hope: The Fragmentation of the Southern Baptist Convention.* Grand Rapids: Eerdmans, 1990.

Lindsell, Harold. *The Battle for the Bible.* Grand Rapids: Zondervan, 1976.

Lolley, W. Randall, Morris Ashcraft, Thomas Henry Graves, and Thomas A. Bland. *Servant Songs: Reflections on the History and Mission of Southeastern Baptist Theological Seminary, 1950–1988.* Macon, GA: Mercer University Press, 1994.

Lovegrove, Deryck W., ed. *The Rise of the Laity in Evangelical Protestantism.* New York: Routledge, 2002.

Lumpkin, William L. *Baptist Foundations in the South.* Nashville: Broadman Press, 1961.

Lumpkin, William L., and Bill J. Leonard, eds. *Baptist Confessions of Faith.* 2nd rev. ed. Valley Forge, PA: Judson Press, 2011.

Maples, Terry, and Gene Wilder. *Reclaiming and Re-Forming Baptist Identity: Cooperative Baptist Fellowship.* Macon, GA: Nurturing Faith, Inc., 2017.

Maring, Norman, Winthrop S. Hudson, and David Gregg, eds. *A Baptist Manual of Polity and Practice.* 2nd rev. ed. Valley Forge, PA: Judson Press, 2012.

McBeth, H. Leon. *The Baptist Heritage: Four Centuries of Baptist Witness.* Nashville: Broadman Press, 1987.

_____. *Celebrating Heritage and Hope: The Centennial History of the Baptist Sunday School Board, 1891–1991.* Unpublished.

_____. *A Sourcebook for Baptist Heritage.* Nashville: Broadman Press, 1991.

_____. *Texas Baptists: A Sesquicentennial History.* Dallas, TX: Baptistway Press, 1998.

McCall, Duke, and A. Ronald Tonks. *Duke McCall: An Oral History.* Brentwood, TN: Baptist History and Heritage Society, 2001.

McClellan, Albert. *The Executive Committee of the Southern Baptist Convention: 1917–1984.* Nashville: Broadman Press, 1985.

_____. *Meet Southern Baptists.* Nashville: Broadman Press, 1978.

McDowell, Edward A. *The Meaning and Message of the Book of Revelation.* Nashville: Broadman Press, 1951.

McGlothlin, W. J. *Baptist Confessions of Faith.* Philadelphia: American Baptist Publication Society, 1911.

McGoldrick, James Edward. *Baptist Successionism: A Crucial Question in Baptist History.* Metuchen, NJ: Scarecrow Press, 1994.

Moody, Dale. *The Word of Truth: A Summary of Christian Doctrine Based on Biblical Revelation.* Grand Rapids: Eerdmans, 1981.

Morden, Peter J. *Communion with Christ and His People: The Spirituality of C. H. Spurgeon.* Oxford: Regent's Park, 2010.

_____. *Offering Christ to the World: Andrew Fuller (1754–1815) and the Revival of Eighteenth-Century Particular Baptist Life.* Waynesboro, GA: Paternoster, 2003.

Morgan, David T. *The New Crusades: Conflict in the Southern Baptist Convention, 1969–1991.* Tuscaloosa: University of Alabama Press, 1996.

_____. *Southern Baptist Sisters: In Search of Status, 1845–2000.* Macon, GA: Mercer University Press, 2003.

Mueller, William. *A History of Southern Baptist Theological Seminary.* Nashville: Broadman Press, 1959.

Mullins, E. Y. *The Axioms of Religion.* Philadelphia: Griffith and Rowland Press, 1908.

Bibliography

_____. *The Christian Religion in Its Doctrinal Expression*. Valley Forge, PA: Judson Press, 1917.

Naylor, Robert E., and Duke K. McCall. *A Messenger's Memoirs: 61 Southern Baptist Convention Meetings*. Franklin, TN: Providence House, 1995.

Nettles, Tom J. *The Baptists: Key People Involved in Forming a Baptist Identity*. 3 vols. Fearn, Scotland: Mentor, 2005–2007.

_____. *By His Grace and Glory: A Historical, Theological, and Practical Study of the Doctrines in Baptist Life*. Grand Rapids: Baker, 1986.

_____. *James Petigru Boyce: A Southern Baptist Statesman*. Philipsburg, NJ: P & R, 2009.

_____. *Living by Revealed Truth: The Life and Pastoral Theology of Charles Haddon Spurgeon*. Fearn, Scotland: Mentor, 2013.

Nettles, Tom J., and Russell Moore, eds. *Why I Am a Baptist*. Nashville: Broadman & Holman, 2001.

Norman, R Stanton. *The Baptist Way: Distinctives of a Baptist Church*. Nashville: B & H, 2005.

_____. *More Than Just a Name: Preserving Our Baptist Identity*. Nashville: B & H, 2001.

Parsons, Mikeal C. *Crawford Howell Toy: The Man, the Scholar, the Teacher*. Macon, GA: Mercer University Press, 2019.

Paschall, Henry Franklin. *Identity Crisis in the Church: The Southern Baptist Convention Controversy*. Brentwood, TN: JM Productions, 1993.

Patterson, James A. *James Robinson Graves: Staking the Boundaries of Baptist Identity*. Nashville: B & H, 2012.

Patterson, Paige. *Anatomy of a Reformation: The Southern Baptist Convention, 1978–2004*. Fort Worth, TX: Seminary Hill Press, 2004.

_____. *Revelation*. New American Commentary. Nashville: Broadman & Holman, 2012.

Patterson, W. Morgan. *Baptist Successionism: A Critical View*. Valley Forge, PA: Judson Press, 1979.

Payne, Ernest. *Thomas Helwys and the First Baptist Church in England*. London: Baptist Union, 1961.

Perry, John. *Walking God's Path: The Life and Ministry of Jimmy Draper*. Nashville: Broadman & Holman, 2005.

Pierard, Richard V., ed. *Baptists Together in Christ 1905–2005: A Hundred-Year Anniversary of the Baptist World Alliance*. Falls Church, VA: Baptist World Alliance, 2005.

Pool, Jeff B. *Against Returning to Egypt: Exposing and Resisting the Credalism in the Southern Baptist Convention*. Macon, GA: Mercer University Press, 1998.

Pool, Jeff B., ed. *Sacred Mandates of Conscience: Interpretations of the Baptist Faith and Message*. Macon, GA: Smyth & Helwys, 1997.

Pressler, Paul. *A Hill on Which to Die: One Southern Baptist's Journey*. Nashville: Broadman & Holman, 1999.

Proceedings of the Conference on Biblical Inerrancy, 1987. Nashville: Broadman Press, 1987.

Ragosta, John A. *Wellspring of Liberty: How Virginia's Religious Dissenters Helped Win the American Revolution and Secured Liberty*. New York: Oxford University Press, 2010.

Richards, Roger C. *History of Southern Baptists*. Rev. ed. Nashville: CrossBooks Publishing, 2015.

Rinaldi, Frank W. *The Tribe of Dan: The New Connexion of General Baptists, 1770–1891: A Study in the Transition from Revival Movement to Established Denomination*. Milton Keynes, UK: Paternoster, 2008.

Rosenberg, Ellen M. *The Southern Baptists: A Subculture in Transition*. Knoxville, TN: University Press, 1989.

Rutledge, Arthur B. *Mission to America*. Rev. ed. Nashville: Broadman Press, 1960.

Sanneh, Lamin, ed. *The Changing Face of Christianity: Africa, the West, and the World*. New York: Oxford University Press, 2005.

213

Bibliography

Scarborough, L. R. *A Modern School of the Prophets: A History of the Southwestern Baptist Theological Seminary, a Product of Prayer and Faith, Its First Thirty Years, 1907–1937.* Nashville: Broadman Press, 1939.

Schaff, Philip. *The Creeds of Christendom.* 3 vols. New York: Harper & Brothers, 1877.

Schepis, Michael E. *J. Frank Norris: The Fascinating, Controversial Life of a Forgotten Figure of the Twentieth Century.* Nashville: Westbow Press, 2012.

Segler, Franklin M. *A Theology of Church and Ministry.* Nashville: Broadman Press, 1960.

Shurden, Walter B. *The Baptist Identity: Four Fragile Freedoms.* Macon, GA: Smyth & Helwys, 1993.

_____. *The Doctrine of the Priesthood of Believers.* Nashville: Convention Press, 1989.

_____. *Not a Silent People: Controversies That Have Shaped Southern Baptists.* Rev. ed. Macon, GA: Smyth & Helwys, 1994.

_____. *The Sunday School Board: Ninety Years of Service.* Nashville: Broadman Press, 1981.

Shurden, Walter B., ed. *Proclaiming the Baptist Vision: Baptism and the Lord's Supper.* Macon, GA: Smyth & Helwys, 1999.

_____. *The Struggle for the Soul of the SBC: Moderate Responses to the Fundamentalist Movement.* Macon, GA: Mercer University Press, 1993.

Shurden, Walter B., and Randy Shepley, eds. *Going for the Jugular: A Documentary History of the SBC Holy War.* Macon, GA: Mercer University Press, 1996.

Slatton, James H. *W. H. Whitsitt: The Man and the Controversy.* Macon, GA: Mercer University Press, 2009.

Smith, Elliott. *The Advance of Baptist Associations across America.* Nashville: Broadman Press, 1979.

Sorrill, Bobbie. *WMU—A Church Missions Organization.* Birmingham, AL: Woman's Missionary Union, 1981.

Staton, Cecil P. *Why I Am a Baptist: Reflections on Being Baptist in the Twenty-First Century.* Macon, GA: Smyth & Helwys, 1999.

Stokes, David R. *The Shooting Salvationist: J. Frank Norris and the Murder Trial that Captivated America.* Hanover, NH: Steerforth Press, 2011.

Stricklin, David. *A Genealogy of Dissent: Southern Baptist Protest in the Twentieth Century.* Louisville: University of Kentucky Press, 2000.

Stripling, Paul. *Turning Points in the History of Baptist Associations in America.* Nashville: B & H, 2006.

Sullivan, James L. *Baptist Polity: As I See It.* Rev. ed. Nashville: Broadman & Holman, 1998.

Sullivan, Regina D. *Lottie Moon: A Southern Baptist Missionary to China in History and Legend.* Baton Rouge: Louisiana State University Press, 2011.

Summers, Ray. *Worthy Is the Lamb.* Nashville: Broadman Press, 1951.

Sutton, Jerry. *The Baptist Reformation: The Conservative Resurgence in the Southern Baptist Convention.* Nashville: Broadman & Holman, 2000.

_____. *A Matter of Conviction: A History of Southern Baptist Engagement with the Culture.* Nashville: B & H, 2008.

Thompson, Evelyn Wingo. *Luther Rice: Believer in Tomorrow.* Nashville: Broadman Press, 1967.

Tie, Peter L. *Restore Unity, Recover Identity, and Refine Orthopraxy: The Believers' Priesthood in the Ecclesiology of James Leo Garrett, Jr.* Eugene, OR: Wipf & Stock, 2012.

Torbet, Robert G. *A History of the Baptists.* 3rd ed. Valley Forge, PA: Judson Press, 1973.

Tuck, William Powell. *Modern Shapers of Baptist Thought in America.* Richmond, VA: Center for Baptist Heritage & Studies, 2012.

_____. *Our Baptist Tradition.* Macon, GA: Smyth & Helwys, 2005.

Tull, James E. *High-Church Baptists in the South: The Origin, Nature, and Influence of Landmarkism.* Rev. ed. Macon, GA: Mercer University Press, 2000.

_____. *Shapers of Baptist Thought.* Valley Forge, PA: Judson Press, 1972.

Bibliography

_____. *A Study of Southern Baptist Landmarkism in the Light of Historical Baptist Ecclesiology.* New York: Arno Press, 1980.

Underwood, A. C. *A History of English Baptists.* London: Kingsgate Press, 1947.

Vedder, Henry C. *A Short History of the Baptists.* Valley Forge, PA: Judson Press, 1907.

Walls, Rodney S. *Calvinism and the Southern Baptist Convention: A Response to Non-Calvinist Objections.* Apollo, PA: Ichthus Publications, 2020.

Wardin, Albert W., Jr. *Baptist Atlas.* Nashville: Broadman Press, 1980.

_____. *The Twelve Baptist Tribes in the USA: A Historical and Statistical Analysis.* Atlanta: Baptist History & Heritage Society, 2007.

Wardin, Albert W., Jr., ed. *Baptists Around the World: A Comprehensive Handbook.* Nashville: Broadman & Holman, 1995.

Weaver, Aaron D., ed. *CBF at 25: Stories of the Cooperative Baptist Fellowship.* Macon, GA: Nurturing Faith, Inc., 2016.

Weaver, C. Douglas. *Baptists and the Holy Spirit: The Contested History with Holiness-Pentecostal-Charismatic Movements.* Waco, TX: Baylor University Press, 2019.

_____. *In Search of the New Testament Church: The Baptist Story.* Macon, GA: Mercer University Press, 2008.

White, Thomas, Jason G. Duesing, and Malcolm B. Yarnell III, eds. *Restoring Integrity in Baptist Churches.* Grand Rapids: Kregel, 2007.

Whitley, W. T. *A History of English Baptists.* London: Charles Griffin, 1923.

Williams, Jarvis J., and Kevin M. Jones. *Removing the Stain of Racism from the Southern Baptist Convention: Diverse African American and White Perspectives.* Nashville: B & H, 2017.

Williams, Michael E., Sr. *Isaac Taylor Tichenor: The Creation of the Baptist New South.* Tuscaloosa: University of Alabama Press, 2005.

Williams, Michael E., Sr., ed. *Witnesses to the Baptist Heritage: Thirty Baptists Every Christian Should Know.* Macon, GA: Mercer University Press, 2016.

Williams, Michael E., Sr., and Walter B. Shurden, eds. *Turning Points in Baptist History: A Festschrift in Honor of Harry Leon McBeth.* Macon, GA: Mercer University Press, 2008.

Wills, Gregory A. *Southern Baptist Theological Seminary, 1859–2009.* New York: Oxford University Press, 2009.

Yarbrough, Slayden. *Southern Baptist: A Historical, Ecclesiological, and Theological Heritage of a Confessional People.* Nashville: Fields Publishing, 2000.

Yarnell, Malcolm B. III, ed. *The Anabaptists and Contemporary Baptists: Restoring New Testament Christianity.* Nashville: B & H, 2013.

Dictionaries

Allen, Clifton J., Davis C. Woolley, and Lynn E. May Jr., eds. *Encyclopedia of Southern Baptists.* 4 vols. Nashville: Broadman Press, 1958, 1971, 1982.

Leonard, Bill J., ed. *Dictionary of Baptists in America.* Downers Grove: InterVarsity Press, 1994.

Simpson, D. P., ed. *Cassell's New Latin Dictionary.* New York: Funk and Wagnalls, 1960.

Treier, Daniel J., and Walter A. Elwell, eds. *The Evangelical Dictionary of Theology.* 3rd ed. Grand Rapids: Baker, 2017.

Journals

American Baptist Quarterly
Baptist History and Heritage
Criswell Theological Review
Oklahoma Baptist Chronicle
Perspectives in Religious Studies
The Quarterly Review
Review and Expositor
Southern Baptist Journal of Theology

Southwestern Journal of Theology
Theological Educator

Annuals and News Outlets

*Annual of the Southern Baptist
    Convention*
Associated Baptist Press
Associated Press
Baptist Messenger
The Baptist New Mexican
Baptist News Global
Baptist Press

Baptist Reflector
Baptist Standard
Biblical Recorder
Christian Century
The Christian Index
Christianity Today
Daily Herald
Houston Chronicle
Religious Herald
Religious News Service
*Southern Baptist Convention Book
    of Reports*
Southern Baptist Texan
The Times Picayune

Index

217

Index

Criswell, W.A. 74–75, 82, 148, 185, 190–91, 193, 209
culture 6, 11, 38, 81–82, 84–85, 92, 96–97, 132, 136–37, 173, 188–89, 193, 200, 210, 214

Day, Michael 105, 194
Deweese, Charles 4, 103–4, 191, 204, 206, 209
Dilday, Russell 95, 120–21, 128, 151, 192, 196–97, 201, 209
Draper, James 57, 87, 110, 187–88, 200–1, 209
Duesing, Jason 184–85, 202, 209, 215

Early, Joseph 182, 186, 191, 199–200, 209
Education Commission 46, 63–64, 99, 102, 104, 188, 211
Elder, Lloyd 57, 75, 95
Elliott, Ralph 36, 57, 85, 90, 95, 120, 127, 143, 153, 189, 198, 209
Ellis, Josh 43, 186
eschatology 162–63, 171, 203
Ethics and Religious Liberty Commission 36, 46, 61–63, 82, 84, 89, 95, 102, 106, 112–13, 129, 166, 168, 188
Executive Committee 33, 36, 46, 48–49, 65–66, 74, 89, 91, 93–94, 97–102, 105–6, 122, 142, 192, 212

Finn, Nathan 71, 173, 181–82, 184–86, 189–90, 195, 203–4, 208
Fletcher, Jesse 49, 60, 71, 172, 181, 185–93, 196, 198, 204, 210
Foreign Mission Board see International Mission Board
Frost, James 35, 54–55, 187
Fuller, Andrew 22, 41, 183, 208, 212
fundamentalism 72, 81, 116, 121, 196–97, 208, 210

Garrett, James Leo 41, 71, 169, 183–85, 189, 200, 204–5, 210, 214
Gateway Seminary 5, 47, 123–25, 197–98, 208, 210
General Baptists 9, 14, 16–17, 20, 22–25, 37, 117, 138–40, 182–83, 208, 213
George, Timothy 41, 137–38, 183, 195–96, 199–201, 210
Golden Gate Baptist Theological Seminary see Gateway Seminary
Graves, Harold K. 124, 197–98, 210
Graves, J.R. 14–15, 31–34, 51, 53–54, 82, 184, 212

Grudem, Wayne 190, 199, 201–2, 205, 210
Guidestone Financial Resources 46, 58–60, 94, 102, 112, 144, 188, 207

Hankins, David 71, 96–97, 181, 183–86, 189, 191–96, 202–4, 206, 208, 210–11
Hefley, James 71, 83, 187–91, 200, 211
Helwys, Thomas 17, 19, 21, 138–39, 167, 182, 209
Historical Commission 4, 46, 56, 64–65, 95, 99–103, 185, 188–89, 211
Hobbs, Herschel 76, 78, 86, 142–43, 147–48, 185, 190, 192, 199–203, 207, 211
Home Mission Board see North American Mission Board
homosexuality 81–82, 84–85, 96, 118, 126, 166
Honeycutt, Roy 75, 78, 95–96, 117–118

International Mission Board 30, 33–35, 45–47, 50–53, 94, 101, 106, 108–10, 129, 144, 169, 175, 177, 187, 194, 210

Jacob, Henry 17–18, 20
Jessey, Henry 18
Johnson, William B. 30–31, 45, 51, 68, 140, 199
Judson, Adoniram 28, 163, 184, 208, 211
Judson, Ann 28, 163, 184, 208, 211

Landmarkism 14, 31–32, 34, 38, 42, 51, 53, 69, 115, 119, 140, 159–60, 162, 173, 182, 184–85, 196, 202, 214–215; see also successionism
Lathrop, John 18
Leland, John 27, 41, 167, 184
Leonard, Bill 9, 71, 86, 181–83, 185, 189, 191–93, 197–98, 200, 202, 212, 215
Lewis, Larry 50, 86, 94, 107, 193
liberalism 36, 72–73, 78–79, 81, 86, 113, 116–17, 127, 198, 204
LifeWay 33–36, 38, 46, 53–57, 66, 72, 75, 87, 102, 110–12, 122, 142–44, 174–75, 187, 194–95, 201, 205, 207, 212, 214
Lord's Day 161, 202
Lord's Supper 34, 40, 159–60, 202, 212, 214

McBeth, Leon 13, 30, 32, 38, 57, 60, 112, 137, 182–89, 194–96, 199, 202, 212, 215

218

Index

Index

Milton Keynes UK
Ingram Content Group UK Ltd.
UKHW032233020824
446485UK00014B/160